Under the Piñon Tree

UNDER the PIÑON TREE

FINDING A PLACE IN PIE TOWN

Jerry D. Thompson

University of New Mexico Press | Albuquerque

Library of Congress Cataloging-in-Publication Data
Names: Thompson, Jerry D., author.
Title: Under the piñon tree: finding a place in Pie Town / Jerry Thompson.
Description: Albuquerque: University of New Mexico Press, 2023. | Includes bibli-
ographical references.
Identifiers: LCCN 2022021910 (print) | LCCN 2022021911 (e-book) |
ISBN 9780826364593 (paperback) | ISBN 9780826364609 (epub)
Subjects: LCSH: Thompson, Jerry D.—Childhood and youth. | Pie Town
(N.M.)—Biography.
Classification: LCC F804.P54 T46 2023 (print) | LCC F804.P54 (e-book) | DDC
978.9/93092–dc23
LC record available at https://lccn.loc.gov/2022021910
LC e-book record available at https://lccn.loc.gov/2022021911

Founded in 1889, the University of New Mexico sits on the traditional homelands of the
Pueblo of Sandia. The original peoples of New Mexico—Pueblo, Navajo, and Apache—
since time immemorial have deep connections to the land and have made significant
contributions to the broader community statewide. We honor the land itself and those
who remain stewards of this land throughout the generations and also acknowledge
our committed relationship to Indigenous peoples. We gratefully recognize our history.

Front cover image adapted from photographs by Russell Lee and Isaac Morris; back cover
image by Russell Lee; photographs by Russell Lee used courtesy of the Library of Congress
Designed by Isaac Morris
Composed in Calluna and Bookmania

CONTENTS

WESTERN NEW MEXICO 1926

AREA DETAILED

Gallup • Santa Fe ☆
Albuquerque (40)

Pie Town •
(25) NEW
MEXICO

(10)
Las Cruces •

N
0   50
MILES

NEW MEXICO

McKINLEY COUNTY

SANDOVAL
COUNTY

ARIZONA

Gallup •
Atchison, Topeka, and Santa Fe

△ *Mount Taylor*
11,305 ft.

Albuquerque •

Zuni •

BERNALILLO
COUNTY

El Malpais VALENCIA
COUNTY

Carrizo Wash

Largo Ck

NORTH PLAINS

Rio Grande

Mangas
Creek

St. Johns •

Salt Lake
Quemado •

**Pie
Town** •

Big Alegres Mtn 10,229 ft.
Little Alegres Mtn

Escondido Mtn
9,869 ft.

△ Mangas •

Datil •

Magdalena •

Socorro •

Springerville •

Fox
Mountain △

GALLO MTS

MANGAS MTS

△ Horse
Springs

PLAINS OF SAN AUGUSTIN

Magdalena
Livestock
Driveway

Atchison, Topeka, and Santa Fe

Aragon •

SOCORRO   COUNTY

Reserve •

CATRON COUNTY
(est. June 30, 1921)

MANGAS VALLEY

On the warm days of summer when I was a boy, I would sit with my grandfather on the front porch of our old house and look out past the mailbox and the dirt road to the meadow and the blue-green mountains. My grandfather related striking stories of the heroism and horrors of World War I and how he and my grandmother and their two children, Twauna Katherine and my father, Jerry Winfield, survived the Great Depression in the mountains of western New Mexico. He was the best storyteller I ever heard, and some of the stories I begged to hear again and again.

We would sometimes stay out for the cool evenings or the startling orange sunsets, watching the moon rise over Little Alegres Mountain, the stars in the night sky, and an occasional meteor streaking through the heavens, its fiery trail gone in seconds. There was nothing like the immutable beauty of the nights in the mountains of western New Mexico. The ocean of darkness in the big sky that surrounded the stars had a special appeal. At 7,400 feet, you were close to the heavens. Those who have never seen the night sky from such an elevation have no conception of its splendor.

I will always remember western New Mexico as a land of endless sunshine, glistening sunsets, crowing roosters, howling coyotes, desert flowers, squeaky windmills, vast forests of piñon and ponderosa pines, and the dark-blue tumble of rugged mountains in every direction. For a young boy, it was a good time to be alive. Life was at its best and a thing of great beauty.

Every June, the air grew warmer and in July, billowing cumulus clouds gathered and boiled up over Mangas Mountain. Great thunderheads, tall and dense, blotted out the sun, as jagged lightning bolts lit up the sky. The thunder rumbled and roared in a chorus of reverberating echoes like giant kettledrums, and made a great impression on a small boy. Grandfather said the display indicated the wrath of God—someone had done something really bad and God was angry. Within weeks, the life-giving monsoon rains transformed the dry, baked, and yellowish-brown landscape into a magically green oasis. But the summers were short. With the frosts of September, the hills and meadow were brown and sad looking again and the woodcutters and Native American piñon pickers came bouncing along the dusty road in their rattling old pickup trucks. Every morning in early November, there was a touch of winter in the air. Hunters in bright-red shirts descended on the land like swarms of locusts in search of deer and turkey, and the sound of their rifles echoed through the narrow canyons and across the eroding hills. At night in the chilly weather, you could see their small campfires sparkling in the mountains like fireflies.

With the dark, bleak, cold days of December, snow covered the meadow and the mountains, and wind whipped the snow into drifts. Winter ruled the land. By early spring, the snow melted, but the sharp north wind, ceaseless and relentless, continued to howl through the piñons and across the meadow. The road became muddy and rutted in the raw cold of early spring before drying out in May. In July, the meadow and the hills turned green, and the cycle of life began all over again. This was the world of my youth in the high country of western New Mexico, in the years following World War II, not far from a place called Pie Town.

HOME FROM THE WAR

One of the first things I remember with any certainty is my father coming home from the war. Before sunup on a cold December day in 1945, a couple of weeks before Christmas, my mother, Jo Lee Thompson, left in the predawn hours with her uncle for the long drive to Socorro and up the Rio Grande to Albuquerque, 160 miles to the northeast, to meet my father, who had telegraphed that he was arriving on the train from New York.

For the occasion, my grandmother was cooking an apple pie in the old juniper-burning stove in the kitchen. "Your daddy will be here soon," she kept saying as she kneaded the dough and glanced out the small window. Through it, you could see down the snowy road that led north through the hills and the piñon and juniper trees in the distance. Retreating with my grandfather to the worn-out couch and the warmth of the big fireplace in the front room, I sensed something special was about to happen. Only the crackling of the piñon logs broke the wintry silence.

Hours later, just as my grandfather was adding another log to the fire, my grandmother rushed into the room, tossing her apron aside and crying out, "They're here! They're here! Your daddy is here!" Beneath her rimless glasses was a grand and wonderful smile. Within seconds, there was the undeniable sound of a car approaching on the packed snow in front of the old log house. As my grandfather rushed to open the door, a handsome stranger who I cannot remember ever seeing before, dressed all in green with shiny black shoes like a mirror, a rainbow of ribbons on his chest, and stripes on his sleeve, came bounding into the room. Excited but painfully insecure, as I was for most of my life, I scurried to the safety of my grandfather's pant legs, only to be grabbed by the stranger and repeatedly tossed into the air. Anxious, I reached to my mother for help, but she just stood there, smiling with tears running down her cheeks.

My father was home from the war, home from the dragon's teeth of the Siegfried Line at Aachen, the horrific death and suffering of the Hürtgen Forest, the snows and bloodletting in the Battle of the Bulge, the race across the Ludendorff railroad bridge on the Rhine River at Remagen, nightmarish memories of the Buchenwald concentration camp, and the bombed-out rubble of what had once been the magnificent city of Berlin. He was one of twelve million Americans who had answered the call to arms.

A few months before my father came home, an event in the New Mexico desert, 135 miles southeast of where we lived near Pie Town, cast a long and dark shadow over the country, the world, and my young life. In the predawn hours of July 16, 1945, at precisely 5:29 a.m., at a remote site on the north end of the Jornada del Muerto, the highly classified Manhattan Project reached a fiery climax. After three years of top-secret planning at the nerve center of Los Alamos on the Pajarito Plateau in the Jemez Mountains, and after monsoon delays, the world's first atomic bomb rose into the heavens.

The war was still an ocean away and I slept soundly through the epic event, but my mother was awakened by the windows in the house rattling. Mystified by what the family thought was a rare earthquake, my grandfather drove into Pie Town the next day, where he read in an Albuquerque newspaper that an army dump near Alamogordo had exploded.

On August 6, 1945, as the bloody war in the Pacific entered its fourth and final year, the secrets of the Manhattan Project were revealed to the world when an atomic bomb was dropped on the Japanese city of Hiroshima, killing an estimated eighty thousand people. Never had humankind witnessed such complete and instant devastation. Three days later, another nuclear bomb was dropped, on Nagasaki, with

My father was on leave from Fort Riley, Kansas, when this photo was taken shortly before he marched off to war. Courtesy of the author.

My father outside Berlin at the conclusion of World War II. Courtesy of the author.

Jerry Winfield Thompson Sr. rose to the rank of first sergeant in the Thirty-Sixth Infantry Division, the famous T-Patchers, during World War I. Courtesy of the author.

equally horrific destructiveness: seventy thousand people perished. Just forty-nine months later, the Soviets detonated an almost identical device in Central Asia, and the nuclear arms race and the Cold War were underway. My young life would never be the same again.

ON THE MIGRANT TRAIL

During the early years of the Great Depression, the Thompson family—my grandparents, Winfield and Quata, and their two young children—lived on the windswept, sunbaked plains of West Texas. My six-foot-two grandfather, the oldest of six boys in the Thompson family, was born in Alabama in 1892, and could remember crossing the Mississippi River in a wagon on a ferry. Sometime before World War I, the family settled in Hico in Hamilton County, central Texas, and it was there that my grandfather was inducted into the army during World War I—the Great War, the War to End All Wars. He served in the Thirty-Sixth Infantry Division, known as the T-Patchers, in General John J. "Black Jack" Pershing's American Expeditionary Forces (AEF). He had been one of five young men who reported to the Hamilton County Courthouse for a physical. Two of the recruits were rejected because of flat feet, and he remembered their sitting on the courthouse steps, crying because they could not go off to war.

Serving during the Meuse-Argonne offensive on the Western Front in the fall of 1918, my grandfather rose to the rank of first sergeant. The fighting in the Meuse-Argonne was the deadliest battle in American history, as the AEF slugged across heavily fortified rough, hilly terrain for forty-seven bloody days. But the American sacrifices helped break the back of the German army.

In many ways, I think the war helped to shape my grandfather as a man. By amazing coincidence, his birthday was November 11, and it was on the eleventh hour of the eleventh day of the eleventh month that the guns fell silent on the Western Front and men came out of the trenches like celebratory rats. After four bloody years, millions of deaths, and suffering beyond imagination, the world caught its breath and the fountains and lights came on all over Europe again.

Back in Texas after the war, my grandfather fell in love with

Quata Veta Deisher, and the two were married in Hico in June 1919. At the same time, Winfield went to work for a well-to-do uncle, A. B. Barrow, who owned a chain of furniture stores and funeral homes across West Texas. At one time or another, Winfield managed stores in Hico, Stephenville, Dublin, Eastland, Odessa, Lamesa, and Rotan, where my father was born in April 1920. Twauna followed a year later in Breckenridge.

When the Depression engulfed the nation in 1929, Barrow began losing money and he closed many of his stores. People were having a hard time buying food, much less furniture. As great black blizzards tore across the Panhandle and the South Plains, sweeping the topsoil away, conditions in West Texas grew particularly grim. Many farmers fled the stingy soil and began migrating west. My grandfather was managing the store in Odessa at the time, which Barrow managed to hang on to until 1931, ultimately closing that store too. Although he lost much of his savings when the banks collapsed, Winfield had scraped together enough money to purchase either a 160-acre chicken farm outside Odessa, where they could try to survive by selling eggs and chickens, or a car. With the car, they could take off for California, as thousands of distraught dirt farmers fleeing the Dust Bowl were doing.

WEST WITH THE OKIES

It was a dark moment in American history. A nation fought for its very existence as dreams became dust in an economic meltdown that left twelve million people unable to find work. After weeks of painful contemplation, with anarchy and violence threatening the country, Winfield bought a 1930 four-door Chevrolet sedan and the family began packing. They first drove nearly 250 miles east to say goodbye to Lucy and Bud Deisher, my great-grandparents, who were trying to eke out a living in Stephenville.

The Thompsons left Stephenville in October 1931, pulling a four-wheel trailer piled with their furniture and everything else they owned—including windows for the cabin my grandfather planned to construct. Canned goods were neatly packed in cardboard boxes, and there were chickens in a coop tied to the top of the car. In the late evenings, when the family camped by the roadside, the chickens would hop down, peck around for something to eat, and climb back into their cage. They even managed to lay a few eggs.

As did so many of the Okies fighting for survival, the Thompson family scurried west like bugs, as Steinbeck wrote in *The Grapes of Wrath*. They joined a great flood of the hungry and homeless, one of the largest such migrations in American history. Early every morning, the dispossessed and desperate arose to try to make their way to what they perceived to be the promised land of California.

The Thompsons slowly pushed across the vast and barren expanses of West Texas and eastern New Mexico, and up the Pecos River to Roswell. Here the family turned west into the mountains toward the Rio Grande. The trip took five long, grueling days. All the roads, still muddy from the late-summer monsoon rains, were dirt at the time, except for a small stretch of asphalt between Socorro and Magdalena. Pulling the heavy trailer, the car frequently overheated. Progress was slow. "I wonder how we ever made it," my father, who was eleven at the time, remembered decades later.

The second night out, the family camped by the roadside on the high divide at the north end of the Sacramento Mountains, between Lincoln and Carrizozo, near the small mountain community of Nogal. It was Saturday night and people from all around had gathered at a local dance hall. Illegal alcohol flowed freely, and in the early morning hours, an argument turned violent as one drunk shot and killed another drunk.

On the verdant Rio Grande, a ribbon of life-giving water that dissects the state from north to south, at the old town of Socorro, Winfield headed the Chevrolet west past the cottonwood-shaded plaza and along the railroad tracks into the Magdalena Mountains. This was the Ocean-to-Ocean Highway, US Route 60, one of the great migrant routes to the West. It had opened in 1917 as the first numbered route across the country, running all the way from Norfolk, Virginia, to Los Angeles, California.

Climbing up and up into the high-desert country, the family paused at Water Canyon Lodge to refill the radiator in the Chevrolet before pushing on around the north flank of the Magdalena Mountains to the bustling railhead and trading center of the same name. From Magdalena, the dusty gravel road continued west through small juniper-crowned hills and across a vast, moonlike tract from the Pleistocene age that had become a rolling sea of grass—the Plains of San Agustin. In the distance in every direction were dim, dark-blue, wondrous mountains. The third night out, the family camped by the roadside in a grove of tall ponderosa pines in picturesque White House Canyon, just east of Pie Town. Nearby was another poor family, much like Steinbeck's California-bound Joads, making their way west.

HOMESTEADING

Across the Continental Divide, past Pie Town, just short of the bleak hamlet of Sweazieville, or what some called Omega, my grandfather

The Thompson homestead in Martin Canyon in the foothills of the Mangas Mountains. The land was later sold and the ponderosa pines clear-cut. Courtesy of the author.

turned the Chevrolet away from California and headed south. He wended down a winding dirt road, past squeaky windmills and vast vistas, toward the Mangas Mountains, eighteen miles in the distance. The summer rains had been plentiful and the grama grass was as high as the belly of a horse. Large herds of white-rumped pronghorn raced about on the open plains, and prairie dogs stood on their hind feet atop their small burrows and barked at the intruders.

In the rocky foothills of the mountains, past the old adobe village of Mangas, on the rough southern edge of the Colorado Plateau, my grandfather purchased 120 acres in the confines of Martin Canyon. The property was on the edge of the Apache National Forest, near the hardscrabble homesteader hamlet of Pipe Springs, about eighteen miles southwest of Pie Town.

Pipe Springs was three miles southwest of Big Alegres Mountain, which towered over the landscape as the highest mountain in the northern part of Catron County. The property was a mile west of Little Alegres, a high volcanic ridge, almost identical to the larger mountain, but smaller and running north–south instead of east–west. More than a hundred homesteaders had filed claims near the two mountains.

Agnes Morley Cleaveland, daughter of rancher Ray Morley and the best writer Catron County would every produce, watched the homesteaders pass by her family ranch near Datil: "They came in family groups, in any sort of conveyance that would roll, their household furnishings piled high and the overflow—washtubs, baby buggies, chicken coops—wired to any anchorage that would hold. In trucks, in automobiles, dragging heavy trailers, the rare exception in horse-drawn wagons, they came, and with them a new order." Their "clearings may be seen with the stumps of the pinyons still showing, or the dust of their plowed fields, blowing across the face of the sky." In many instances, Cleaveland struggled to disguise her disdain for this "new order."

Instead of California, the Thompson family wound up in the mountains in western New Mexico, simply because my grandfather had heard a rumor that there was cheap land near Pie Town, where the family could homestead. Several years later, Winfield returned to Texas to visit two of his brothers and drove by the chicken farm near

Jerry Winfield Thompson Jr., Twauna Katherine Thompson, and Jerry Winfield Thompson Sr. at the Thompson homestead in the winter of 1932–1933. Courtesy of the author.

Odessa he had contemplated buying. Out his window, six pump jacks were pulling crude oil out of the Permian Basin.

PIPE SPRINGS

On the property in Martin Canyon, there was a small, two-room log cabin with a split-log and dirt roof. In the *Catron County News* for October 8, 1931, it was noted that "Mr. Thompson and family moved into the G. W. LeCroy house Wednesday. The two children entered school here Thursday morning."

Oklahoman and Texan neighbors helped the family replace the windows in the makeshift cabin and Winfield began hauling rocks for a fireplace since it was growing cold in the mountains. In early January 1932, the family was pleasantly surprised, the county newspaper announced, when several neighbors arrived with food for a social gathering.

My grandmother joined twelve other women in what they called the Ladies' Club that met weekly for a quilting bee. In some communities of Okies, there was a distinction between those who filed or "proved up" on their property through hard work, and those like my grandfather who bought relinquishments or finished what others had started. But at Pipe Springs, there seemed to be little difference. All the homesteaders had one thing in common—they were dirt poor, desperate, and struggling just to put food on the table.

The Thompsons had brought and hoarded enough supplies to get through the first winter, but times were tough. During a break of good weather in March 1933, there was a "logrolling" at the Thompson cabin and eleven neighbors arrived to help with the construction of a new cabin. The homesteaders, almost all of them from West Texas and Oklahoma, came from a land of dust and bank foreclosures and ruined farms, and they were all willing to assist one another. In a land shaped by rugged individualism, communitarianism ruled the day. In fact, the family was astounded by the degree of cooperation at Pipe Springs and the willingness of neighbors to assist one another. A belief that this was one's moral duty seemed contagious.

The spirit of camaraderie at Pipe Springs and nearby Pie Town prevailed for more than a decade. Every family seemed to know the joys and pains of the other families, and they unified in times of crisis. They mended fences together, looked after their neighbors' children, and gathered for funerals, birthdays, church services, and Saturday-night dances. At the same time, the newcomers were in many ways as self-reliant as if they were living a Thoreauvian dream.

The quaint log cabin in the grove of ponderosa pines in Martin Canyon was a world from the comfortable home the family had enjoyed back in Odessa. Eking out a living from the land was backbreakingly difficult. It was radically different from selling furniture. But the family adjusted.

No sooner was the original cabin complete in the late fall of 1931 than the snows came. The long, cold winter that followed proved to be one of the worst in a decade. The temperature dropped to well below zero, the Chevrolet would not start, and everything froze solid. Well into January 1932, the storms continued; the snow piled higher and higher. Although the snow finally melted in the spring, my father would never forget that particularly brutal winter, of being forced to sleep in the car for weeks at a time, wrapped in blankets to escape the leaking dirt roof of the old cabin and the mountain cold.

As the local newspaper had observed, less than a week after the Thompson family arrived, eleven-year-old Jerry and ten-year-old Twauna enrolled in Pipe Springs Elementary School, a crude, one-room log cabin the homesteaders had built on the flats at the mouth of Martin Canyon, a little over a mile northwest of where the family huddled. Here a rutted road led to Mangas and another wound north around Big Alegres to Pie Town. A third road, the community's lifeline to the outside world, twisted east across the Continental Divide and beneath the jagged north face of Little Alegres to the crossroads ranching village of Datil.

Considering the era in which it was built, the school was more than welcome. For winter warmth, families took turns carrying wood for a large cast-iron potbelly stove in the back of the school. Children sat on split-log chairs before split-log desks. Vera Jeanette Laidlaw, who my father thought an absolute saint, taught all eight grades. Often in the winter, Jerry and Twauna waded through waist-deep snow for more than a mile to get to the school. Other children walked or rode horses or mules from as far away as five miles. Winfield constructed a small, V-shaped snowplow pulled by two mules that he used to forge a path to the school. Lunch was carried in a half-gallon syrup bucket with holes poked in the top for ventilation.

For many years, long after the school had disappeared, a sturdy log privy stood by the roadside. Every time my family drove by the small structure, Winfield would coax him to reveal how he had once been in trouble there. I could not imagine how an old outhouse could get someone in trouble, but my grandfather kept teasing my father, who remained silent, and the conversation always drifted off to another subject. About the fourth or fifth time my grandfather mentioned the outhouse, my father, a bit irritated, relented.

As it turns out, he and another student, the preacher's son, Ralph Hollums, had been determined to get even with another student they accused of being a bully, a show-off, and a snitch. One day after school when the student went to use the privy, the two pranksters jammed the door shut, crawled to the roof, and proceeded to urinate on the poor student through the large cracks in the split-log roof, having little pity for his cries for help as he scurried from one side of the privy to the other. The deed gained my father and Hollums a paddling. Learning of the dastardly deed, which was deemed beneath any good Christian boy, my grandfather and grandmother hurried to apologize to the parents of the aggrieved student and to Vera Laidlaw, with promises that their son would never do anything so disgusting again.

A HOMESTEADING LIFE

The family had not envisioned anything like the harsh winters in the mountains of western New Mexico. One winter, the temperature dropped to forty degrees below zero and many small animals, especially pigs and calves, froze to death. Had it not been for by grandfather's monthly $12.50 pension for his service in World War I, the family might not have survived. All the homesteaders were poor. Everyone was having a hard time, often just focused on staying alive. "We were dirt poor but didn't know it," a young homesteader, Doris Caudill, remembered years later. "Come on out. This is a poor man's country," another homesteader wrote to a niece back in Texas, "[but] you can get started here."

A year after arriving, Winfield bought a milk cow and built a small shed for the cow. He acquired two mules and built a chicken house out of logs. For the first time, the family had fresh milk and eggs. He also purchased a couple of hogs and built a pigpen. In the late spring, Quata planted a garden, and Winfield used his span of mules to clear several acres in the bottom of the canyon, where the family planted pinto beans and corn. The narrow canyon was littered with boulders, and they spent as much time clearing and hauling rocks as they did plowing and planting.

There was a small spring in the bottom of the canyon near the cabin, but in the summer, the seepage dried up and the family was forced to haul water in barrels in a wagon from Pipe Springs, three miles away. Electricity and indoor plumbing were only a dream. Clothes were washed on a rubboard. Travel was on foot or by horseback, except in times of an emergency, when the ill or injured were rushed off by car to the doctor in Quemado or Magdalena.

The harsh winters and difficult travel caused most families to stock up on supplies, including flour and sugar in one-hundred-pound sacks and coffee and lard in giant cans. For many of the homesteaders, the trek to Magdalena in late fall to purchase groceries and supplies became an annual ritual.

There were two preachers at Pipe Springs, Reverend E. H. Bird and Reverend C. W. "Charley" Hollums. Frequently, the "preachins" at the schoolhouse or a private residence would last all day and into the night. In June 1934, a church was built of logs on a small rise near the springs. During the construction, workers paused frequently to sing and pray, and families often enjoyed a sparse lunch together. A few months later, Reverend Hollums brought a piano all the way from Albuquerque.

Dances were held every Saturday night at someone's cabin, but most of the time at George and Belle Burns's home, since they were good musicians. Someone would play the fiddle and the guitar, and Mrs. Burns would pound on the piano. My father remembers once piling into the E. Norton family wagon and traveling across the Continental Divide for a dance at the Sayward Gordanier place near Greens Gap, ten miles to the east. Couples danced through the night, and the sleepy Thompson family did not return home until the afternoon of the next day. The great sense of community among the homesteaders led to the establishment of a reliable and resilient social network that became the very heart of the Pipe Springs community.

CHAPTER TWO

THOSE WHO CAME BEFORE

In the early summer of 1934, during one of the worst drought years on record, the Thompsons joined four other Pipe Springs families for a camping excursion. Traveling westward in wagons, they wound up a mountain road across the rimrock to Slaughter Mesa and through the forest to the headwaters of Largo Creek. The campsite was near where the American Valley Cattle Company once had its headquarters and Quemado Lake was constructed decades later. Here families who had come from the dried-out lands of Texas and Oklahoma vacationed at a sparkling mountain spring at the base of a small peak for several days before returning to Pipe Springs. "They all came back terribly impressed with that part of the country," the *Magdalena News* remarked.

The family was always amazed at the number of arrowheads near El Caso Spring, and I would go there many times with Winfield and Quata in the years to come. There was no greater joy for a young boy than finding a perfectly shaped obsidian arrowhead. On one excursion, I struggled to the summit of the small peak that overlooked the spring, the peak my family had camped beneath in 1934. A circular ruin of large volcanic rocks stood at the top, evidence that Native Americans had been there centuries earlier. I often wondered what life had been like on the top of that small peak for those who had carried all those rocks to the high point. There was little doubt that whoever had built the structure was fearful of intruders. I would later discover two other identical structures on similar conical peaks near Mangas.

INDIGENOUS PEOPLES

Some of the first inhabitants of the region were the Mimbres, a branch of Mogollon peoples, who migrated up from the south in the tenth and eleventh centuries, along with the Ancestral Puebloans, who moved in from the Colorado Plateau to the north. These First Americans built small, primitive dwellings of adobe and rocks along the area's creeks and valleys. Their homes were covered with logs and dirt roofs. When I was a child, you could still see the outlines of their tiny rooms clustered together in small villages, always built on the southeastern slopes of the low hills. A severe drought from around 1275 to 1300 drove the inhabitants to abandon their homes and migrate to the Rio Grande Valley. Their villages fell into decay until all that remained were piles of adobe and rocks, yet their arrowheads, grinding stones, and broken pottery continue to litter the landscape. I was always fascinated by the colorful shards.

In the centuries that followed, the Mangas Mountains, the vast grasslands of Slaughter Mesa, and the Gallo Mountains seemed to form a dividing line between the Diné (Navajo), who inhabited the vast expanses of the Zuni Plateau to the north, and the Chiricahua Apache, who roamed the rough, broken Mogollon Rim and the desert uplands to the south.

Violent change came with Spanish colonization in the sixteenth century and for centuries after, and Mexican independence and American conquest in the nineteenth. Vicious raids, often retaliatory, engulfed the regions during Spanish colonization, and Native American slaves were carried off by the hundreds. Later, during the American Civil War, the violence against the Diné and the Apache intensified. Calvary patrols from Fort Craig on the Rio Grande and Fort Wingate near El Malpais to the northeast penetrated the area, burning hogans, razing wickiups, killing livestock, and destroying what little agriculture existed. El Sordo, a local Navajo clan leader who was the brother of Delgadito and Barboncito (head chief of the Navajo), went to Fort Wingate to make peace but the army responded by destroying his camp near Rito Quemado. While scouting through the area, many of the soldiers, most of them Hispanic, took a liking to the vast grasslands, small creeks, and towering mountains.

RITO QUEMADO

One of those soldiers was Pvt. José María Madrid. Madrid had fought in the First New Mexico Cavalry and had been on several expeditions into the area. At the end of the Civil War, the twenty-six-year-old married Antonia Padilla from the village of El Rito Colorado, east of Laguna Pueblo. About 1873, in the midst of a vicious Apache war, he established a little village near the headwaters of a small creek. Rito Quemado, it was said, took its name from the Navajo or Apache having burned the sage and rabbitbrush along the creek. According to the founders of the small community, the name came from an Apache chieftain named El Quemado, who lived in the area for many years and got his name from being very dark skinned. From a large spring that bubbled out of the arid tablelands, the creek wound westward for a mile through bone-dry hills to join Mangas Creek, northeast of Escondido Mountain. The area had long been known as the homeland of a band of Navajo headed by José Largo.

Antonia Padilla's brother, José Antonio, who had served in the territorial militia during the war and had scouted the area, arrived from Belen with a large herd of sheep and was thought to have started the livestock industry in the area. Another brother, José Francisco Padilla, arrived shortly thereafter with another herd of sheep.

In September 1879, only a few years after the village was established, five men were killed by Apache between Rito Quemado and the Sierra Datil. By 1886, enough herders and cattleman had moved into the area and a post office was established. Although many in the village remained poor, a few prospered. A wealthy merchant, José María Baca, was able to send his son, Damacio Baca, to St. Michael's College in Santa Fe.

By 1883, the *Albuquerque Journal* charged that Rito Quemado had become the "rendezvous for a bad gang of outlaws." The time had come, the newspaper asserted, for the outlaws to be "cleaned out." There is little doubt as to the lawlessness of the area. When a prospector named Thomas Culligan passed through the small community that same year and made the mistake of showing off his money and a watch, the saloon-keeper, Doc Warner, and a sheepherder followed the man twelve miles east the next day, robbed him, and killed him with an axe. In September 1888, Socorro County sheriff Charles Allen was summoned on a four-day ride to the village after Jesus Baca seriously wounded Desiderio Jaquez in a quarrel over "a woman." A few years later, in December 1891, Frank Blake made off with five hundred of Manifor Romero's sheep in broad daylight. A posse pursued Blake but the rustler fought them off. A few days before Christmas in 1893, José Romero, the mail carrier between Rito Quemado and Datil, was killed, his coyote-ravaged body found beside the road by two prospectors. Gun battles were common as late as 1911, when Antonio Marquez seriously wounded Carlos Telles.

Besides its violence, Rito Quemado became notorious for its fraudulent voting. So much confusion existed in the western part of Socorro County that for almost two decades, the area was thought to be part of Valencia County. Newspapers joked that not only did dead people vote in Rito Quemado but so did the sheep. "We do not object to New Mexico sheep voting that have gained a residence, but it is hardly fair to drive them in from Arizona," the *Socorro Sun* quipped. In 1882, in the disputed race for territorial delegate to the US House of Representatives between Tranquilino Luna and Francisco Manzanares, there were so many fraudulent votes in the Rito Quemado precinct that several citizens were called into court to testify. Although his name was on the pollbook as having voted, José Francisco Padilla testified he had been in Belen at the time of the election and could not have voted. José María Madrid, Prudencio Padilla, and Antonio Ochoa, all of whom were registered as having voted, had also been in Belen. In fact, several dead people also voted. Although Luna was declared the victor and took his seat in Congress, there were so many fraudulent votes, especially in Valencia County, that the state legislature annulled the results and declared Manzanares the winner.

Only a few years after Rito Quemado was established, seven families, including those of José María Madrid, Pablo Piño, Pedro Baca, Manuel Baca, and Silverio Padilla, moved twelve miles southeast into the more verdant Mangas Valley. In this small valley at the foot of the Mangas Mountains, three rock-and-adobe villages were established. The main village, Mangas, was located on a slight rise on the east bank of Mangas Creek, less than a mile from where I came of age. Here the creek formed an expansive, lush green *vega*, or meadow, where large herds of cattle and sheep grazed. An impressive adobe Catholic church with a small bell tower was built facing the village and the vega.

By 1883, there were fourteen families living in the valley, more than at Rito Quemado. A post office was created in 1905 and a few years later a school. By this time, the valley had as many as one hundred families and the main village boasted a saloon and a sizeable mercantile house. Most of the families were dependent on the vast herds of sheep that roamed the valley and the nearby hillsides and mesas. At the height of the livestock boom, Mangas was one of the largest voting precincts in Socorro County. Everyone, most of them Republican, voted at the home of José Ygnacio Aragon.

The village of Mangas got its name from the great Chiricahua Apache chief Mangas Coloradas, remembered for his sagacity, diplomacy, and six-foot-six-inch height. He was known to have roamed over the area before soldiers in the California Column took him prisoner during peace talks near Pinos Altos and murdered him at Fort McLane in January 1863. His body was mutilated—his head cut off, his skull boiled in a pot of water and sent east for scholars to examine.

Some names reflected the history of the land. There were names of mountains and canyons that dated back hundreds of years, names that endured through time, such as Caballeriza, Gallinas, El Toro, Alamocito, Descalso, Cañon del Buey, Cañon del Macho, El Caso, and Valle Tio Vinces, as well as canyons named after early settlers such as Padilla, Gabaldon, Baca, and Salvador.

When English-speaking outsiders came to the mountains, many of the names changed. For example, Las Mesitas became Castle Rock, Siete Canovas became Seven Troughs, and La Angostura became the Narrows. From this era came Skunk Canyon, Nester Draw, Pumpkin Flat, and of course, Pie Town.

Many of the names the homesteaders and ranchers gave to the places in the county have been lost with the passage of time, but others remain. There was one racist and demeaning name from the late nineteenth century, N—— Head Butte, that did not survive. Obviously embarrassed, Forest Service cartographers changed the

José Ygnacio Aragon (1850–1929), Petrita Baca Aragon (1860–1916), and two of their eleven children, Rafaelita (1889–1942) and Honorata (1896–1909). Aragon was the first mayor of Magdalena, a banker, businessman, leading entrepreneur, and one of the largest sheep barons in western New Mexico, running as many as forty thousand head of sheep in the Mangas Valley and adjacent mountains and mesas. Courtesy of Cristine Romero Ellis.

name of the small knoll to the less racist Negrohead Butte. South of Pie Town, Sally's Pine was named after Sally Mickey, who donated property for a school, and for the big ponderosa that grew nearby. A small, oblong mountain near where we lived at Mangas, and which I frequently climbed, was Tater Hill. There was Poverty Pool north of Pie Town, where several homesteaders settled near El Malpais. North of Quemado, there were several homesteaders along Nester Draw.

My favorite place-name was for a place north of Glenwood called Gut Ache Mesa, allegedly named by some cowboys who became deathly ill after eating some green mesquite beans. To this day, locals refuse to give Mogollon its proper Spanish pronunciation and insist on calling it "Mug-e-on" instead of "Mog-o-yon." But the name that seemed to generate the greatest curiosity with outsiders was always Pie Town.

One of the more prominent sheepmen in the valley was José María Baca, who ran a mercantile house and became postmaster, just as he had at Rito Quemado. Another well-to-do sheepman was Manuel S. Pino, a politically influential Republican. When the post office was first established, the community was called Pinoville in his honor before the name reverted back to Mangas a few years later.

JOSÉ YGNACIO ARAGON

Two miles south of Mangas was another settlement, the village of San José. The community was nestled around a big, bubbling spring that gave the valley life. Here the large whitewashed ranch headquarters of José Ygnacio Aragon looked out over a large open vega toward the Mangas Mountains. A hundred yards to the northwest stood a small Catholic church constructed of stone and plastered with mud. Aragon also built a store and several small rock dwellings where his herders and their families resided. When Rancho de San José was first erected, Indian raids were common, and family members placed small figurines, or santos, in the windows of the hacienda to ward off Indians, who were thought to be superstitious.

Aragon was born in 1850 at the village of Valencia, twenty miles south of Albuquerque, into one of the old Spanish families that proudly dated their heritage back to Juan de Oñate. Given a small herd of sheep when he was young, he grew his herds over time into the thousands in the tablelands west of Belen. Expanding his holdings into the Mangas Valley, Aragon, who was cousin of the notorious Elfego Baca, become the undisputed king of the Socorro County sheep industry and one of the wealthiest and most influential men in New Mexico.

One of five brothers, Aragon invested in the prosperous Gustav Becker–John Sinclair Mactavish mercantile house in Magdalena, and despite his inability to converse in English, became vice president of the First National Bank. He owned the Hotel Aragon on Main Street, a dance hall, and a theater, and allowed his home to become the first hospital in the town.

After an Atchison, Topeka and Santa Fe Railway spur reached Magdalena from Socorro in 1885 to transport cattle and sheep, as well as timber and ore, the town bragged that it had become the largest livestock shipping point west of Chicago. When the community decided to incorporate in 1918, Aragon was selected as the first mayor. He was also thought to have owned the first automobile in New Mexico.

At the time, Magdalena was rough and violent. Trail drivers dusted off their chaps, sought strong drink, and often fought with hard-rock miners from nearby Kelly. The situation was explosive, and Aragon witnessed more than his share of gunfights and hangings. While he was at the First National Bank in 1921, the bank was robbed of $800, though the thief was apprehended, hiding at the stockyards, within hours.

Aragon insisted on paying his herders personally, and once a month he made the long drive from Magdalena to Mangas, always insisting that he travel alone, calculating that if he were robbed, no one would be in danger except himself. When not living in the high country at Rancho de San José in the summer, Aragon frequently took his family on monthlong vacations by rail to St. Louis or Mexico City.

WOOLLY BACKS

The sheep industry shaped life in the Mangas Valley in the late 1800s and early 1900s. At the height of his empire, Aragon grazed as many as 54,000 woolly backs and employed as many as fifty herders. Each herder, or pastor, was paid a living wage and was responsible for 1,200 to 1,500 sheep. A caporal oversaw several herders. During lambing season, extra herders were hired. Sheepmen such as Solomon Luna, José Ygnacio Aragon, and Frank Hubbell, were always looking for *bureros*, or burro boys, to work alongside the experienced herders. Boys no older than ten could earn fifteen dollars a month by helping to tend camp, pack burros, keep an eye out for coyotes, and move the flock.

Shearing was usually in early June, and thirty to forty freight wagons carried the wool by way of Tres Lagunas and down the Rio Puerco to Belen for shipping to textile mills in the East. After the railroad arrived in Magdalena and there was adequate storage in the town, the wool was sent across the Plains of San Agustin. One of the more exciting times in the valley was when the wagons returned from Magdalena loaded with provisions and ranch supplies.

By 1897, with his herds producing as many as six hundred bags of wool annually, only Aragon's rival to the west, Solomon Luna, produced more—nine hundred bags a year. The two quarreled frequently over territory, water, and grazing rights. Tragically, only four months after New Mexico became a state, Luna died by drowning on the night of April 29, 1912, in one of his dipping vats south of Big Alegres Mountain.

The Thompson store at Mangas in the late 1930s. Courtesy of the author.

Thirty miles south of Mangas, on the headwaters of the Tularosa River, Melquiades Aragon, a brother of José Ygnacio, also ran vast herds of sheep. Here, near old Fort Tularosa, he built a house identical to that of Rancho de San José. When Melquiades applied for a post office, he was told that New Mexico already had a community named Tularosa and he would need a new name. Aragon it was.

A mile up Mangas Creek from Rancho de San José, in a large grove of cottonwood trees, stood the spacious home of another sheep-herding family—that of Pedro and Antonia Gabaldon. Here were large sheep corrals, a spacious, two-story residence, and a whitewashed barn. Like the Aragons, the Gabaldons lived in Magdalena during the cold winter months, but they always returned to the high country for the mild summers. By 1900, the Gabaldons were running thousands of head of sheep across Slaughter and Baca Mesas and the adjacent grasslands. By the late 1930s, Gabaldon had so many herders that a small school was established at the ranch.

DECLINE OF THE SHEEPMEN

With the introduction of synthetic material during World War II, the wool market went into serious decline. A prolonged drought stretching well into the 1950s did not help either. Moreover, after World War II, large numbers of the Aragons' and Gabaldons' herders began moving away, taking higher-paying jobs in the Morenci, Arizona, copper mines. With little choice, the sheepherding families were forced to sell their sheep and convert to cattle raising. Sheep country became cattle country. Decades earlier, in the 1880s, Texas cattlemen had moved into the high country, as did Mormons from the West, claiming vital sources of water and pushing the Hispanics off their land. Eventually, the Aragons and Gabaldons gave up their cattle and the population of the Mangas villages declined rapidly.

Farther up the canyon, at the foot of Mangas Mountain, just inside the forest boundary, was another spring. The Forest Service erected a two-room "ranger station" and corrals, and it was here that my grandfather, when not on fire-lookout duty, frequently spent the summer with my grand-mother. Just down the creek was the third of the Mangas villages, called

San Antonio. It consisted of several small rock-and-adobe dwellings, and was where the Gallegos family lived. Between San José and San Antonio, other families such as the Castillos lived in a large grove of cottonwoods.

At Mangas, my grandfather and father often conversed with Eliseo Baca, one of the last sheepmen in the valley. Born shortly after the turn of the century, Eliseo and his wife, Margarita, knew as much history of the valley as anyone. Eliseo fondly recalled the heyday of the sheep industry in the valley in the early part of the century. By 1920, he said, only eighty thousand head of sheep were run through the dipping vat at Rancho de San José. By 1940, he said, the number had plummeted to only ten thousand.

Thirty miles north and across the Continental Divide to the east, the Frank A. Hubbell Company had acquired 67,000 acres of vast grasslands and continued to pasture thousands of the woolly animals. In 1922 alone, Hubbell sent to market 12,000 lambs. As late as 1940, the company had an annual clip of more than a hundred bags; in 1950, the company was still using the Magdalena Livestock Driveway to drive thousands of head of sheep to Magdalena every year. When the government outlawed the use of poison against coyotes in the 1950s, the coyote population exploded. In 1968, and after almost ninety years of running sheep, the entire Hubbell lamb crop was wiped out by coyotes. The Hubbells, too, converted to raising cattle.

The Magdalena Livestock Driveway, five to ten miles wide, and two hundred square miles total, had seen as many as 150,000 sheep and 21,600 cattle driven to the railhead in 1919 alone. By the 1950s, however, trail drivers had been replaced by the far more efficient and faster cattle truck.

By 1950, there were only a few sheep left in the Mangas Valley, but shearing time in early June was always exciting. I would pedal my bicycle down to the village to watch the shearers at work. With large electrical clippers, they could quickly sheer a sheep. Other workers hustled to pack the dirty, brown wool into oversized cloth bags that were loaded onto a big truck as the strikingly white sheep, after being dipped, went bleating off into the meadow. I had no idea I was witnessing the passing of an era.

CHAPTER THREE

TOM CAT COUNTY

I often wondered about the early history of the area around Pie Town and the Mangas Valley. In the late 1800s and early 1900s, most of the newcomers to the western part of New Mexico where I grew up were Hispanic. They were the sheepmen and their families who established the villages in the Mangas Valley. That changed in the early to mid-twentieth century with the passage of the 1916 Stock Raising Homestead Act. Unlike President Lincoln's 1862 Homestead Act that promised 160 acres of "land for the landless," the Stock Raising Homestead Act gave settlers a full section of land—640 acres—for ranching purposes. In the western part of Socorro County, where my family would move fifteen years later after it became Catron County, the passage of the act was met with the chagrin of ranchers, who had grazed their herds on the public domain for decades. That land would now be available to homesteaders wanting to establish their own ranches and farms.

Grazing on public lands was already regulated by the time of the 1916 Stock Raising Act. As early as 1900, drift fences were being replaced by barbed wire, and the days of the open range, when ranchers grazed their cows over vast expanses of government land without restriction, was over. For the first time, windmills dotted the landscape. In fact, it was the windmill, not Remington or Colt, or the introduction of barbed wire, that won the Southwest.

In 1922, N. G. Baca, the US land commissioner in Quemado, a new community six miles west of Rito Quemado, reported that homesteaders by the hundreds were arriving to "look over the north part of the county with the intention of becoming permanent residents of that section." As many as ten land claims were filed every week. The new settlers were mostly "Texies," farmers from the South Plains and Panhandle of the Lone Star State. The influx of prospective ranchers drew other stock workers in subsequent years. "Texas is becoming well represented in the county with cowboys arriving looking for work," the *Reserve Advocate* remarked in November 1921.

The land was rife with the potential for conflict. Ever since the Republic of Texas had tried to gain control of New Mexico and the Santa Fe Trail in 1842, and the Confederate States of America had attempted to seize the entire Southwest in 1861–1862, most Hispanics in New Mexico greatly distrusted most Texans. But in the decades preceding World War I, and the years that followed, there was little they could do to stop the inrush of homesteaders.

Two years after the act started bringing new ranchers to the area, the cattlemen were hit with a severe blow: a killing drought that lasted from 1918 to 1925. The drought dried up the food supply for the cattle, and thousands of them died all over New Mexico. Conditions were particularly bad on the large ranches in the western part of Socorro County. The cattle that survived were driven or shipped across the border to the Mexican state of Chihuahua, where there was abundant grass and forage. Ray Morley and Theodore Gatlin sent 2,165 cattle to Mexico. But the drought didn't affect only cattle. In 1922, the Frank A. Hubbell Company shipped sixty-seven railway cars of sheep to graze in Colorado in the longest train ever seen in Magdalena.

After decades of isolation, on February 25, 1921, Catron County was formed out of the western part of Socorro County, with Reserve (formerly Upper Frisco) as the county seat. Residents wanted the county to be named Frisco, but at the last minute, friends of Thomas Catron had the name changed to honor the former US senator. A sturdy, two-story adobe courthouse was constructed on Main Street in Reserve, land records were transferred from Socorro, and county officers were elected for the first time. When Socorro County lost another large chunk of territory to Sierra County following a special election in 1950, Catron County, with 6,929 square miles, became the geographically largest county in the state. At the time, it also had the fewest people. Caught in the migration from rural to urban areas during and after World War II, the county lost 28 percent of its population in a decade, while Albuquerque grew by 173 percent.

At first, many politicians in Santa Fe jokingly referred to the county as Tom Cat County. My father, an employee of the Forest Service for many years, often joked that he worked for the "Funny Service" in "Cartoon County." Life there was frequently like being in a Looney Tunes cartoon, with plenty of Wile E. Coyote shenanigans, he said.

GUN FIGHT AT MIDDLE FRISCO

The county seat of Reserve had originated as one of three small villages along the San Francisco River. As had been the case at Rito Quemado and Mangas, after the Civil War, Hispanos from the Rio Grande Valley settled the string of villages, naming them Upper, Middle, and Lower Frisco. At one time, the villages boasted of a dozen bars and bordellos. Upper Frisco was sometimes called Upper San Francisco Plaza, or Milligan's Plaza—named for a rough Irish army sutler, Bill Milligan—but was then renamed Reserve around the turn of the century, after the vast forest reserve that lay next door.

When Texas cowboys first began flooding into the area in the 1880s to work on and establish their own cattle and sheep ranches, tension between the Hispanic villagers and the Texans reached a breaking point. Many of the Texans brought long-held racial prejudices against Hispanic peoples with them, and, from the perspective of the villagers, the Texans' arrogance and assertiveness seemed to know no bounds. Many of the Texan ranchers and cowboys had a hard time adjusting to life in a place where Hispanos dominated politics. The ranchers also resented the vast herds of Hispanic-owned sheep that competed with their cattle for water, land, and food.

Tensions reached a violent climax in Middle Frisco in October 1884. It all started when an unimposing, mustached, five-foot-seven-inch-tall nineteen-year-old deputy sheriff from Socorro named Elfego Baca arrested a cowboy named Charlie McCarthy for disorderly conduct. "I will show the Texans there is at least one Mexican in the county who is not afraid of an American cowboy," Baca allegedly said. The arrest sparked the siege of a small jacal, where Baca took refuge, by a drunken gang of as many as twenty of John Bunyan Slaughter's rowdy cowboys. Slaughter owned a large ranch in the area and his cowboys were known to resort to their guns to settle disputes, especially with the herders and cowboys of Solomon Luna. Baca successfully stood off against Slaughter's cowboys, who riddled the adobe building with bullet holes for thirty-three hours before surrendering.

Over time, Baca's courageous defense became legendary, one of the most famous gun battles in the history of the American West, celebrated in the 1950s Walt Disney television series *The Nine Lives of Elfego Baca*. Baca brought justice, at least for a few days, to the raw, restless territory.

THOMAS BENTON CATRON

Catron County got its name in 1921 from Thomas Benton Catron, a Missouri native and University of Missouri graduate who had served as a Confederate artillery officer during the Civil War. Catron was instrumental in getting New Mexico admitted as the forty-seventh state in 1912, and served as one of the state's first US senators.

Catron came to what was then New Mexico Territory after the Civil War, learned Spanish, studied law, and was admitted to the bar. Part of a group of notorious land speculators called the Santa Fe Ring, Catron was able to gain an interest or clear title to thirty-four old Spanish land grants totaling more than three million acres. By 1900, he was the largest landowner in the state. In state Republican politics, he also allied himself with the notoriously corrupt Albert B. Fall of Teapot Dome infamy.

Catron was one of the investors in the American Valley Cattle Company, which ran twelve thousand head of sheep on the vast grasslands in western New Mexico from its headquarters south of Quemado at the head of Largo Creek. American Valley was just another questionable alliance on Catron's part. On May 6, 1883, five hired gunmen from American Valley murdered in cold blood two homesteaders, Alexis Grossetete and Robert Elsinger, near Gallo Springs, on the south side of the Gallo Mountains. The company had realized, as did others before them, that whoever controlled the water in the area controlled the land. Gunmen from the company also pushed many Hispanic settlers off their land.

HENRY COLEMAN

After World War I, the most feared man in the northern part of the county was the striking and debonair Henry Street Coleman. Coleman would stand in front of the justice of the peace office in Quemado, quick-draw his pistol, twirl it around several times, ask someone to throw a tin can in the air, and shoot three holes in the can before it fell to the ground. Although he was popular with many of the Hispanics in and around Quemado, several ranchers accused him of rustling their cattle.

Coleman was considered the black sheep of the well-to-do Hudspeth family of West Texas. His father had been sheriff of Bandera County near San Antonio, and his brother Claude served in the US Congress and as a prominent El Paso attorney.

With his Texas-born wife, Jennie Clarintha "Clara" Potter, Coleman drifted north from Deming, New Mexico, around 1912, and filed for a homestead along Largo Creek, not far from Quemado. After a stormy divorce, in December 1918, Clara and her hired hand, Don Oliver, were found brutally murdered. Some blamed Coleman for the dastardly deed, but he was able to prove he was in Magdalena at the time. In turn, Coleman put the blame on a neighbor, Frank Bourbonnaise, who lived across Largo Creek from Clara, and gunned him down in cold blood. Claiming self-defense, Coleman was acquitted by a sympathetic judge in Socorro in a directed verdict.

After World War I, when Coleman's cattle rustling became brazenly obvious, several ranchers near Quemado decided they had had enough. On October 15, 1921, a posse led by Thomas M. Curtis and "Salty" John Cox obtained an arrest warrant and rode to Coleman's Goat Ranch, west of Zuni Salt Lake in Catron County. Spotting Coleman approaching the ranch on horseback, the posse shot him off his horse, though Coleman managed to drag himself to a dry arroyo, where he exchanged gunfire with the posse and laid through the night. When one of the posse members gathered enough courage to crawl to the arroyo the next morning, Coleman was found dead, leaning against a juniper tree, his revolver still in his hand and pointing to the heavens. He had been shot in the leg and had bled to death. Many of the residents of Quemado proclaimed the posse heroes. Others in the village mourned Coleman's loss. His body was carried to Quemado, tied over his saddle like a sack of flour. As to the actions of the posse, "We all do things that we are not proud of," Curtis was heard to say.

Coleman was carried in a car to Magdalena for burial. Stories of his rustling days and the circumstances of his death, often exaggerated, permeated the county for decades.

SPANISH FLU

Not all of the deaths in Catron County in the early part of the twentieth century were due to clashes between Hispanics and Texans or outlawry. Even before the end of the War to End All Wars, the brutal Spanish flu swept across the nation. As many as seven hundred thousand Americans, seven times the number of doughboys who died in the war, perished in the pandemic of 1918–1919. Worldwide, as many as twenty-one million were thought to have died. In the United States, schools, theaters, businesses, churches, and banks closed their doors. Everyone wore a face mask. Those inflicted had fevers that shot to 105 degrees within hours; every muscle seemed to ache, pneumonia ensued, the lungs filled with liquid, delirium set in, and death quickly followed. In Quemado, twelve-year-old Eliseo Baca watched as his mother died a painful death. His father was stricken but survived. During the pandemic, the Baca children were whisked off to relatives in Mangas, which was more remote and thought to be safer than Quemado.

Twenty-eight individuals perished from the contagion in the Quemado area alone. Every town and village in New Mexico was struck in one way or another, but none as hard as the congested mining community of Mogollon in the southern part of Catron County, where hundreds of miners and their families clustered together in makeshift mining cabins that clung to the steep mountainsides. The second and deadliest wave of the flu was likely carried to the town from Silver City.

In Mogollon, graves could not be dug fast enough. The community quickly ran out of coffins, and corpses piled up like cordwood in a warehouse on Main Street. Young Hispanic miners, many in their late teens and early twenties, were hit particularly hard by the influenza, as was the Native American population in the state. In Mogollon in October 1918, six members of the Bustamante family died within eighteen days; their caskets were carried thirty minutes along an ascent to a cemetery on a steep, rocky ridge above the town.

A PLACE CALLED PIE TOWN

On October 27, 1922, a thirty-year-old Texas-born bachelor and World War I veteran, Clyde Lee Norman, filed a claim to what he called the Hound Pup Lode in the Palisades Mining District. The claim was astride one of the picturesque, rocky dikes that ran from southeast to northwest in the northern part of Catron County. The claim was 1,500 by 600 feet. Norman's real intent was not mining, although he dug a small hole in the side of the dike. Instead, he was hoping to benefit from the increasing number of travelers passing along the Ocean-to-Ocean Highway and the settlers in the remote northern part of the county.

Born at Brownwood in Brown County, Texas, on July 14, 1891, Norman was orphaned at an early age, losing his mother when he was five and his father when he was eight, after which he was scuttled off to live with relatives and make his way through the world largely on his own. Returning from war in May 1919, he had gone west to Datil, where he worked as a ranch hand and trapper. While in Datil, he received the news of the death of his older brother and closest living relative, William Henry, back in Brownwood.

The ungraded and gravel-less highway, later known as Route 60, ran through Norman's claim. At an elevation of 7,796 feet, the claim sat in the middle of the Magdalena Livestock Driveway that ran 126 miles from Springerville, Arizona, to Magdalena and was only a mile from the Continental Divide. Norman constructed a crude structure of upright piñon logs twelve feet high on each side with a roof of poles covered with brush and dirt. He chinked the structure with mud and built a tiny lean-to in back for a kitchen. Norman dug a well near the dike and found at a shallow depth good water, which he drew to the surface in a bucket with a rope and pulley, and later with a hand pump.

Watching cars and trucks pass by on the Ocean-to-Ocean Highway, Norman went to Magdalena and purchased two barrels of gasoline, a barrel of oil, another of kerosene, and a hand-siphon gasoline pump. He painted a sign that read "NORMAN'S PLACE," and in smaller letters "Gas and Oil for Sale—Free Water for Radiators," nailed the sign to a piñon tree, and waited.

In Datil, Norman made friends with Helen McLaughlin, who had come to the high country from Texas for her asthma. McLaughlin was a good cook and made cakes, pies, and doughnuts for the tourists at the Eagle Guest Ranch. Norman bought some of the pastries and began reselling them at his place. He also developed a crush on McLaughlin and asked her to marry him, but she politely declined, and when she learned he was reselling her doughnuts and pies, she told him to make his own pastries. Norman professed ignorance, and in time, she relented and began teaching him the craft.

Norman sold so many doughnuts to travelers that he also began selling dried apple pies. In time, he mastered pie making, especially for a recipe he had known back in Texas, and word quickly spread that he had some of the best pies in the county. Everyone began calling Norman's Place "Pie Town," and Loraine Reynolds and McLaughlin painted him a new sign that read "PIE TOWN." Cowboys, sheepherders, truckers, and anyone else traveling along the dirt track that ran east across the Continental Divide to Magdalena and Socorro, or west through Quemado to Springerville, stopped at Pie Town for apple pie, or perhaps a doughnut and a cup of coffee. A village was born.

PIE TOWN OR NO TOWN

A year later, Norman became business partners with an auburn-haired Texas transplant named Harmon Leroy Craig. Born in Jacksboro, Texas, on March 1, 1877, the wily Craig was an army veteran with a fifth-grade education. One of seven children born to William James Craig and Nancy Jane Blackerby, Harmon had enlisted in the army at Dallas, Texas, in 1902 and was assigned to the Hospital Corps, largely because he had once worked in a drugstore. Five-foot-seven-and-a-half with a ruddy complexion, he had been discharged at San Francisco in 1905, only to reenlist at Seattle a few months later. Sent to Cuba with the occupational forces, he was discharged at Havana in October 1908.

Craig first came to the high country at the beginning of World War I, when he and his brother, Charlie, drove a herd of cattle from Texas to the rich grasslands around Big Alegres Mountain. Large tracts of the land were still open range at the time, and the brothers saw unlimited opportunity. The winter of 1918–1919 proved a disaster, though. The Spanish flu was sweeping across the country and the winter was one of the worst on record, with snow three feet deep. The snow and freezing temperatures took a terrible toll on livestock and people. Some old-timers said the winter was as bad as that of 1892–1893, which wiped out many of the ranchers in the western part of the state.

Harmon and Charlie did all they could to save their herd, but the animals either starved or froze to death. With little money, Charlie settled in Magdalena before eventually going back to Texas, but Harmon went to work on several large ranches in the area, including the vast W-Bar Ranch, headquartered a few miles south of Pie Town and owned by Swedish-born William C. "Bill" Dahl. For a time, Dahl was so wealthy that he financed his own private school at the ranch for his two daughters and two sons.

In 1924, Harmon Craig began assisting Norman at Pie Town and the two became partners. Norman continued to make apple pies, and Craig dished up some delicious chili con carne. Craig built a log cabin high on the dike on the north side of the highway that consisted of two bedrooms, a kitchen, and a large room that doubled as a restaurant and grocery store. On the galvanized tin roof, Craig painted "Pie Town" and "Groceries" in large letters.

In 1927, Craig applied for a post office, but authorities in Washington told him that "Pie Town" was too ridiculous a name, that he needed to find a more conventional one. Craig insisted it was Pie Town or no town and told the post office inspector to "go to hell." On May 14, 1927, he was granted a post office, and Craig was named the first postmaster. Frank Hubbell, of the sprawling Frank A. Hubbell Company that controlled thousands of acres of land near Pie Town, was said to have mailed the town's first letter.

In the early 1920s, Craig began courting a widow named Theora Baum. The two had first met when Baum, who had cooked for several of the large ranches in the area, went to work at the fashionable Magdalena Hall Hotel. They had a lot in common. Baum had arrived to the area with her family in two covered wagons and homesteaded northwest of Quemado.

Craig and Baum married in 1924, and she and her two daughters from her previous marriage, Oleta and Faye, along with the family's Jersey milk cow, moved to Pie Town. It was not long before Theora and her daughters were running the restaurant and baking pies—mostly apple, cherry, and raisin—and the reputation of the village was enhanced. A few months later, Craig purchased Norman's share of the business for $700, including two cows and two calves, and Norman's Hound Pup claim.

Norman returned to Brownwood, Texas, where in June 1928 at the age of thirty-six, he married a widow, Alice Blackwood. She was living with her young son, Nathan, and her elderly father, Arthur Cohen. Norman lived for a while at Indian Creek, ten miles south of Brownwood, eking out a living as a farmer. Decades later, Clyde Lee Norman, the founder of Pie Town, died on March 3, 1985, at the age of ninety-three in Brownwood and was buried in Greenleaf Cemetery.

In a few short years, Craig became known as the "maker and owner" of Pie Town. Because the community was located on the Livestock Driveway, Norman and then Craig were unable to get a clear title to the property. Finally, in 1927, Craig persuaded Senator Bronson Cutting to intervene with the Department of the Interior in Washington, DC, and Craig was permitted to file a claim to 160 acres in the northwest quarter of Section 19, and the property was withdrawn from the Livestock Driveway. Six years later, in 1933, Craig was given a clear title to the property, with President Franklin D. Roosevelt (FDR) signing the deed.

"NICE CLEAN CUSSING"

Theora Baum Craig recalled years later how her cowboy entrepreneur husband "cussed a lot," but he "cursed nice clean cussing," she insisted.

Perhaps more importantly, she went on to say, "Old H. L. Craig could make a little money." It was Craig who made the town what it was.

Craig's wife and stepdaughters turned out as many as fifty apple, cherry, and raisin pies a week. With the flood of refugees passing through during the Great Depression, Craig put in some real gas pumps across the street from the store, enlarged the Pie Town Hotel, and built a garage, tourist cabins, campground, and a large two-story bean house, where pinto beans—the primary crop of the area, due to climate and favorable growing conditions—could be cleaned and stored.

"Mr. Craig, the maker of the city, is now installing hot and cold showers. A new double cabin and garage. That makes our place modern. We have a big department store, hotel, café, garage, post office, and plenty of nice clean cabins. All is quiet at the little log schoolhouse," a Pie Town correspondent for the *Catron County News* wrote in April 1931.

This rare image of Pie Town looking west along the Ocean-to-Ocean Highway was taken by an unknown photographer at least a decade before Russell Lee visited the village in 1940. On the dike at the top of the hill is the Pie Town Hotel and on the right is Harmon Craig's garage. On the south side of the street is Craig and Joe Keele's gas station and mercantile store that doubled as a post office. Courtesy of the author.

For a small fee, desperate newcomers fleeing the Dust Bowl were permitted to stay in the "tourist court" until they could find land of their own. The court was actually three small cabins constructed near the dike, at the back of the store. Craig even allowed these refugees to charge groceries and other supplies until they could get back on their feet. Instead of camping by the roadside, migrants on their way to California could camp across the street and down the hill from the small business district where there was a privy and picnic tables. Pie Town is "one busy place," the *Catron County News* recorded in August 1937, and when the census enumerator showed up three years later, Pie Town boasted a population of twenty-seven.

The Republican in overalls, as Craig was known, seemed to have a personality that caused the homesteaders to trust him. And he trusted them

Russell Lee made this image of the hardworking Pie Town entrepreneur Harmon Leroy Craig handing homesteader Peter Marshall Leatherman a sack of nails. Lee labeled Craig the "first and foremost" citizen of the town. Courtesy of the Library of Congress, Prints & Photographs Division, Farm Security Administration / Office of War Information Black-and-White Negatives; call number LC-USF34-036750-D.

in return. Craig sold town property at fair market prices, loaned greenbacks with no collateral or interest, and sold groceries on credit. He also taught the rawest homesteaders survival skills, such as how to make harnesses out of old tires. By the front door of the store, he kept a bucket of water and a dipper so that anyone who came into the store could get a drink.

Craig also dug a well near his store and gave the farmers free access to water. In her recollections of homesteading near Pie Town, Doris Caudill asserted that Craig was little more than an "old buzzard," who never "gave anybody anything." He always "demanded blood," she claimed. Her remembrances are at odds, though, with those of others who recalled Craig going out of his way to help numerous desperate homesteaders. He was "glad to help those who worked and tried to help themselves," Colita Schalbar remembered. Bobby Ray McKinley recalled, "Everyone thought the world of Craig"—he was a "really fine guy." My aunt Twauna Thompson, who worked for Craig as a clerk for a few months, remembered him as being "kind and gentle" and someone who never "raised his voice."

The undeniable and underlying principle that allowed Pie Town to survive and function was the homesteaders' determination to improve themselves. Most of the Dust Bowl refugees had known bitter poverty back in Texas and Oklahoma, and they were forced to become innovative. Some of the dirt floors of the dugouts were covered with gunny sacks sewn together as carpets. "For the first time in their lives these people own their land, and they feel they've got a future here," Craig said. "Sure, it's hard going, but a man can make it if he's willing to work."

Pie Town would always be Craig's town. Even after he retired in 1938, Craig could still be seen walking the streets of Pie Town, according to the *Quemado News*, "encouraging the farmers to plant beans and corn."

MERCHANT PRINCE OF PIE TOWN

During the Depression, Craig met a mild-mannered refugee of the Dust Bowl named Jack (Joe) Keele. Originally from Tennessee, the bespectacled Keele had moved to Dimmitt, Texas, where he ran a chicken farm and tried to make a living selling eggs. When his wife, Evelyn, tragically died in childbirth in 1923, Keele married her sister, Carrie.

To escape the black northers and blinding dust storms that engulfed the Texas Panhandle during the worst years of the Depression,

Carrie and Joe Keele headed west in 1933 in a worn-out 1928 Chevrolet truck. With only six cents to their name, the "busted" Keeles settled on 640 acres of land in the Mountain View community, fourteen miles northwest of Pie Town. While Carrie taught at nearby Mesa School, Keele tried farming but complained he couldn't keep the neighbor's cows out of his crops. It was about this time that the courteous and respectful Keele went to work for Craig as a carpenter. Craig purchased the lumber, and Keele constructed the two-story bean warehouse, the largest building in the town, and several other structures with the help of a few people from the community. Other Keele structures included the Farm Bureau building and a teacherage.

Craig was so impressed with Keele's skills and energy that he

Jack Keele, hard-luck Texas farmer turned grocery man—the "Merchant Prince of Pie Town"—slices bacon for a homesteader. Photograph by Russell Lee. Courtesy of the Library of Congress, Prints & Photographs Division, Farm Security Administration / Office of War Information Black-and-White Negatives; call number LC-USF34-036832-D.

brought him in as a business partner, and the grocery store was expanded to include feed and hardware. In time, Keele became the president of the Catron County Farm Bureau, a promoter of 4-H clubs, and a vibrant and active pillar of Pie Town society. He and Carrie built a house in Pie Town, just up the street from where Harmon and Theora Craig lived and across the street from the Craigs' beanery.

One homesteader remembered the earnest and likeable Keele as a "bighearted person who threw open wide the doors of his grocery store to farmers and ranchers of the surrounding area. Their credit was good until the next bean harvest. If it hadn't been so, a lot of people would have starved out and had to hunt greener pastures." Another bean farmer recalled Keele as a "nester's friend." He "fed my family

The center of the small Pie Town business district was Craig and Keele's grocery and hardware store. Photograph by Russell Lee. Courtesy of the Library of Congress, Prints & Photographs Division, Farm Security Administration / Office of War Information Black-and-White Negatives; call number LC-USF34-036796-D.

The Pie Town Café was operated during most of the Depression by Oklahoma-born Lois Staggs and her husband, Harvey. Photograph by Russell Lee. Courtesy of the Library of Congress, Prints & Photographs Division, Farm Security Administration / Office of War Information Black-and-White Negatives; call number LC-USF34-036773.

when I couldn't get groceries anywhere else," the farmer remembered. "You could owe him $100 or more and take a few sacks of beans or take some piñon nuts to him, he would weigh them, pay you the cash for them, you could take the money and walk out, and he wouldn't say a word about what you owed him." The *Catron County News* proclaimed Keele the "merchant prince of Pie Town." Craig and Keele probably had the best-stocked grocery store in the county.

Their general store, along with the Pie Town Café and curio shop, looked much like an Old West movie set. During the latter years of the Depression, Oklahoma-born Lois Staggs and her husband, Harvey, ran the café. For a time, Guy Melton operated a barbershop and J. C. Wythe ran a taxidermy. "At Your Service: Hotel and Camp in the Pines— Home Cooking, Cottages, Cold Mountain Water, Tourist Supplies and

Pie Town Hotel atop the dike where Russell Lee and his wife, Jean Smith Lee, rented rooms in 1940. Photograph by Russell Lee. Courtesy of the Library of Congress, Prints & Photographs Division, Farm Security Administration / Office of War Information Black-and-White Negatives; call number LC-USF036875-D.

General Merchandise" was how Craig advertised his growing village. During the early years of the Depression, the Standard Oil Company donated buckets of paint and the entire town was painted a patriotic red, white, and blue.

At the entrance of Craig and Keele's store were two signs depicting other towns and cities, near and far: to the east, Datil was 22 miles away, Magdalena was 63, but Dallas was 802; to the west, Quemado was 22, Phoenix was 312, and Los Angeles, 825.

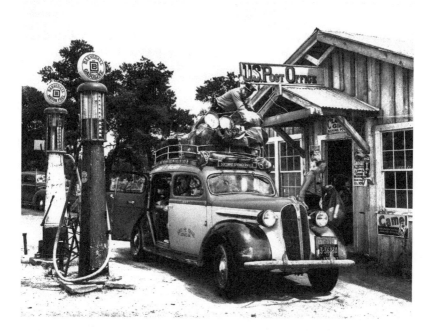

Carrying mail, baggage, and passengers, the Santa Fe Trails Stages limousine operated Monday through Saturday between Socorro, New Mexico, and Springerville, Arizona, and was Pie Town's lifeline to the outside world. Russell Lee took this image of travelers waiting patiently as postmaster Arch E. McPhaul helps unload the mail at the Pie Town Post Office. The original photograph was taken on Kodachrome color film, which Lee was experimenting with at the time. Courtesy of the Library of Congress, Prints & Photographs Division, Farm Security Administration / Office of War Information Black-and-White Negatives; call number LC-USF34-036719-D.

The shelves and the counter in the general store and the café were made of split logs. Even the pie cabinet was constructed of split logs, with a screen to keep the flies away. There was no electricity, telephone, or physician in the community. In the early 1930s, Craig also donated land for a cemetery on the northwest side of town. Local farmers built a Baptist church on the Ocean-to-Ocean Highway. Not to be outdone, the women in the community constructed a large privy for the church. Since the church was the only one in town, all faiths were welcome to worship there. A few years later, the church burned to the ground, but the faithful rebuilt it at the same location.

Baptists were the largest group in Pie Town, but there also were Methodists, Presbyterians, Catholics, and even members of the Church of Christ and the Church of Nazarene. Regardless of their church affiliations, the homesteaders frequently gathered in schools or homes. Some children began their spiritual journey in a dirty stock tank. One Pie Town settler never forgot her first church service, when she witnessed the scene of a four-year-old boy "puffing clouds of smoke from a huge pipe while the preacher brought the word of God to the small congregation of mountain people," as David Wallace Adams wrote in his *Three Roads to Magdalena*. One Pie Town mother recalled how the family walked three miles to church until the birth of her son, after which they rode horseback. "I would put a pillow in front of me on the horse, then lay Douglas on the pillow. He grew up going to church on horseback."

A big woody station wagon, driven by a uniformed Santa Fe Trails Stages driver, made the trip through Pie Town from Socorro to Springerville every day except Sunday. Bringing passengers with their luggage roped to the roof, along with the mail, it was the community's only reliable contact with the outside world. The cry "The mail is in!" was always welcomed.

Although Pie Town never had many inhabitants, it was the center of the region's homesteading country, which ran sixty miles east to west and fifty miles north to south, roughly from Datil in the east to Red Hill, west of Quemado, and from Fence Lake and El Malpais in the north to Apache Creek and Horse Springs in the south.

TWO COWS, TWO CHILDREN, AND TWO DOLLARS

In 1938, a legendary Pie Town homesteader, Roy McKee, pulled a sixteen-foot wagon—built on car axles and loaded with household goods—with his 1929 John Deere tractor four hundred miles, all the way from Lamesa, Texas. Putting along at sixteen miles an hour, McKee remembered, "I had everything we owned—which wasn't much—in that trailer. The tractor ran on gas or coal oil and it didn't have any lights, so I just stopped and camped at night." Everywhere you looked, McKee said, "there was somebody broke down. Okies. Dusted out like me." Arriving in Pie Town, McKee traded an old car for a small piece of land just across the dike from the community, built a dugout, and began clearing the land. Using a team of mules and a walking plow, McKee cleared forty acres the first year.

There was little work in the community, McKee recalled. "You couldn't get a job. Nobody had anything for you to do. Everybody was just alike. Nobody had any money." Working as a sawmiller or ranch hand paid $1.50 a day, barely enough to feed a hungry family, and the work was hard and long.

In *From the Top of the Mountain*, Kathryn McKee Roberts, the daughter of Roy McKee and Maudie Belle McKee, recorded the recollections of many Pie Town homesteaders, including those of Texas-born Alma Ruth Giles, who settled with her husband, Campbell P. Giles, near Pie Town in 1934. "Life was really hard," Alma recounted. "When we arrived at Pie Town, we had two horses, two cows, two children and two dollars, so two was our lucky number." The family spent four long years living in a "half dugout" built approximately five feet underground and three feet above, lined with logs and then topped with a roof of dirt and straw. Because they could be built quickly and inexpensively, the dugout was often homesteaders' dwelling of choice, even when better times allowed otherwise. But living in a dugout involved a constant war against dirt. Rinse water from the laundry was thrown on the dirt floor to help pack it down.

Economic struggle was the norm. "Our house was not very well built," one Pie Town woman recalled, with only "mud between the logs and as it dried and shrunk, the rats would come in. Daddy would sit up and wait for them to come out. They would get in the shadow of the water bucket, thinking they were hid, then he shot them with his .22." One Pie Town mother remembered that the mud-and-brush ceiling in the family's homestead was so infested with rats that "it came to the point where we never sat down to dinner without the .22 rifle at the table." On one occasion, spying a large rat, she said, "I reached over carefully and slowly for the gun and shot the rat, which fell in the middle of the table, ruining our dinner."

Most of the homesteaders had a milk cow but few other livestock apart from a horse or two and some mules. Some had pigs that could be sold for as much as a dollar each. All the homesteaders had gardens, where they grew carrots, radishes, cabbage, green beans, peas, okra, onions, pumpkins, and tomatoes. Everyone put in a few acres of corn, too, both for animal consumption and the table. But the cash crop the

Faro and Doris Caudill's recently completed dugout a few miles north of Big Alegres Mountain. Many homesteaders near Pie Town lived in dugouts during the Great Depression and into the 1950s. Courtesy of the Library of Congress, Prints & Photographs Division, Farm Security Administration / Office of War Information Color Photographs; call number LC-USF35-371.

homesteaders were primarily dependent on was the pinto bean. They plowed and cleared the land with, in most cases, teams of horses and mules; a few of the homesteaders used old or improvised tractors.

Usually in early March, as soon as the soil began to thaw, the farmers would begin plowing. Late-season snows were a blessing, providing much-needed moisture; in 1933, a snowstorm dumped several inches of snow the second week of May. In late June of each year, the farmers would begin to plant. Since the growing season was normally less than ninety days, the timing for planting was critical. Light rains were welcome at this point, but a rain of two inches or more could wash out a crop and force farmers to replant.

Some homesteaders farmed only a few acres, while others maintained as many as one hundred. Roy McKee, perhaps the champion of the Pie Town bean farmers, grew beans for eighteen consecutive years, and indeed remembered once planting more than a hundred acres of the crop.

The price of beans in the late 1930s and early 1940s was five cents a pound. A good farm could yield as much as three hundred to five hundred pounds of beans per acre. An industrious farmer could make as much as $1,000 a year from beans, a subsistence income at the time. The homesteaders did this with minimal water available, and many of the dryland farmers were certain their beans were superior to those grown elsewhere with irrigation.

In addition to the threat of heavy late rains, porcupines gave the homesteaders fits. When they were not feasting on the bark of piñon and ponderosa pines, porcupines devoured the buds and blooms of the young bean plants. A porcupine could wipe out an entire row of beans in a single night. The homesteaders hated the porcupines, hunting and killing them with as much vigor as they trapped and poisoned coyotes and prairie dogs. Sam McKee (brother of Roy McKee), who farmed a plot of land on the northeast slopes of Big Alegres Mountain, said he once killed seventeen porcupines in a single afternoon. Some homesteaders had dogs that were trained to kill porcupines, but after a dog did its work, its owner often had to spend a careful hour or more with a pair of plyers to extract the quills from the hurting canine.

Although the growing season in Pie Town was short, the summer days were long, and the beans grew fast. At about the time of the first frost, usually in early September, the bean farmers would begin to plow up their beans, leaving the plants out to dry. Once the beans were dry, the plants would be thrown into piles by a machine or with pitchforks. The bean plants were then hauled out of the fields and placed in a thrasher to separate the beans. Few farmers could afford a thrasher, so as many as a half dozen farmers would form a cooperative to share the cost and equipment. Many of the small farmers were also dependent on their neighbors' help at harvest time, so the bean harvest was usually a communal activity. Winfield Thompson and family "helped Archie Bowers plow up his beans and pile them last Tuesday and Wednesday," the *Catron County News* recorded in early November 1933.

The neighbors were "always willing to come in and help, and you was the same way with them," Roy McKee remembered. "If you run into any kind of problems, why, the neighbors always come in." After the beans were cleaned, they were sacked and taken to the bean house in Pie Town, where they were recleaned and sold.

REPUBLICAN COUNTY CONVENTION

As war clouds descended on the world in the late summer of 1939, several hundred people arrived in Pie Town at the invitation of Harmon Craig and Joe Keele for the county Republican Party convention. More than one hundred cars—many of which were from Mogollon, Reserve, Glenwood, and the southern part of the county—lined the Ocean-to-Ocean Highway. Many homesteaders parked their cars in a grove of trees behind the Farm Bureau building so that if the state police happened by, the owners would not be ticketed for not having any license plates.

It was the first time either the Republican or Democratic Party in the county had held its convention outside of Reserve or Aragon. Sam Norris, one of the village's more successful bean farmers, gave a welcoming address. Much of the dialogue at the gathering centered on the Taylor Grazing Act of 1934, which had turned millions of acres of public land over to the big ranchers, "taking it from the poor who needed it the most."

Other topics raised at the meeting included the location of the county seat. Some of the convention goers wanted the seat moved from Reserve to Datil, and a petition was circulated to that effect. If the argument about the location of the seat when the county was created had been that Socorro was too remote, so was Reserve, they claimed. Roads to Reserve were inadequate, they said; the small community had no telegraph, much less a decent telephone connection with the outside world. Sometimes it took days to contact the sheriff or anyone else in county government.

Some of the Pie Town homesteaders hoped to make their community the county seat, or at least to create a new county in the north. The idea of changing the county lines was brought up by at least one other convention goer, and someone in Reserve called the Pie Town homesteaders a "radical bunch of know-nothings," who should be placed, by force if necessary, in a county by themselves. Many of the inhabitants of Pie Town agreed. "OK," was the response. "Draw the line. We are ready to withdraw at any time."

Although several roads met at the small community, and it was centrally located in the county, it did not even have its own voting precinct as late as 1938. Horse Springs, Greens Gap, Mangas, and Alegres, south of town, all did, as did Prairieview, Midway, Cow Springs, and Trechado, north of town. On the census, Pie Town citizens were listed as residents of "Trinchera [sic]." For many people in the state and county, Pie Town was little more than a wide place in the road.

CONFLICT AND DEFIANCE

In Catron County, as more and more open land was subdivided for homesteading in the 1920s and 1930s, ranchers grew increasingly uneasy. Many came to hate the homesteaders, whom they called nesters, sodbusters, squatters, outsiders, and intruders. Echoing the comment of the Reserve resident at the convention, many of the ranchers considered the recently arrived homesteaders ignorant, desperate Okies straight out of *The Grapes of Wrath*. The ranchers wanted all homesteading stopped. Reflecting the passionate attitudes of the large ranchers and blaming the homesteaders for her father's financial problems in the 1930s, Agnes Morley Cleaveland asserted that the homesteaders cut the stockmen's fences, butchered their steers, and hauled water away from their wells. Moreover, she argued, the ranchers paid the majority of the taxes for the roads and the schools that educated homesteaders' children.

For the nesters, on the other hand, it seemed unfair that the ranchers had grazed herds of cattle on the public lands for decades without paying a cent. In some instances, homesteaders filed on land in the middle of the large ranches, and demanded access to the land. Ranchers frequently responded by chasing settlers off at gunpoint. "They didn't like us at all," homesteader Roy McKee remembered. Cattlemen around Pie Town, who found themselves in the minority, thought the government land was theirs, but "it belonged to the people," McKee went on to say. "They tried to run you out every way they could," he recalled. He had several confrontations with Bill Dahl, whose sprawling W-Bar Ranch was adjacent to McKee's homestead. "I had a little bit of fence . . . and an old boy said he'd take my fence down . . . and I told him he wouldn't take my fence down." The man "didn't come back anymore," but not before shooting McKee's porcupine-killing dog. The big ranchers "run worlds of [homesteaders] out," McKee added. "They sent people here three or four times when I first come here, claimed they was workin' for the government . . . and they was gonna move us out. I told 'em, well, I'd be here when they come back with a government official." Sure enough, a "government official" arrived but told McKee, "It don't look like you fellas are botherin' anybody."

Several homesteaders north of Pie Town were forced off their claims, and the threat of violence hung heavy over the land. In March 1926, northwest of Pie Town in Valencia County, Hugh Moore, a prominent rancher who ran a store and the post office at Trechado, was stabbed in an altercation by homesteader Oscar Nicholson. Nicholson was hauled into court in Reserve and forced to pay Moore $500.

In June 1931, in front of the Trechado post office, Moore shot and killed another homesteader, R. D. Wilson, with a shotgun. The two had been quarreling over water and grazing rights for months. Moore was charged with first-degree murder and taken to Los Lunas, the Valencia

County seat, for trial. In September, a jury deliberated through the night before finding him not guilty. Although Wilson was unarmed at the time of the shooting, Albuquerque attorneys successfully argued that Moore thought Wilson was drawing a pistol and that his life was in danger, a defense strategy frequently used in such cases. Wilson had chased Moore's cattle off his land several times and even shot at the rancher, the attorneys argued.

Before the hotly debated Taylor Grazing Act passed in 1934, closing public lands to homesteading, hundreds of farmers in and around Pie Town tried to push back. Led by Harmon Craig and Joe Keele, they met frequently at the Farm Bureau building to write as many as 270 letters to their congressmen and senators in opposition to the act. But it was to little avail. The ranchers were better organized, had more political clout, and were wealthier. They lobbied harder and won over almost all the western senators to their side.

On June 28, 1934, with one of the worst dust storms in the nation's history settling on Washington, DC, FDR signed the act into law. Ranchers around Pie Town were jubilant. The complex and far-reaching law gave the Department of the Interior absolute control over grazing lands in the public domain in the American West and withdrew, with minor exceptions, land for homesteading.

Although the Taylor Grazing Act was touted as a soil conservation effort, it replaced the Stock Raising Act and effectively ended homesteading in the American West. As many as eighty million acres were designated as permanent livestock grazing land under the act, and ranchers were given preferences in leasing the lands for a small fee for ten years, with the lease being easily renewable. Thousands of homeless families who were hoping to homestead would remain on the long list of the "forgotten." Around Pie Town, not only did Washington and Santa Fe pay the homesteaders little heed, but county officials in Reserve basically ignored them as well.

Elsewhere in the West, cattle and sheepmen protested that they were no longer able to graze their herds on government-owned lands. Ranchers, in the meantime, became more organized. There had been a New Mexico Cattle Growers' Association for decades, and Ray Morley had served as president from 1916 to 1918. Then, in 1938, the owners of as many as 150 large ranches in Socorro, Catron, and Valencia Counties formed the Western New Mexico Livestock Association. W. C. Hanna of San Marcial was elected president, while Bill Dahl from Pie Town and George D. Farr of Datil were selected as vice presidents. The ranchers were adamant that the recently designated Taylor Grazing Act land not be opened to homesteading. Ranchers in the county were also antagonistic toward the Forest Service, which restricted their use of forest lands.

For homesteaders in Catron County, this was all more of the same; they had always been at a disadvantage. Almost all county officials were from the southern part of the county and were under the influence of the large-ranch holders and the Mogollon mining interests. Even the commissioners in the northern part of the county during the Depression, such as J. J. McPhaul and Bill Dahl, were ranchers.

TWO-GUN COW COUNTRY

Frequently, the violence in northern Catron County seemed to rival that of Mogollon and Magdalena. In October 1931, a "strange young man, heavy built, dark complexioned, and wearing a dark cap," knocked the Tres Lagunas postmistress senseless and fled with seventy-five dollars.

In some instances, the bloodshed in the county caught the attention of the national press. On May 10, 1941, my father drove into Quemado to purchase some supplies and thought it strange that no one was around, until he spotted two bodies covered with bloody sheets lying on the ground on Main Street. It was a sight he never forgot.

That case of violence took place after sixty-three-year-old Louis C. Wilson, along with his thirty-one-year-old wife, Mildred, came to Quemado from Hansford and the heart of the Dust Bowl in the Texas Panhandle. They had rented a small house on a hill three miles west of town, where he worked as a blacksmith. Wilson claimed that neighboring ranchers John M. Garrison, sixty-three, and Garrison's son Arthur, thirty-four, who had arrived from Jack, Texas, by way of Clapham in Union County, were stealing from him. A breaking point came when Wilson asserted the younger Garrison had stolen $261, which had been hidden in a baking powder can under the floor of his blacksmith shop. He also claimed that the Garrisons had taken a roll of barbed wire from his neighbor Reuben Boone. Arthur Garrison has also been indicted in Reserve for "malicious injury to animals."

Wilson had no doubt that Arthur Garrison had taken his money, and he was furious. "I got my pistol and my wife and started hunting for him," he admitted.

Wilson found the Garrisons on Main Street that May day and began cursing and threatening them. He said that the older Garrison got out of his car with a pistol in his hand, whereupon Wilson shot him twice. "You asked for it! Now you are going to get it!" he said. At the same time, Arthur Garrison took a swing at Wilson with a car jack and Wilson fired two shots into his body. As Arthur stumbled and fell, Wilson shot him again and then emptied his pistol into the fallen father. Still cursing, Wilson threw his pistol into his car, pulled out his rifle, and continued to shoot into the dead and dying Garrisons. "I wanted to be sure them fellows was dead," Wilson said. According to witnesses, Wilson then sat in his car, threatening to kill anyone who tried to retrieve the bodies. Still furious, Wilson finally walked down Main Street, threatening to kill anyone who came outside. "I was just as crazy as a blacksmith can get," he admitted.

By the time law enforcement officials arrived, Wilson had left Main Street and barricaded himself and his wife in their small residence west of town. "I won't go to jail," he shouted, saying he would "kill the first officer who enters the gate." When Fred Balke, the popular Catron County sheriff whom Wilson knew and trusted, finally got to the scene, Wilson agree to talk as long as the sheriff came into the house unarmed. Wilson admitted to killing the Garrisons but said he had done so in self-defense and refused to give himself up. Although they had the house surrounded, police were reluctant to rush the residence after they learned that Wilson had several shotguns, a few pistols, and plenty of ammunition. One neighbor warned the state police that Wilson could split a fence post with a pistol at a hundred feet. With his wife helping him to stay awake, Wilson held out for two days and two nights. When the state police said they were preparing to dynamite his house, which would kill his young wife, Wilson finally surrendered and was rushed off to jail in Socorro and then Albuquerque. "It was them damned state police I was afraid of," Wilson said. The red-eyed, stubble-faced Wilson, in his farmer overalls and railroad engineer cap, was photographed as he entered the Bernalillo County jail.

After relatives arrived from Clovis to help post his $15,000 bail, Wilson stood trial in Reserve in October. Officials and residents feared trouble as passionate homesteaders and ranchers, some in overalls and others in cowboy hats and spurs, crowded the small town. Uncle Bill's Bar on Main Street did a booming business. Sheriff deputies were brought in from adjacent counties, and everyone entering the small adobe courthouse was searched. The state attorney general's office assisted with the prosecution. Eight witnesses were called, including schoolteachers and ranchers, several of whom had witnessed the violence. More than one witness said the Garrisons had been unarmed and were gunned down in cold blood.

Facing a death sentence, Wilson took the stand in his own defense. He claimed that John Garrison was armed and that he had felt his life was in danger. Wilson admitted during the trial that his real name was B. F. Durham, and that he had changed his name sixteen years earlier in Texas, when "kin folks" began forging his name. A jury of ranchers and miners quickly convicted Wilson of first-degree murder, and he was sentenced to life in prison. Wilson accepted the verdict calmly, asking only that Sheriff Balke escort him to prison in Santa Fe. Seven years later, on May 15, 1948, Kentucky-born New Mexico governor Thomas Jewett Mabry reduced Wilson's sentence to fifteen years and granted him a conditional release.

On December 8, 1941, the day after the shocking news that catapulted the United States into World War II reached Quemado from the distant Pacific, "the little cowtown's second double slaying" occurred less than a hundred yards from where Wilson killed the two Garrisons a few months earlier, shaking the community to its roots. The double homicide had its origins in a running feud between Texas-born, blue-eyed Leland Walter Simpson, "a 46 year-old cripple" who ran a filling station and a small garage in Quemado, and two Dust Bowl brothers,

William "Joe" and Willis "Ellis" Killen. All were respected members of the community. The Killen brothers, both World War I veterans, were homesteading eight miles north of Quemado, where they farmed a few acres and ran a small herd of cattle. The older brother, Joe, also drove a school bus and sat on the local school board. Ellis was known to be "simple minded" and several of the young men in town, as young men were known to do at the time, enjoyed teasing and harassing him. This agitation appears to have gone too far when they began to hint that his wife, Lizzie, was carrying on an extramarital affair, that the father of his soon-to-be-born child was not Ellis but a mysterious lover.

On the day of the bloodshed, the Killen brothers drove into what the *Albuquerque Journal* called a "country village," to Simpson's gas station, which was across from his mother's store, on the west end of town. At the time, Simpson was sitting in a barber's chair, holding his infant daughter. Both the unarmed Simpson, who tried to flee while clinging to his daughter, and a highway department worker, Jack L. Wininger, who was in the station at the time, were shot and killed. A second highway worker was shot but managed to escape.

Promptly arrested, the Killen brothers were hauled off to jail in Socorro, where bail was denied. Two months later, in February 1942, a Reserve jury took less than thirty minutes to find the brothers guilty of first-degree murder; they were sentenced to life in prison. In 1951, Governor Edwin L. Mechen commuted their sentences to fifty years in prison, and in 1955, they were paroled. Joe Killen died in Clovis in 1969 at the age seventy-three, while younger brother Ellis lived to be eighty, dying in Amarillo, Texas, in 1982.

THUNDER MUGS AND BEAN FARMERS

℘he man who put Pie Town on the national map was Russell Werner Lee, an Illinois-born, itinerant documentary photographer working on behalf of FDR's Farm Security Administration (FSA). Lee was, in fact, one of the more prolific photographers working for the New Deal, and one of the best. His car loaded with cameras, boxes of flashbulbs, and other photography equipment, Lee crisscrossed the nation during the Great Depression. From the Iron Range of Minnesota to the cotton fields of the segregated South, he photographed a troubled nation and a troubled people.

While Lee was working in San Augustine, Texas, in early April 1939, his boss in Washington, DC, Roy Stryker, suggested he head out to New Mexico, where he was certain to find "a hell of a good thing." In the Land of Enchantment, Stryker said, "we are going to have a lot of most interesting work for you." Stryker was sure Lee would "get quite excited about that part of the country and [we] will want you to stay there for a long time." In particular, Lee was to "do some small town pictures."

By the time Lee arrived in Pie Town, FSA photographers had sent enough images of suffering Depression-era citizens to Washington to shock the country. Now, Lee's supervisors insisted, it was time to show the successes of the New Deal, and how people were reshaping their lives. Stryker hoped Lee could find some "better farms" to work in with the "bad conditions which you have already covered so successfully." In New Mexico, Lee was to "put on the syrup and white clouds and play on the sentiment." Perhaps Pie Town was the place.

Although Lee planned to arrive in New Mexico by mid-May 1939, his schedule was interrupted by the publication of John Steinbeck's epic *Grapes of Wrath*, which Lee considered one of the best novels he had ever read. For his part, Stryker was suddenly "bubbling over with ideas" of how to "exploit the public excitement over this whole thing." Lee was off to Oklahoma to get some shots of "families departing . . . and [of] Hoovervilles." New Mexico would have to wait.

By late 1939, after several weeks of work in eastern Oklahoma, Lee finally headed west to Amarillo, Texas, and across the Llano Estacado to scout out the high country north and south of Taos. There he photographed Costilla and Questa before returning later in the spring of 1940 to cover Chamisal and Peñasco.

It is not certain how Lee first heard of Pie Town. In an article in *U.S. Camera* that featured a number of what Lee thought were his best Pie Town photographs, he recalled first hearing of the community at the FSA regional office in Amarillo and immediately writing to Stryker "for permission to undertake a photographic survey in this Pie Town section." In a later interview, however, Lee said he became interested in Pie Town when he and his second wife, Jean Smith Lee, spotted the name on a road map. "I wondered what sort of place would call itself Pie Town," Lee recounted. Parts of both versions of the story are possible.

Regardless, in April 1940, as a stricken America struggled into its eleventh spring of the Great Depression and war clouds descended on Europe and spread across Asia, the thirty-six-year-old Lee steered his 1939 Plymouth around the cottonwood-shrouded plaza in Socorro and headed west into the mountains. Past Magdalena, along the lonesome two-lane ribbon of asphalt, Lee passed the Civilian Conservation Camp on the eastern edge of the vast, windswept Plains of San Agustin and arrived in the crossroads hamlet of Datil. There he paused to ask questions and snap a few photographs of the Eagle Guest Ranch, as well as the Navajo Lodge a few blocks away, which Lee called an "old ranch house" and where he and Jean spent the night.

After passing through White House Canyon, by the Sawtooth Mountains, and crossing the Continental Divide, Jean and Lee pulled into Pie Town. Lee immediately noticed that all the buildings in the community were painted red, white, and blue, thanks, he learned, to the Standard Oil Company. While Lee was eating a sandwich at Lois

Staggs's Pie Town Café— the only café in town—Joe Keele walked up and introduced himself. Keele said that within fifteen miles of the town, 250 Dust Bowl refugees were eking out a living by dryland farming pinto beans and corn and raising small herds of cattle. Small, makeshift satellite communities, often with schools and a post office, had sprung up north, south, and west of the town.

On June 6, 1940, the *Magdalena News* noted Lee's arrival in Pie Town: "Mr. Lee of Dallas, Texas, is staying in Pietown [*sic*], taking pictures of most anything he can find. Mr. Lee is a photographer for the United States Department of Agriculture. Most of the farmers are planting beans this week."

In the high country, where the growing season is short and the winters are long and cold, Lee reported that the farmers had claimed plots of land ranging from 30 to 640 acres and lived in log cabins or dugouts. The Dust Bowl refugees, and at least seventy-five families who had come before them as early as World War I, used the Stock Raising Homestead Act to claim up to 160 acres of designated grazing land, which they promised to improve and farm and "prove up."

As he explored and photographed northern Catron County, Lee may have felt as if he were stepping back in time. There were no paved roads, banks, telephones, or indoor toilets, and there were only a few battery-operated radios. (My grandfather bought a radio in 1936, and it was such a significant event that it was mentioned in the *Magdalena News*.) The nearest physician was twenty-two miles to the west in Quemado, and the nearest railroad was fifty-nine miles to the east in Magdalena. In fact, Catron County was the only county in the state that had never known a railroad, although one had been planned in the 1920s, dissecting the county from south to north.

THE LAST FRONTIER

The region was truly, as Keele told Lee, the "Last Frontier." From the beginning, Pie Town seemed to have a strange gravitational pull on the photographer. The more he learned, the more Lee became fascinated with the town and its dryland farmers. Pie Town was, he told Stryker, an area that had to be photographed. By late 1940, he had taken more than six hundred black-and-white images and some equally beautiful ones in Kodachrome, an experimental new color film.

After sleeping at the Pie Town Hotel his first night in town, Lee headed west to Quemado, a lively village on the windswept east bank of Largo Creek, before continuing west, past vast vistas and rough

PIE TOWN AND SATELLITE COMMUNITIES, 1940

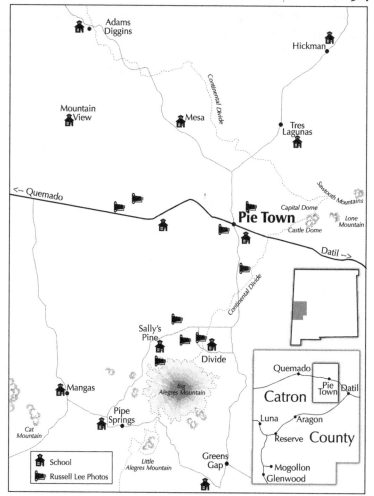

volcanic mesas to Springerville, Arizona. Lee watched cattle graze the irrigation-flooded meadows along the Little Colorado River before they were driven south into the White Mountains for the summer. Lee hoped to photograph the rough lumber and sawmill town of McNary in the heart of the White Mountains on the Fort Apache Indian Reservation, but the snow was deep in the high country and the roads were impassible. Lee kept pressing west and south through the "magnificent country" of the Salt River Canyon to the "Valley of the Sun." From Socorro to Phoenix, he traveled through "about all the extremes you could imagine—sandstorms, rain, dust-storms, sleet, driving snow, and finally tropical heat."

With Pie Town still on his mind, Lee hurried on to Tucson, Tombstone, Bisbee, and Douglas, Arizona, and then east to Silver City, New Mexico. Lee wanted to be back in Pie Town by the latter part of May. He especially wanted to be there by June 1, the first Saturday of the month, when there would be a "meeting of the whole community." Driving north, past the towering western summits of the Mogollon Mountains and the Gila Wilderness (the largest designated wilderness in the United States), Lee paused in Glenwood for a day or two of relaxation and "a little fishing."

After climbing along a narrow, frightening tract of road carved out of sheer cliffs, with one hairpin turn after another, he spent several days in the picturesque old gold and silver mining town of Mogollon. Nestled along a deep gorge on the western slopes of the rugged mountains, with rickety miners' cabins clinging to rocky hillsides, the community dated back to 1889, when gold and silver were discovered there. Lee chatted with one of the storekeepers and a saloon owner and became convinced that he should return for several days of work in the community, hopefully on June 15, the next payday, when Lee was told there would be fights, drunks in the gutters, and everything one might associate with a mining town. Lee badly wanted to depict the lives of the miners.

Pressed to be in Pie Town, Lee continued north to the Catron County seat of Reserve. Located more than one hundred miles from any railroad, Reserve looked "every bit like you might expect it," Lee wrote.

While in the village, Lee spotted a poster advertising a rodeo in Quemado on June 9, and he made plans to attend. Slated for amateur participants only, the rodeo would be held along Largo Creek, a few miles south of the community, where camping was available in a large grove of cottonwood trees. "I believe it should be the closest approach to an old fashioned country gathering that we could find out here," Lee reported.

Back in Pie Town, Lee rented two rooms at the three-room Pie Town Hotel, using one of them as a darkroom by covering the windows with a blanket. The small log dwelling, perched atop the easternmost dike in town, had once been the community's only store. Rooms had no running water or bathroom—only a bed, a table, a chair, a wash-basin, and a "thunder mug," otherwise known as a chamber pot. "I think there's going to be a good story here—it certainly looks like the last frontier," Lee wrote. While Lee was in Mogollon, rumors reached Pie Town that he was a German spy, but few residents believed an undercover agent would spend his time making photographs of lowly homesteaders in such an out-of-the-way place.

The dryland farmers Lee met in and around Pie Town were, as he put it, "characterized by rugged individualism, hardiness, materialism, need to master nature, love of personal freedom and low regard for races and religion not their own." Most were Texans, but a few were Oklahoma cotton, soybean, and corn sharecroppers. Fleeing droughts and unemployment, many of them had visions of jobs in the orchards of the golden state of California, but, like my grandfather, found them-selves in this remote corner of the Southwest instead.

It was the "Great Depression and we had decided to get out of Texas," Ed Jones, one of Pie Town's legendary homesteaders and sto-rytellers, recalled. "High dry winds blew from the west. Clouds of red dust filled the skies. Blue northers came day after day. Cows lay dead everywhere. Banks foreclosed on farms and ranches. We lost almost all. My father, mother, me, and Jess, the family bulldog, left in a Model A, off to what promised to be a new life for all. . . . We arrived in Pie Town on July 4, 1933."

Most of the people arriving in Pie Town were without any money, Harmon Craig told Lee. "Usually they brought their kids, their personal belongings, some articles of furniture, some family heirlooms. They came in cars which barely made the grade. Once they arrived, our people helped them to locate the land to be homesteaded."

The community was unincorporated and had no formal government, although it was "thoroughly democratic," Lee concluded. Craig was the "unofficial representative of the community in county and state politics." He was in a "perfect position to become the economic dictator," Lee noted, but he was not authoritarian "in spirit or fact." His motives, Lee went on to say, did "not seem to be economic, nor completely altruistic. The only way to describe it is to compare them to his bookkeeping style, which consists of two old fashioned spelling tablets. In one he puts down what he spends, and in the other what he takes in."

DEPICTING THE HOMESTEADERS

The more time Lee spent in Pie Town, the more he came to admire the homesteaders and their survival instincts. In turn, the settlers accepted him and invited him into their homes and lives. Accustomed to working from sunup to sundown, the refugees talked freely of having left a land of great sorrow and suffering to find hope in the bean fields they grubbed out of the rabbitbrush and carved out of the woods, far from the black blizzards and the deadly dust pneumonia of the Dust Bowl. Some, like John Evan Lacy, had escaped to the high country too late. Lacy, who suffered from dust pneumonia ever since his family left Texas, died in May 1935, long before Lee set foot in the town, and was laid to rest in the Taylor Cemetery near the small outpost of Adams Diggings, seventeen miles northwest of Pie Town.

As Lee witnessed firsthand, many of the farmers in the small hamlets around Pie Town lived in dugouts. A dugout was little more than a hole in the ground, anywhere from three to six feet in depth, and lined with piñon or ponderosa siding. Jack Whinery, who settled near Pie Town, built a dugout in ten days. His only cost was thirty cents' worth of nails. "The dugouts," Lee recorded, "are quite light and airy and are cool in summer and warm in winter." People utilized all sorts of items for dugout construction, such as automobile windshields for windows. Automobile doors were recycled as doors in houses and sheds. Lumber slabs discarded by local sawmills were given to anyone who would haul them away; they were then used for fences and barns. Homesteaders never bought anything they could make themselves. Lee took one image of Laura Edith Whinery sewing a flyswatter.

All the women homesteaders quilted. My mother and grandmother would lower a crude quilting frame from the ceiling of a bedroom, sew on the quilt all day, and then raise the frame back to the ceiling in the evening. Lee photographed Atis Staggs with a quilt she had sewn that featured the forty-eight states. Some of Lee's best photographs are of a dance at the Staggs residence. His image of Olie McKee holding a can of beer while dancing a jig is unforgettable.

At a small homestead, less than a half mile south of Pie Town, Lee took several photographs of Jack Whinery and his wife and five children. Like many of the homesteaders, Whinery had established a garden and built a fence around his yard from the ponderosa-log slabs given away by local sawmills.

Lee also took considerable interest in one of the more successful homesteading families—the Huttons. In 1931, George Hutton Sr. had led the family west from Pottawatomie County, Oklahoma, to claim eighty acres in the piñons and junipers eight miles northwest of Pie Town, where he built a comfortable home. Hutton had grown cotton near Maud, Oklahoma, but simply wanted to get away. "I just couldn't stand the noise and all the people," Hutton told Lee. "We've liked it out here and now there's nothing I'd rather see less than an old oil field or a cotton field." Unlike most of the homesteaders around Pie Town, the Huttons were Catholic.

With the help of his son, George Hutton Jr., Hutton built a small machine shop, a cistern from which the family drew water, and a windcharger to generate electricity. Lee spent an entire day with the Huttons, snapping images of the family at dinner and of Bessie Hutton using a makeshift electric washing machine her son had built from scratch. My father thought highly of George Jr., who ran a machine shop and could "make damned near anything." Another Lee image shows Bessie hard at work in the family garden. Another has her reading a book beneath religious images and a sign stating, "Believe In the Lord Jesus Christ and Thou Shalt Be Saved." Lee even snapped a photograph of the family's rock fireplace. "Russell Lee was all over the country," George Hutton Jr. remembered forty years later. "He came out here and spent almost one whole day with us. Made all kind of pictures. He had a 35-mm camera and he had a four-by-five regular photographer's camera. . . . I can say one thing for him—he was one hell of a good photographer, that man was. Russell and his wife was [sic] very, very likeable people, very likable."

Ed Jones remembered Lee as a "great big . . . real jolly fella. I'd be cooking in the café when I'd look up and see Russell come down from the hotel for his breakfast. He was a real nice gentleman." Colita Schalbar, whom Lee photographed at an all-night dance and who went on to teach elementary school in the community, remembered Lee as a "really nice person . . . not snobbish or stuck up."

My grandfather remembers seeing Lee at the rodeo in Pie Town and then a few weeks later at the rodeo in Quemado, but he does not appear in any of Lee's photographs. He saw Lee again when the photographer returned to Pie Town one last time to exhibit some of his images at the Farm Bureau building.

RUSSEL LEE AND PIE TOWN FAMILIES

The homesteaders who seemed to have captivated Lee's imagination the most were Doris and Faro Caudill and their five-year-old daughter, Josie. Lee had obtained the names of several homesteaders from Keele, and "armed with a crude map," he recalled, "I put the camera in the car and drove into the country in the general direction of one of the farmers. The lighting happened to be good for some general long shots of the terrain and countryside, so I took a few pictures. As I was driving down one side road, I noticed a farmer and his horse, resting from plowing his field, and looking in my direction. I stopped the car, waved to him; he waved back, and I walked across the partially-plowed field and introduced myself. He was a young man, about thirty, named Faro Caudill—a homesteader."

Caudill, whose father and uncle were said to have been cattle rustlers back in Texas, showed Lee around his property and introduced him to Doris, his wife of seven years, "a tall Texas girl a few years his junior." Doris had come to Pie Town from Sweetwater, Texas, in the summer of 1929 and married Faro at the height of the Depression in 1933; the two had moved into a dugout shared with her father-in-law and her husband's twelve-year-old sister. With no running water or electricity and only a dirt floor and a mud roof, the family managed to eke out a living some twelve miles south of Pie Town at what homesteaders were calling Divide.

Inside the Caudill dugout, Lee heard a remarkable story of survival and perseverance. "We don't have too much to do with. We came without money, we've had to grub and clear out land, dig our wells, build our corrals and barns as well as our houses," Faro Caudill recalled. "Plowin' always was the easiest work for me . . . it gives me time to think," he went on to say. "It isn't an easy life we got here. But we don't go hungry."

Besides several family portraits, Lee photographed Doris working in the garden, ironing, milking cows, sewing, straining milk for cream, and carefully examining the prized family stores of canned vegetables. Doris remembered Lee and his new wife, Jean, who would "come early and stay all day." Doris said she "loved both of them. They were real nice people. They were so down-to-earth, our kind of people. They weren't snobbish or high-toned. . . . The Lees were just real good people."

Lee also photographed Faro Caudill planting beans and constructing a new dugout on a site he found closer to water at the foot of Big Alegres. But Lee was particularly taken with Josie, a "pert and pretty five year old." Perhaps his most poignant images are those of Josie playing with several small dolls on the floor of the dugout in front of the family's worn-out couch. Of Lee's 619 black-and-white photographs of Pie Town and its environs, almost 100 are of the Caudill family.

During one of his last visits to Pie Town, Lee carefully observed and photographed the community singing contest at the Baptist church. "'Safe in the arms of Jesus,' rang out in the small frame church building during the all-day sing, despite a pounding rain and clap and roar of thunder outside," he recorded. Homesteaders had "come in from the surrounding farms—afoot, on horseback, in wagons and cars." In addition to "group singing," there were "duets, quartets, and solos until noon, when all would adjourn to the grove outside for dinner and then back to the church [where] they would sing again until early evening." The community also boasted of a literary society that met regularly.

Lee also spent some time with James Samuel (Sam) Norris and Ellie Norris and their four children, Granvill, Rex, Jimmy, and Betty, on the family homestead just north of Pie Town. After the youngest son, Jimmy, was diagnosed with asthma in 1933, the Norris family was told to move from Texas to a higher, drier climate. They left Mason County, Texas, and moved to Artesia, New Mexico. Two years later, they packed their belongings into their Model T and a four-wheel trailer and headed west to Pie Town. Living in a big army tent east of town, the family had $4.80 to their name. Only two weeks after arriving, Sam and his two oldest boys, Rex and Granvill, each got work for $1 a day, the going wage at the time, doing odd jobs on the George Rigsby ranch north of town. When those jobs petered out, they went to work at the W. R. Thomas sawmill near Big Alegres south of town.

In the summer of 1936, Sam Norris and his sons acquired a homestead northeast of Pie Town. Jimmy rode the school bus, a Model A with a tent over the back, to Quemado High School, while Betty went to school in Pie Town. One Kodachrome image shows the father working in a cabbage patch. Other images show the family posed with canned goods, the sons tying corn into bundles while harvesting their crop.

Both my father and grandfather thought highly of Rex and Granvill, who were hardworking and trustworthy. During World War II, Rex fought in the Pacific and Jimmy served in the Army Air Forces. Our families frequently hunted and prospected together. I remember one fatiguing sojourn into the canyon lands northeast of Pie Town near the Bell Mountain peaks to see a fossil site Rex and Granvill had discovered. For some strange reason, no one had thought to bring any water, and after about six hours of hiking up and down canyons and over mesas, everyone began to suffer intensely, until Granvill found a small, stagnant, putrid pool of water full of algae and hundreds of tiny tadpoles in the bottom of one of the canyons. Little was said while everyone dropped to the earth and began gulping vociferously. How many tadpoles were swallowed that day will never be known.

In early autumn of 1940, Lee was also back in Pie Town in time for the two-day Northern Catron County Fair in the pines around the Farm Bureau building and the beanery. The fair included agricultural exhibits from 4-H clubs in the small communities around Pie Town, as well as produce from individual farmers and ranchers. On display were quilts, rugs, embroideries, fresh and canned vegetables, and, of course, pies. Those attending the fair also took in free barbecue at the rodeo that Lee photographed. As had been the case for the past few years, the rodeo, which was open to cowboys from all over the state and country, was a big success, with hundreds in attendance. There were even two quarter horse races. On Friday and Saturday, enormous crowds danced the night away with "lots of music, lots of people, and lots of fun with barbecue for all." The second evening, rains drove eighty-five dancing couples from the dance platform to Chartier's Dance Hall, three miles west of town. Ed Jones, the secretary for the fair, had little doubt the festive event was on its way to becoming one of the "great successful and useful county fairs of the state."

By this time, the summer monsoons had made the countryside green and inviting. The "valleys, the hillsides, and even the tops of the mountains where rocks usually abound . . . are covered with generous covers of green verdure," one observer wrote. It was perhaps the wettest summer in twelve years, a pleasing respite for the Pie Town homesteaders after years of suffering. The big, puffy, white cumulus clouds that Stryker had promised are visible in a few of Lee's images.

During Lee's last visit to Pie Town in the early autumn, he displayed some of his photographs at the Farm Bureau building. He seemed to be happy when people gathered to glow over the images and ask how they could obtain copies.

During much of the summer of 1940, in the calm before the storm of war, Lee observed the Pie Towners at work and at play. He photographed them in their fields and in their homes, and at meetings at the Farm Bureau building; he photographed barefoot children at school and hardy farmers singing and dancing, playing 42, praying, and eating their Sunday dinner by the light of kerosene lamps. "I wanted to show people in other parts of the country how Pie Town lived," Lee would say

DEATH AND LIFE

The Depression was hard on the Pie Town homesteaders, and especially the years 1935 and 1936. Conditions were better in 1937, when farmers produced a bumper crop of pinto beans, but in 1938, it was dry again. The next year was good, but 1940 was even better, one of the wettest in memory. With abundant rain, "the valleys, the hillsides, and even the tops of the mountains, where rocks usually abound . . . are covered with generous covers of green verdure," one observer noted. Green grass blanketed the landscape. "It's a delight now for any New Mexican to drive out over Route 60 and look at the green valleys and verdant hills, everywhere furnishing feed in unlimited quantities for everything that feeds on grass and foliage," the *Quemado News* reported.

Agricultural products exhibited at the Pie Town Fair in 1940 were the best anyone could remember. Pie Town pinto beans even won three of the top four awards in the farm produce category at the New Mexico State Fair in Albuquerque that year.

Beans and cattle were the backbone of the fragile Pie Town economy. Every year, thousands of head of cattle from the big ranches near the small community were driven to market. Cowboys herded the animals from the W-Bar Ranch a few miles south of town and from the Double Circle in the foothills of the Datil and Sawtooth Mountains to the east, using the Livestock Driveway that stretched from Arizona to the railhead at Magdalena. As many as sixteen cowboys could drive a herd as large as 2,200 head from the W-Bar to Magdalena in three weeks, moving at a pace of three to five miles a day. But the days of the cattle drive were coming to an end.

Ultimately, weather conditions, and growing conditions for plant life and livestock—and people—linked the residents of Pie Town and its surroundings to the land. In the 1930s, their lives and deaths, and those of my family and friends, played out against the backdrop of snowstorms and sunshine, monsoons and drought.

PIÑON NUTS

Although bean farming and cattle ranching supported most of the inhabitants of Pie Town, another boost to the local economy came from piñon nuts. A record $700,000 in piñon nuts were harvested in New Mexico in 1936, and in 1937, the harvest was said to be worth $500,000. Taught by the Diné to harvest the nuts, New Mexicans sent hundreds of thousands of pounds of piñons to market every year. New Mexico had the largest piñon pine forests in the nation. No county had more of the trees than Catron County, and the mature groves around Pie Town were among the very best.

After the bean harvest was complete each fall, entire families of homesteaders rushed into the woods to pick piñon nuts to supplement their meager family incomes. Working hard, a single individual could gather as many as forty pounds of nuts in a day. Some families could collect two thousand pounds in a few weeks.

The practice popped up in area newspaper accounts each fall. "Several of the town people have been out for nuts during the past week," the Socorro Chieftain reported from Reserve in October 1938. A few years earlier, in October 1931, the only bustle around Quemado was from piñon pickers who "[go] out in the morning early and come back at night." That year in Datil, the Catron County News reported that everyone was so busy with piñons there was "no time for bridge." The Merino Springs store, north of Quemado, handled twenty-two thousand pounds of piñon nuts in 1931 alone. Two years later, in November 1933, a correspondent for the Alegres column wrote in the county newspaper, "Nearly all of the folks here are picking piñons while the weather is still pretty." The Clovis Evening News-Journal reported in October 1935, "It's piñon gathering time in Quemado," and Piñon Ridge near town was "dotted with picturesque Zuni Indian camps." In 1936, the Bear Canyon column in the Quemado News noted that Ben

Christian, one of my grandfather's friends, had been out "a week or two near Pie Town gathering piñons."

Picking piñons would continue well into the winter. At Pipe Springs in early November 1933, when Chloe Oldham received word that her grandfather had died back in Texas and school had to be canceled for several days, the children scurried out into the woods to gather piñons. In the *Catron County News* Alegres column in January 1934, it was reported that "truck loads of Indians were passing by every day going to pick piñons." At Mangas several weeks later, the county newspaper noted that the "Leyba family came in last week from picking piñons." In October 1936, as many as a hundred Diné were picking piñons on the Ed Clubb ranch at Mangas; one of the Diné died during the effort and was buried in the local cemetery.

Piñon nuts are harvested from the cones of piñon pines. The trees are unpredictable when it comes to their crop, as they rarely bear cones two years in a row. Sometimes the trees go seven years without producing cones. In a good year, one branch might contain three to four cones in a cluster, with each cone yielding twenty to twenty-six small nuts.

Some of the dryland farmers did not wait for the cones to dry on the trees but rather picked them green. The farmers would then lay cones in the sun to dry for up to three weeks or until the cones began to crack open. The green burs were covered in a sticky resin, one farmer remembered, and were "one son-of-a-gun to pick." Working with the green cones caused pickers' fingers to get stuck together; they had to clean their hands with fine sand. Invariably, many of the nuts in these cones never developed and turned out to be light colored and rotten. My grandfather always picked the nuts after they had dropped and would dump the nuts into a water bucket; the ones that floated were scooped out and thrown away.

Often on weekends in October and November, I would walk, bucket in hand, with my grandmother to a small grove of piñon trees less than fifty yards from the old house where we lived. Sometimes we would head off into the hills. Quata seemed to prefer nut gathering in a quiet spot near the family's old homestead, about three miles away, near the mouth of Martin Canyon. Here were several mature groves of piñon trees, where the nuts were large and plentiful. You could shake the small trees and force the nuts to fall, but the more mature trees required climbing or using a ladder, which was time consuming and difficult. Our usual method of procuring the nuts was the old-fashioned method of crawling around on hands and knees and picking them up from the ground.

Frequently, Quata would pack a lunch and we would stay out until the sun went down. One of my great joys was sitting in the shade of a large piñon tree in the cool days of October, without a care in the world. One fall, we gathered more than 150 pounds of the precious nuts, which we sold for fifty cents a pound to Wayne Hickey, who ran a small grocery store in Pie Town. Having seventy-five dollars was like being rich.

When my grandfather came along, he always took a large tarp and a long fishing pole. Winfield would spread the tarp under a tree my grandmother carefully selected, and pound the limbs and burs with the pole. Nuts, burs, small dead limbs—everything—came tumbling to the ground, where we separated the nuts from the burs and threw aside the small limbs and debris. The Diné sometimes used a similar practice but would sweep everything into wood-frame screens before separating the nuts from the rubble.

Another method of procuring the nuts was outright theft. Pack rats would often make nests from small pieces of wood and other forest wreckage in the forks of a juniper tree, near an old log, or at the base of a large piñon tree, in which they stored several pounds of nuts for the winter. Nut-seeking humans would rip into the nests, often killing the rats before making off with their precious nuts, which could total several pounds. I often wondered how long it took the poor rodents to gather all those nuts that my grandfather whisked away in minutes, but I did not dare tell anyone that I sympathized with the rats. They carried diseases and were to be killed on sight, but I still worried that in the winter they would go hungry and die a slow and terrible death. Taking their food supply seemed unnecessarily cruel. Why I developed empathy for animals at an early age, even animals as lowly as rats, I will never know, but it persisted over time.

My father said that when the family had the grocery store at Mangas, they would buy as many as one thousand to two thousand pounds of the nuts every year from Diné, Zuni, and Acoma pickers, who gathered the nuts in the vicinity of Pie Town and Mangas. Winfield paid eight cents a pound and then hauled the nuts, one pickup load at a time, sixty-five miles to Magdalena, where they were sold for twelve cents a pound. (A man from Magdalena frequently roamed the area around Pie Town, offering ten cents a pound in cash, and once bragged of purchasing five thousand pounds in under two weeks.) Often Native Americans traded the nuts for food and supplies. They would also exchange their colorful woven blankets for staples. Indeed, piñon nuts were often used as barter. The *Catron County News* announced in November 1933 that Corbin LeCroy had traded Wallace Phipps (both men were friends of my grandfather) some piñons for a young pig.

The income generated by Pie Town homesteaders and Native Americans from picking piñons was equal to that of local stock raisers. Harmon Craig told Clay W. Vaden, a field writer for the Works Progress Administration (WPA), that from September 20 to November 25 of 1936, he purchased $16,000 worth of piñons. Within twenty-five miles of Pie Town, between five hundred to a thousand Native Americans, mostly Diné and Zuni, were working for thirty local "white men," Craig said. Ninety percent of the piñons picked in the area were purchased by the Charles Ilfeld Company in Magdalena, who shipped them to a roasting plant in Albuquerque, before they were sent on to New York and sold to retailers.

PERILS OF WINTER

If there was money in picking piñons, there was tragedy, too, on both human and socioeconomic levels. Many of the large ranchers, such as Ellis McPhaul (part of the J. J. McPhaul ranching family), who owned a spread northeast of Pie Town, realized there were profits to be made in the tiny nuts, and they began hiring pickers from as far away as Mexico. "Noble red men" from the reservations were also employed, the *Catron County News* reported, using the stereotyping terminology of the day; the Native Americans worked long hours for meager wages. At one time, McPhaul had more than a hundred Native Americans working for him during the piñon harvest. "The Indians are kept in camps, supplies given them at exorbitant figures, and about all they make is robbed from them," the *Catron County News* proclaimed in 1937. "Then the heavy snows perhaps catch them in the mountains and freeze them half or entirely to death." A reporter for the *Quemado News* agreed, writing that "white men profiteer over them like a lot of buzzards."

The paper had it right. Tragedy struck during the 1931 harvest, with a terrible blizzard on November 10. A storm brought deep snow to the mountains and plateaus in the western part of the state. Two feet of snow fell in Pie Town and Mangas, and more in the mountains as the temperature dropped well below zero. In some places, there were drifts five and six feet high. As many as five hundred Diné, Zuni, and Acoma piñon pickers were caught and isolated in makeshift camps in the pine forests of Catron and Valencia Counties.

Many of the Native piñon pickers, including women and children, did not have warm-enough clothes for the debilitating conditions, and only scant supplies of food. Though there was plenty of wood to burn, their only cover was their wagon sheets. As their food supplies dwindled, many consumed the nuts they had picked and hoped to sell. In desperation, some killed their horses for food. In the frigid cold, they suffered intensely. Some of those stranded starved; others froze to death.

A relief party of fifty Navajo men set out from Crownpoint but they were stopped by eight-foot-high snowdrifts that blocked the roads. Realizing their friends and relatives were in desperate straits, another two hundred Navajo set out on horseback for Atarque, where several parties were known to be stranded, but the rescuers were hindered by the cold and the snow and forced to turn back. Weather conditions prohibited airplanes from dropping supplies.

After several weeks, supply trucks behind snowplows finally reached many of the Native American piñon pickers and brought them to safety. The following spring, a homesteader from Fence Lake saw one of the trails in the woods lined with dead ponies and "dead Navajoes in the forks of the piñon trees wrapped in blankets." The exact death toll was never known. Many of those who survived had to have their feet amputated as a result of frostbite.

It was a bad winter, the winter of '31. Every rancher lost stock. A large herd of sheep on the Magdalena Livestock Driveway on the

Plains of San Agustin froze to death. On the Navajo Nation, twenty-four thousand head of sheep and goats perished. By early February 1932, as much as seventy inches of snow had fallen.

Five years later, in January 1937, another blizzard hit the northwestern part of the state. Again, Native American pickers—this time, several thousand Diné—were trapped in the mountains and forced to survive on horse meat and piñon nuts. Snowdrifts reached eight feet high, and the temperature dropped to ten below zero. But this time, airplanes were able to drop supplies, and, later, trucks behind snowplows were able to reach most of the starving Navajo. Still, the tribe lost twenty thousand sheep.

While the experiences of the piñon pickers were extreme, winters were exacting on all the people of the high country. It was a season that could easily bring death to families. In January 1918, a trapper and prospector named Otto Davis froze to death after he was caught in a blizzard in the Gallo Mountains while looking for a team of horses. His ravaged body was not found until the spring thaw, after which he was buried in a lonely grave behind the Jewett Ranger Station, in what was then the Datil National Forest.

A couple of decades later, in January 1938, a fourteen-year-old boy from Mule Creek named Ted Adams was desperate for work and set out across the Mogollon Mountains on foot. He went by way of Willow Creek and the high country and was out three nights and four days in two feet of snow without food or matches to start a fire. Adams finally stumbled, half-alive, out of the mountains to a ranch near Beaverhead. His feet were black, badly frozen.

Struggling through deep snow, ranchers carried young Adams to Reserve for medical aid. The sheriff, Tom Summers, rushed the boy to the hospital in Silver City. Glancing at his frozen feet, physicians quickly concluded that both had to be amputated. Moreover, the boy's life was in danger. People from all over Catron and Grant Counties prayed for young Adams's recovery. Following the amputations, the lad held on for two weeks, but died suddenly on January 24.

A little over a month later, in February 1938, Mrs. Diego Gonzales started out to visit relatives, walking along the Zuni Salt Lake road that led northwest from Quemado. Caught in a blinding snowstorm, the worst in a decade, she failed to show up the next day, and as many as twenty-five people from Quemado hurried north to look for her. They searched for two days, finally finding her body near Nations Draw. She was dead, but her body was still warm. It was thought she had been dead for less than an hour. Gonzales had walked more than twenty miles. That same month, Prajedes Jaramillo, who suffered from dementia, strayed from home and died from exposure to the cold.

A year later, in early February 1939, a forty-two-year-old bachelor named William Burgess, who ranched on the Plains of San Agustin between Beaverhead and Horse Springs, set out walking from his house to his mailbox a few miles away. Caught in a blinding snowstorm, the most severe of the season, he became helplessly lost and staggered around for seventy-five miles in a circle before collapsing from exhaustion. A few days later, the state police found his frozen body twenty-five miles from his house.

One of the more tragic stories is that of Virginia Lopez, who left Aragon in the middle of the winter, shortly after World War I. With her infant daughter and two sisters, Lopez was hoping to visit her husband, who was in a sheep camp on the western edge of the Plains of San Agustin. On the way, the travelers were caught in a blinding blizzard, one of the worst in memory. Unable to see more than a few feet ahead in the glaring whiteout, the car Virginia was riding in slid into a ditch and the women were stranded. Thinking they were not far from the sheep camp, the three sisters commenced walking. Exhausted as the storm grew in fury, Virginia made a cave beside the road and left her infant wrapped in her coat and the daughter's blanket. With the snow still pounding and now coatless, Virginia became wearied, her hands and feet freezing. Knowing the sheep camp could not be far, she urged her sisters on through the storm. When the rescuers arrived, Virginia was still alive but died within hours, although her infant daughter, Anita, was safe in her wintry cave and lived to adulthood.

SUMMER STORMS

Blizzards weren't the only weather-related threat to people and their livelihoods in Pie Town. In the high country during the monsoon season, usually beginning in late June or early July, lightning storms were dangerous. Everyone seemed to know someone who had died from being struck directly or at least knocked down by lightning. At high noon on July 20, 1925, Eloy Sedillo was killed near Quemado. Lightning hit him on the head and went out the right foot of his badly burned body. In Demetrio Canyon on the north slope of Fox Mountain, southwest of Quemado, ten-year-old Lorenzo Chavez was attempting to retrieve a kitten from beneath a clothesline in a rainstorm when lightning struck and killed him.

One of my grandfather's closest friends and neighbors was Aaron Elisha "Shorty" Norton. Most people called him E. Norton, but my grandfather affectionately called him Shorty. They were about the same age and had both had seen combat during the Great War, my grandfather in the Thirty-Sixth Infantry Division and Shorty in the field artillery brigade of the Thirty-Fourth Infantry Division.

Born in Quanah, a small town just south of the Red River in north Texas, Norton went west at an early age with his father. They landed in Sierra Blanca, in the rugged and arid expanses of the Trans-Pecos, where Norton worked on a cattle ranch for several years. He was working at Rincon in Doña Ana County when he was drafted into the army during World War I. After the war, Norton made his way to the Mangas Valley, and in December 1923, he married Sarah Emma Naomi Mickey (who went by Naomi), twelve years his junior.

The Nortons rented property in Greens Gap before homesteading 160 acres on the Pipe Springs flat, where Shorty farmed several acres of beans and a small field of corn, and ran a small herd of cattle. Norton also became the unofficial keeper of Pipe Springs, frequently cleaning the springs, the only water supply for many of the homesteaders. In winter, he used his span of mules to pull the mail car through the snow over the Continental Divide at the north end of Little Alegres Mountain. A son, Ellis Aaron, or Ellie as the family called him, was born in 1926; a daughter, Thelma Naomi, followed three years later.

My grandparents' interaction with the Nortons is reflected in newspaper stories from the '30s. "The Thompsons and Nortons pulled and brought in their turnips Saturday. They had several large wagon loads," the *Catron County News* reported in November 1933. At the same time, "J. W. Thompson and E. Norton took a load of piñons to Pie Town Friday," the newspaper went on to say.

Although Norton could be stubborn and rough, my grandfather liked him. They would often travel together to Pie Town and to Magdalena for groceries and supplies. They worked for the Public Works Administration (PWA) on the Pie Town–Horse Springs road and the new Pipe Springs schoolhouse. Winfield also helped Norton dig a well and, on occasion, trap prairie dogs.

Norton could be defiant and combative. For some reason, he objected to a church being built across the road from his cornfield. During church services, my grandparents remembered, he would harness his mules and commence plowing the field only yards from the church, often cursing the mules in such vile language that any good Christian would be embarrassed and the church services would be interrupted or suspended. No one seemed to have the nerve to confront Norton.

Once, when Norton was squabbling over a property line with a neighbor, Francisco Sanchez, the two men resorted to fisticuffs and Norton was charged with assault and battery. The sheriff hauled him off to the justice of the peace in Aragon. When Norton refused to post bond, he wound up in the county jail in Reserve, where my grandfather bailed him out. Another time, Norton got into a feud with a different neighbor, Jim Stagner, and on January 2, 1943, Norton filed charges with the justice of the peace in Quemado, claiming Stagner had threatened to kill him. Justice of the peace records in Reserve indicate my grandfather also helped to pay Stagner's $300 bail. Two weeks after his arrest, Stagner filed charges against Norton, claiming his life had been threatened. Neither man appeared in court to testify, and the charges in both cases were dropped. For years, both men carried a revolver and neighbors feared the worse.

His confrontational characteristics aside, Norton could be sociable, and his family often hosted Saturday-night dances and pie suppers. In 1936, for example, the Nortons held an "old time country dance" on New Year's Eve to celebrate the end of leap year. The dance was lady's choice, and the men were responsible for bringing cakes. For several years, Norton also hosted goat-roping contests every Sunday.

Tragedy struck the Norton family during the monsoon season on August 13, 1943, shortly before my father went off to war. With tears streaming down his cheeks, sixteen-year-old Ellis came whipping his horse up to the front door of our old house. The horse was sweating heavily, gasping for air, and foaming at the mouth.

Ellis said his father had been struck by lightning. Norton and his son had been gathering some cows on horseback in one of the pastures, not far from their homestead on the Pipe Springs flats, when a sudden bolt of lightning struck the father. Through tears and muffled wailings, Ellis said he thought his father was dead. Through a rainstorm, my father rushed to the scene in the family pickup with the terrified son crying by his side. Norton lay dead, just as the son had said, his wife and daughter kneeling and praying by his side.

Norton was badly burned, his horse dead on the ground only yards away. In the late-afternoon mist, the saddle was still smoking. The horse's metal shoes had melted and the smell of burnt hair and flesh permeated the air. There was little my father could do but offer comfort. Other neighbors arrived and placed Norton's body in the family wagon, covered it with a sheet, and carried it to the Norton homestead less than a half mile away.

There was no cemetery at Pipe Springs, so Naomi decided to bury her husband in the Divide cemetery, near where her family lived on the north side of Big Alegres. Norton's friends gathered to dig a grave, but they hit solid rock after only a few feet and were forced to use dynamite to open a hole. A long funeral procession of neighbors, friends, and grieving family, some on horseback and others in wagons and cars, wound their way to the cemetery. E. Norton, a real character if there ever was one, was buried in the juniper-and-piñon-scented forest in the shadow of Big Alegres Mountain.

My grandfather's friend was, unfortunately, not the only person to succumb to this unlikely fate. When my family first settled in Martin Canyon, my father heard the tragic story of a young man named Willis B. Ditmore, a Forest Service employee who was struck by lightning and killed on Mangas Mountain. Not long after the turn of the century, the newly established Forest Service had erected a wooden tower on the mountain and a small cabin just below the tower. Ditmore was standing in the doorway of the cabin late one evening when he was struck and killed instantly. When the Forest Service had not heard from Ditmore in several days, they went to investigate and found his body.

There was only a rough trail to the summit of the mountain at the time, and Ditmore's body had to be tied over a mule and carried off the mountain like a sack of flour. "Your son's sudden death was a great shock to the organization, particularly coming as it did but a few days after another lookout on a distant mountain also lost his life in the same manner," district ranger Frank C. W. Poole wrote Ditmore's family.

OTHER TRAGEDIES

These deadly lightning strikes were just some of many accidents and other tragedies that claimed the lives of people in and around Pie Town. My father and grandfather were in Pie Town on February 17, 1947, when a fifty-three-year-old bean farmer, George Nichols, was killed by a falling tree. A month later, nine-year-old Boyd Peterson was run over by a road grader, his skull crushed. The following month, Elmo Bell, son of the popular Dr. M. C. Bell, committed suicide in Quemado.

At the Point of the Malpais, north of Pie Town, Gus Rainey and his Mexico-born wife, Myrtle, lost their two boys, Hale, sixteen, and Oriel, fourteen, when the sons went swimming in an earthen tank near the family homestead. The Raineys became alarmed when one of the boy's horses returned home without a rider. Their sons' hats and lunch were found on the edge of the pond and the family immediately feared the worst. The water was drained and the bodies of the two boys were found less than ten feet apart.

PASSING OF AN ERA

For the ranching industry in the Pie Town area, the decade of the 1930s represented the passing of an era, as several of the large ranch holders—the area's old-timers—passed away.

In June 1932, William Ray Morley Jr., who struggled for years to hang on to the vast Drag A Ranch near Datil, died in Pasadena, California, at the age of fifty-six. A former All-American football player and coach at Columbia University, he was a legend in the Datil area and a backbone of the ranching community. Despite her disdain for homesteaders, Morley's sister, Agnes Morley Cleaveland, authored one of the great classics set in the county, *No Life for a Lady*.

In August 1933, Peter Henry Goesling, one of the area's more popular and respected cattlemen, died at his Double Circle Ranch just east of Pie Town. Born in Herford, Germany, in November 1867, the legendary Goesling came to the United States and started in the sheep business in Texas and Oklahoma. In 1893, he moved to Colorado, where he operated a livery stable. Four years later, he moved to Springerville, Arizona, where he worked for a local merchant, Gustav Becker. After a few years, he had gone back into the sheep business at Winslow, before moving to the high country and investing in cattle.

Anastacio Baca, a wealthy pioneer who wielded a lot of political power in Quemado and who once ran large herds of sheep and cattle around Mangas, died in Albuquerque in late February 1934, after a long struggle with diabetes. Baca was widely known for his "kindness and charity." Relatives and friends packed the small Sacred Heart church in Quemado for his funeral mass.

In May 1936, Vess Jones, who owned the sprawling NH Ranch in the Gallo Mountains south of Quemado, died in an Albuquerque hospital at the age of fifty-two. Jones was in the process of shipping several head of cattle to Magdalena when he complained of not feeling well and was encouraged to see a doctor. He had said he did not have time, and died shortly thereafter.

In December 1937, another old-timer, Albert Steele, died at Horse Springs, alone, as he had lived for most of his life. Born in Joplin, Missouri, Steele went west after his parents passed away and quickly took to life on the range. At one time, Steele served as the supervisor of the large V Cross T Ranch; he claimed he drove more cattle to Magdalena than any other man. Between 1913 and 1915, he trailed fifty-four thousand head to market. Steele was also known as a respected cattle inspector.

On December 18, 1939, Bill Dahl, owner of the W-Bar Ranch south of Pie Town, a county commissioner, and a political force in the community for many years, died of a brain hemorrhage in an Albuquerque hospital at the age of fifty-two. Dahl had come to the United States from Sweden when he was fifteen, and over time became one of the wealthiest men in Catron County. Although he quarreled with his homesteader neighbors, he was elected county commissioner several times. Dahl sold his ranch and he and his wife moved to the Pacific Northwest, where he had first lived when he immigrated to the United States, but his Texas-born wife, Bessie, had insisted they return to the sunny Southwest. The couple and their four young children had settled near Albuquerque.

BLESSINGS OF THE NEW DEAL

The people of Pie Town and Catron County—the homesteaders, Native peoples, Hispanics, ranchers—all dealt with hardship and adversity as part of life in the high country. Facing tragedies brought on by natural disasters and other calamities, they were survivors. Life brought them blessings even as it brought challenges. Perhaps the greatest godsend the Pie Town homesteaders ever received came from afar. FDR's New Deal not only helped to restore the morale of a broken nation but also gave a distressed and downtrodden people, a citizenry who had little hope, a glimmer of confidence.

In December 1933, my grandfather went to work for the PWA on the Pie Town–Greens Gap road and the road to Mangas that wound around the wooded northern flanks of Big Alegres. It was the largest government project in the county. In May 1935, several hundred unemployed people in the county signed up for the WPA for similar work projects.

At one time, as many as 250 men were employed in the county on PWA or WPA projects. Wages were $3.20 cents a day, and Winfield got another $2.80 a day for his team of mules. The roads were built with mule-drawn fresnos and a road grader pulled by six mules. During the week, the workers lived in tents and did their own cooking; they went home to their families on the weekends.

Once the road projects were complete, several men, including my grandfather, began construction on a new Pipe Springs schoolhouse. A new site was selected across a dry arroyo on a small rise about three hundred yards north of the old school. The new school was built of hewn pine logs that were cut and dragged from the nearby hillsides.

In 1936, Public Works Administration workers pause while building the Pipe Springs schoolhouse. Grandfather Winfield is fifth from the right, leaning against the log structure. Others in the image include Les Thomas, Jake Dodson, Fred Caudill, George Rigsby, and Campbell P. Giles, among others. Only the foundation of the school remains today. Courtesy of the author.

For many years, my family proudly displayed a photo of my grandfather posing with several other workers in front of the half-built structure.

Besides the school at Pipe Springs, PWA workers built elementary schools, most of them one-room log structures, all over the northern part of the county at Mesa, Greer (not to be confused with the other Greer in Arizona, southwest of Springerville), Dyke, Greens Gap, and Divide (or what the homesteaders called Pumpkin Center). They constructed a school at Mangas out of adobe, with a big set of windows that looked south toward the adobe church and the mountains beyond. Although the structure was a lot more durable than the log schools, it took a lot longer to construct. PWA workers also constructed the Quemado–Trechado road and built a small, sturdy jail in Quemado. They also dug twelve community wells, improved cemeteries, and made war on prairie dogs. Many of the homesteaders also took advantage of the Soil Conservation and Domestic Allotment Act of 1935, which paid them to retire land that was windswept or badly eroded and to put it in a soil bank.

CIVILIAN CONSERVATION CORPS

The New Deal program that perhaps had the biggest impact on Catron County was the popular Civilian Conservation Corps (CCC). The CCC took unemployed and unmarried young men between the ages of eighteen and twenty-five, mostly from the large eastern cities, and put them to work conserving the nation's abundant natural resources. CCC recruits received thirty dollars a month, but twenty-five dollars of their pay was sent to support their families. Enrollees received military-style green uniforms and were supervised by army officers, who insisted on military discipline in their camps. What FDR was really doing, critics charged, was preparing young men for war. Although there was no evidence for these accusations, when World War II arrived in 1941, former CCC workers seemed always to be selected as corporals and sergeants.

The CCC did much to help develop the tenants of the modern environmental movement. In fact, it turned out to be the greatest conservation movement since Theodore Roosevelt put millions of acres of land into national forests, parks, and monuments. CCC camps in New Mexico provided more than fifty thousand young men from the state and across the nation opportunities to help their families financially and to learn new skills.

One of the high country's earliest CCC camps, Camp Chaffee, was established in the spring of 1933 in a large grove of ponderosa pines along the south bank of Tularosa River at the small Apache Creek community. Hundreds of young men from the camp toiled to construct roads in the national forest and to string thousands of miles of telephone lines. In 1934, they built a lookout cabin on Fox Mountain, southwest of Quemado, and forty-foot steel towers and cabins on El Caso overlooking Slaughter Mesa. They also constructed a steel tower on Mangas Mountain that replaced the old wooden tower erected by the Forest Service two decades earlier. The CCC had yet to complete a road to the summit of the mountain at that point, and the steel beams and lumber for the cabin were carried by pack trains of mules. My grandfather spent several summers spotting fires from the tower, and I worked there the summer after graduating from high school.

A camp dedicated primarily to soil conservation was constructed at Quemado in April 1939. Many of the young CCC workers who arrived in the area were from Pittsburgh, Pennsylvania. Brought to Magdalena by train, they were then taken by a dozen trucks to Quemado. The enlistees were "a nice-looking lot of youngsters . . . nice kids," the local newspaper noted. At Quemado, they joined seventy young men who had transferred from the Cuchillo camp in Sierra County.

One of the largest CCC camps was at Glenwood, sixty-seven miles northwest of Silver City; the camp opened in May 1936. The Glenwood camp had subsidiary camps at Willow Creek, in the heart of Gila country, not far from where Geronimo, the legendary Bedonkohe Apache leader, was born in June 1829. Because of heavy snows in the mountains, the Willow Creek camp was only operational in the summer.

In the summer of 1938, from a camp up Whitewater Creek, a CCC crew began constructing the Catwalk trail along the cliffs and giant boulders above the creek. The spectacular walking path was built mostly of planks secured on a large metal pipe that had once been used to supply a power mill constructed in 1893. The Silver City office also supervised a CCC camp in Reserve that was established in June 1933. At the same time, camps were inaugurated in Arizona at Blue, Springerville, and Buffalo Crossing, and in early 1938 at Greer, Arizona. A camp at Los Burros, Arizona, three miles north of McNary, was also established.

One of the last camps to be established in the area was on the eastern Plains of San Agustin, sixteen miles west of Magdalena. Many of the young men there were from Edinburg, Texas. Beginning in January 1936, the enlistees began fencing a sixty-five-mile stretch of land along the fabled Magdalena Livestock Driveway, also known as the Beefsteak Trail, so the ranchers in the western part of Catron could better drive herds to the stockyards and railhead at Magdalena. Varying in width, the stock driveway encompassed eighty thousand acres of land, mostly on the Plains of San Agustin. The CCC workers dug wells at ten-mile intervals to provide water for the thirsty herds traversing the dusty trail. The San Agustin CCC workers even had a basketball team that once competed with the Horse Springs Prairie Dogs and were victorious 16–9.

Continental Divide Altitude 8.300 Ft.
Near CAMP SANITARY Quemado, New Mexico.

During the Great Depression, Franklin D. Roosevelt's Civilian Conservation Corps offered employment to many young men from eastern cities. This image is between Pie Town and Datil, some thirty miles east of Quemado. The Continental Divide was later determined to be a mile east of Pie Town at an elevation of 7,796 feet. Courtesy of the author.

Camps such as those at Apache Creek and Glenwood taught both academic and vocational classes. Young men could enroll in courses in mechanics, carpentry, tractor operation, road construction, forestry, or even the use of dynamite, along with arithmetic, reading, and writing. More advanced students could take algebra, geometry, English, or sociology and psychology.

Many of the CCC recruits were able to return east to join their families for Christmas. Those who could not travel were taken in by the residents of such places as Quemado and Glenwood. One of the recruits from Pennsylvania assigned to the camp at Apache Creek fondly remember the Christmas of 1938: it was all quiet on Christmas Eve when the camp bugler sounded the well-recognized church call.

Several CCC trucks rolled up to the camps to take Protestant men to services in Reserve, while the Catholic men went to the small chapel upstream at the picturesque village of Aragon. There the parishioners huddled around a large bonfire in front of the Santo Niño de Atocha church, where the men smoked hand-rolled cigarettes and the villagers spoke in hushed tones. Women offered coffee and homemade pies. As midnight approached, several nuns led a line of schoolchildren, all dressed in their best Communion clothes, to the church, where they sang "Silent Night" in Spanish. Everyone applauded, after which one of the CCC truck drivers jumped onto the tailgate of one of the trucks and clapped his hands, prompting the English-speaking enrollees to sing their version of "Silent Night." "If I live to be a thousand, I do not think I will ever hear [that song] sung with such reverence and so much heart," the young recruit from Pennsylvania recorded. "There was not a dry eye in the crowd." Afterward, the enrollees joined in Mass and a grand procession around the church.

Apart from the federal programs operating in the region during the 1930s, some unemployed people in the county found work with one of the area's many sawmills. Sawmill owners at this time were clear-cutting private lands, leaving scars that would last a hundred years, especially around Pipe Springs and on the north slope of Big Alegres. There were also large timber sales in the national forests, especially in what had become the Apache National Forest south of Mangas and near Jewett Gap. In 1939, J. W. Tyra of Alamogordo received the bid to cut more than a million board feet of lumber in the Jewett Gap area alone. Tyra was hoping to supply the railroads with 750,000 crossties that he agreed to deliver to the railhead at Magdalena. A few of the homesteaders cut and shaped ponderosa pines into railroad crossties and dragged them to wagons and trucks at the base of Big Alegres, where the timbers were hauled to Magdalena and sold for twenty cents each. Some of the area's inhabitants cut fence posts from the scrubby juniper and were able to make as much as four dollars a day selling them to the large ranchers.

Both my father and grandfather took advantage of the seasonal work the Forest Service offered in fire suppression and on lookout duty at Mangas Mountain, El Caso, and Fox Mountain.

"STRAIGHT-OUT SOCIALIST OUTFIT"

Although many of the homesteaders took advantage of and relied on New Deal programs, others cursed FDR and Eleanor Roosevelt and everything the New Deal stood for. One of the more controversial New Deal programs was the 1933 Agricultural Adjustment Administration (AAA).

Grandfather Winfield (*left*) visits with one of his best friends, Whitey Reid, on Mangas Mountain. Three generations of Thompsons worked the lookout. Courtesy of the author.

Roosevelt's "brain trust" in Washington, DC, following the concept of supply and demand, concluded that the only way to drive agricultural prices higher was to drive production down. The government purchased cattle of drought-stricken ranchers and farmers, either to send to the market or to be killed and buried. Of an estimated 1.7 million cattle in New Mexico, the AAA purchased 95,713, about half of which were shot and the other half shipped to slaughterhouses. Many of the Pie Town homesteaders were given a slaughtered beef from one of the big ranches, which, one farmer commented, was much better than eating rabbit.

In February 1936, J. S. Bruton, who lived six miles south of Pie Town, wrote a lengthy letter to the *Magdalena News* criticizing the AAA. Farmers had not farmed all their lives to suddenly sit down and "let some college graduate come along and tell them what to do and how to make a living," Bruton argued. The New Deal had "ruined the younger generation," who had "lost confidence in themselves," he went on to say. The prevailing mood of those on the dole was that "the government owes me a living and I'm going to have it." FDR and the entire New Deal was a "straight-out Socialist outfit from beginning to end." Agnes Morley Cleaveland, a close friend to the wife of President Herbert Hoover and a noted author, had little doubt that the New Deal was destroying traditional American values and leading the country straight into a dictatorship.

MOVING TO MANGAS

My father was fifteen when the high school at Pipe Springs closed. Unable to attend high school in Quemado and too young for the CCC, he went to work for W. R. Thomas, felling logs with a crosscut saw on the north face of Big Alegres. That same year, Winfield sold the Martin Canyon property to a man named Walter Whinery and, with his friend Buford Badget, purchased a small, two-room log store just south of the village of Mangas, along with 120 adjoining acres, from F. A. Blake and Frank Christian. Within a year, my grandfather bought Badget's interest in the store. Filimon Baca once ran a store in the village, but it had been closed for several years, and for a few years the Thompson store prospered as the only option in the village.

Winfield added a bedroom, a kitchen, and a large front room to the back of the store, and even a small second story on top. He also dug a well, built a fireplace, and helped my grandmother fence a garden. Nearby he used his two mules and a wooden sled to clear rocks from twenty acres on a gently sloping hillside, where he planted beans and corn. On the north side of the kitchen, he constructed a small, homemade cooling box where food could be stored; damp cloths were sometimes wrapped around the milk to cool it quickly.

Winfield added gas pumps and made weekly trips to Magdalena to purchase wholesale supplies from the Charles Ilfeld Company. The Ilfelds were Jewish pioneer merchants who had played a major role in the social and economic development of nineteenth-century New Mexico.

As a result of their Texas roots and their love of FDR, the Thompsons were dyed-in-the-wool Democrats who attended local party meetings at Mangas and the county convention in Reserve. In contrast to later years, the county at the time was predominantly Democratic. I remember the family enthusiastically voting for Harry Truman in 1948, but the 1952 presidential race was different. In 1951, Truman had fired General Douglas MacArthur, a World War II hero, after the general took his argument for enlarging the war in Korea and even bombing China to the US Congress. The American public did not take kindly to Truman's decision, and as many as 7.5 million New Yorkers packed the streets to cheer MacArthur upon his return to the United States. Back in New Mexico, my father was similarly furious and gave me an "I Like Ike" button and told me to wear it. I asked him why he was supporting General Dwight D. "Ike" Eisenhower instead of the Democrat, Adlai E. Stevenson, and he said he had fought with Ike in Europe and the general was a good and honest man. I think my father also feared being dragged back into the military and was hoping Eisenhower would end the war in Korea, as he was promising.

CULTURAL BAGGAGE

Most of the homesteaders who arrived in the high country brought a lot of cultural baggage with them from Texas and Oklahoma. Prejudices, racism, and stereotypes abounded. In 1936, a "Negro minstrel" concert was well attended and enjoyed by all at the Collins School at the mouth of Bear Canyon near Pipe Springs. A "Negro program" at the Farm Bureau building in Pie Town in August 1939 drew a large crowd, who enjoyed the show. Exactly what this "Negro program" was is uncertain, but it is likely to have been a show by a traveling team of white people in blackface who performed comic skits and dances that lampooned African Americans as dim witted, lazy, superstitious, and happy-go-lucky, as most minstrel shows had done for decades. The blackface comedy skits were not unique to Pie Town—Sunny Slope and Trechado also indulged in the racist and dehumanizing humor.

When I was growing up, ghosts from the past frequently reared their ugly heads. Once, Quata was flipping through an old photo album of images of the family back in Texas. There were happy hunting scenes in the Big Bend, several places where the family had lived when my grandfather sold furniture for his uncle, and a camp on the Llano River where the Thompsons and their neighbors went fishing in the summer. Several of the photographs were of Quata proudly posing with a much taller, darker woman. "Who is that?" I innocently asked. "Why, that is N——Jane." Quata responded. "She loved fishing and she always went with us. She was one of the nicest persons you could ever meet. We just thought the world of her. She was just like family."

Once, an adjoining rancher bought a small herd of Black Angus cattle and my grandfather expressed concerns that the "n——" bull in the herd might get through the fence and breed with his Herefords. This came from a man who denounced segregation and idealized Jackie Robinson and the legendary Leroy Robert "Satchel" Paige, who, at that time in the early 1950s, was still pitching at the age of forty-seven. I vaguely remember Quata and Winfield talking about having attended the lynching of a black person somewhere in Texas. It was gruesome and they had regretted it, they said.

One of the wealthy Texas oilmen who came to hunt deer around Pie Town every year was Jake Hancock, a staunch conservative who made no effort to hide his racist thoughts. During the uranium boom of the early 1950s, Hancock formed a small exploration company, GeTex, with a dentist friend from Georgia. Hancock purchased a green jeep and an expensive scintillator, and hired my father and grandfather to help him scour the northern part of the county for uranium. On October 10, 1955, I had tagged along, as usual, when they were prospecting the sandrock country about twenty miles north of Pie Town. They gathered for lunch around a transistor radio to listen to the first game of the World Series. Once again, the Brooklyn Dodgers were challenging the New York Yankees. My grandfather was a big Dodgers fan, largely because of Jackie Robinson, while Hancock was a rabid fan of the Yankees, largely because they had no "Negro" players, he said. An ardent segregationist, Hancock hated Eleanor Roosevelt and thought Franklin D. Roosevelt was a socialist and that his New Deal had ruined the country forever.

My grandfather and Hancock wagered five dollars on the game, a lot of money at the time. It was the top of the eighth inning; the Yankees were leading by two runs and the Dodgers were batting with two out and Jackie Robinson on third. Robinson made a daring dash for home against the Yankee left-hander Whitey Ford. The Yankee catcher, Yogi Berra, made the tag but Robinson was safe. "Anyone who would let that goddamned n—— steal home ought to lose!" Hancock angrily blurted out, throwing his hat on the ground. "Black son of a bitch." I will never forget the anger and hate in his face. Although the Dodgers lost the game and my grandfather lost five dollars, the Dodgers went on to win the series in seven games, their first championship in franchise history.

Around Pie Town, in the mountains of New Mexico, the Old South never seemed to be far away. Many of the homesteaders spoke in slang and used Southern idioms. When I sometimes set goals that seemed excessive, my grandfather would remark that I was "whistling Dixie." Or, if he had a laborious task, it was a "long row to hoe." Someone who was young and short was "knee high to a grasshopper." If you were doing something exceedingly slow, you were "slower than molasses in the winter." If you were doing something rapidly, such as eating fast, you were "goin' to town." If the family had a steady income, we were in "tall cotton." Anyone perceived as hypocritical or to be practicing a double standard was like the "pot callin' the kettle black." If the task at hand was difficult, Winfield could only get it done if the "Lord was willing and the creek don't rise." One of the idioms I particularly

My mother, Jo Lee, and I shortly after World War II. My mother never mentioned her mixed-race Cherokee father, who robbed more than fifteen Oklahoma banks and five trains, and spent fourteen years in Leavenworth Federal Penitentiary. Courtesy of the author.

before being relegated to the privy when a new set of catalogs arrived in the spring. It was always great fun to look through the catalogs and dream of a more luxuriant world beyond Pie Town and Mangas.

When most of the homesteaders moved away during and after World War II, my grandfather was unable to sustain his small store. Instead of the weekly trips to Magdalena for wholesale goods from the Charles Ilfeld Company, at the end of the fire season, my grandparents and I made an annual August pilgrimage to Socorro. The weather in the Rio Grande Valley was always warm, and the Socorro plaza was a delight with its green grass and tall cottonwood trees. There were benches where I would pause with Winfield and Quata and just watch the world go by. There was a theater on the west side of the plaza, and on rare occasions, we attended an early matinee. On the east side of the plaza was a bar and a Buster Brown shoe store where I once got a pair of new shoes. On the south side was a variety store and a drugstore.

In front of the drugstore, Winfield once found a large money bag containing several hundred dollars and countless personal checks. It was obvious someone had been on their way to make a bank deposit and lost the bag. We walked a few blocks to the bank and the tellers were able to identify the individual attempting to make the deposit. I had never been as proud of my grandfather in my life. I often thought of how easy it would have been to just take the cash and throw the checks in the trash.

One of the biggest delights during the Socorro trip was the stop at Evett's drugstore in Magdalena on the way home. We would be winding our way slowly up Sedillo Hill toward the Magdalena Mountains when Winfield would ask the magic question that he always asked: "How about we stop in Magdalena for something to eat?" Winfield and Quata would order hamburgers, but I always had a grilled cheese. Equally delightful were the foaming fountain Cokes served in a large, bubble-shaped glass. Sometimes Winfield would stop at Salome's Store on the west side of town for a loaf of bread and a few groceries. My grandfather liked Salome, a Syrian immigrant who had come to Magdalena in 1911 and was one of the town's more successful entrepreneurs.

DAMNED BANKERS

Largely because of the collapse of thousands of banks during the Great Depression, which resulted in millions of families losing their savings, my grandfather never trusted banks or bankers. "Someone dressed in a suit has to be up to no good," he would often say. "They think of themselves as better than you are and they will try to cheat you." He would frequently quote Woody Guthrie's poetic ballad of the outlaw Pretty Boy Floyd:

> Yes, as through this world I've wandered
> I've seen lots of funny men;
> Some will rob you with a six-gun,
> And some with a fountain pen.

Every time my grandfather earned a few dollars, he would take the money and bury it. "You can never tell what might happen," he would say, fearing another depression. Winfield kept track of every penny he spent and every dollar he made, and he seemed to worry about money all the time. He had a deep fear of being poor again and losing all he possessed. He saved everything, including tin cans he hammered flat and placed in cardboard boxes. He would straighten rusty nails he pried out of boards and store them in coffee cans. "You never know," he would say. "We may need them someday." He even saved string and paper bags. He and my father built a garage out of rusty roofing tin they received as compensation for putting new tin on the school in Pie Town.

Just as the fear of another economic catastrophe haunted my grandfather, decades after he passed away, I could see this trait in my father too, who would store cases of sardines, Vienna Sausage, and potted meat. If we ate at a restaurant and someone didn't eat everything on their plate, he would become upset, often referring to the family surviving on beans and corn bread during the Depression. He always saw security in material objects. When he finally got a steady job with the county and then the Forest Service, and was able to purchase a new car, he never drove it. It just sat there in the driveway while he drove his old, beat-up, worn-out pickup truck. I once asked my father what he planned to do with all the food he had stored. Parroting what he had learned from my grandfather, he commented, "You never know what might happen." The Depression had inflicted deep psychological scars on my family that never healed, as was the case with many American families.

Another trait my grandfather passed on to my father was punctuality. It was always better to be thirty minutes early for a meeting than five minutes late. Once when my father had some business at the courthouse in Reserve, we left Mangas before sunup and arrived in Reserve at seven in the morning. We waited on the street for over an hour for the courthouse to open. One year when we went to the state fair in Albuquerque, my father insisted that we leave at three o'clock in the morning. When we approached Magdalena, it was still dark, and I remember being half-asleep and looking out the window, seeing all the lights in the town and thinking that it had to be the largest city in the world.

BRAVE NEW WORLD

After hunting season was over and all the hunters had gone back to Texas and Oklahoma, I always looked forward to Christmas. A few days before the magical day each year, my grandfather would take an axe from the toolshed and we'd head off into the woods, often tramping through snow. He would cut a small piñon, and I had the honor of dragging the tree back to the house. My father would attach some boards to the base of the tree and place it under the large windows in the front room, not far from the fireplace.

My mother was always in charge of decorating the tree. We never had any electric Christmas lights, even after we acquired electricity, but she would hang handcrafted ornaments and some aluminum icicles on the branches. For Christmas dinner, we usually had a turkey left over from hunting season. Santa Claus always left me socks or underwear, or, in a good year, a shirt, mittens, or even a coat.

When I was about five or six, I woke up early one Christmas morning and rushed into the front room, where my grandfather always had a roaring fire going and in the warm glow, the Christmas tree would glimmer in the morning light. I could always judge how the family was doing in a particular year by the number of presents under the tree.

Under the tree that year, Santa Claus had neatly arranged fifteen small plastic soldiers, each about two inches tall, all lined up and ready for battle. For years to come, these brave soldiers waged war against the "Krauts" and the "Japs," terms that would not be used today. The battles were contested in a dry arroyo, where the sand was soft and aerial attacks were easy. Here was my D-Day, my Battles of the Bulge, Iwo Jima, and Okinawa, all wrapped into one, all as ferociously fought as the battles had been in the real world a few years earlier. In every confrontation, the Americans decisively defeated the Germans or the Japanese, who were represented by sticks in the sand. I don't remember a single American soldier ever being killed or wounded in a battle. But the enemy always took a terrible beating. Small rocks and clods of earth, pine cones, or whatever else I could find rained down on the enemy. In the warm summer days after school was out, the fight would take an hour or more, but the enemy always lost.

COYOTES

The first week of the summer recess in early June when I was about six or seven, I approached the arroyo with my plastic soldiers ready for a major battle and saw something that remained etched in my brain forever. The breeze must have been in the right direction and I must have made little noise in approaching the arroyo. My trusty dog Rusty was probably sleeping at the house or distracted or just taking the day off. As I looked down into the arroyo, there was a female coyote with two nursing pups. Nearby, the coyote had dug a den halfway up the side of the arroyo. The pups were scampering about on my sandy battlefield, joyfully snapping at one another, while their mother stood watchfully by. At times, they tried to indulge the mother in their play, but she just stood there. After a few minutes, they gave up their game and went back to nursing. Something in the gray eyes of the coyote was grand and joyful. If there could be elation in an animal's demeanor, this had to be it—it was my *National Geographic* moment.

When I got back to the house, I was careful not to say anything to reveal what I had seen. This was an era when all predators were considered enemies of farmers and ranchers, and with the encroachment of civilization, government hunters and trappers lurked about. For years, the government had paid a bounty for killing predators. The AAA was continuing to pay ranchers to eradicate prairie dogs. "Greens Gap and Oak Springs ranchers are all busy poisoning prairie dogs," the *Quemado News* reported in July 1937.

One of my father's friends from Pie Town was a government hunter who not only killed coyotes and prairie dogs but trailed mountain lions with his pack of dogs for days before the dogs would tree the frightened lion and he would shoot the animal. Among an abundance of mounted antlers, photos of proud hunters posing with their dead lions or bears hung on restaurant walls in Pie Town, Datil, Quemado, and Reserve. Such scenes were the ultimate public display of masculine prowess.

I once listened to the Pie Town government hunter relate to my father how he poisoned coyotes and prairie dogs. Fears that the hunter would come and shoot or poison the coyote and her pups near the house haunted me for weeks. But I kept my secret, and a month or so later when I trekked down to the arroyo, the mother and her pups were gone.

LAST GRIZZLY BEAR

Undoubtedly, the most admired hunter in the county was Montague Stevens, a one-armed pioneer who had once owned a sheep and cattle ranch in Catron County the size of the state of Rhode Island. Stevens also brought the first grand piano to the county.

The son of a British army general, born in India in 1859 and educated at Cambridge, Stevens came to the United States in 1880. He was immediately attracted to the awesome beauty of the mountains and vast grasslands in the western part of New Mexico, the last unsettled area in the territory. Although a hunting accident cost him his left arm, Stevens seemed to enjoy killing with a frenzy that rivaled that of Ernest Hemingway or Theodore Roosevelt. In 1893, Stevens took part in the "sport" with Frederic Remington and Nelson Miles, and in 1943, he published a macho account of his hunting attributes, *Meet Mr. Grizzly: A Saga on the Passing of the Grizzly Bear*, that went through several editions. For ten days in 1895, Agnes Morley Cleaveland hunted with Stevens in the Datil Mountains; she proudly posed with one of the two grizzlies Stevens killed.

Texas folklorist J. Frank Dobie, who also praised the hunting exploits of another Catron County resident and noted trapper and hunter, Ben Lilly, found Stevens's *Meet Mr. Grizzly* to be a superb set of recollections by the "most mature" of any ranchman in the West at the time. Hunting magazines acclaimed Sevens, who hunted on horseback with a pack of hounds and boasted of killing as many as nineteen grizzlies. According to these publications, Stevens was a "brilliantly innovative 1890s houndman" and a "hero of the Gila country."

For decades, cattlemen and sheep raisers were determined to exterminate the grizzly. Even the government got into the act of extermination, placing the grizzly, along with prairie dogs, mountain lions, and wolves, on the death list and offering a bounty for their carcasses. By the end of World War I, there were fewer than sixty grizzlies in the Southwest. A decade later, it was estimated there were only twenty-eight, and a decade after that, they were down to ten—and then the great bear was gone. Winfield and many others were convinced that Stevens killed the last grizzly in the state, but it appears the bear held out in the remote recesses of Gila country into the 1930s.

In *Meet Mr. Grizzly*, Stevens included a photo titled *The End of the Trail*, depicting a massive old bear he called the Jewett Gap Grizzly lying dead near the summit of Fox Mountain, his enormous head and nostrils half-buried in the snow. Of all the animals that once inhabited the state, none elicited more respect and fear than the grizzly bear.

Sometime after 1902, after a neighbor trying to kill coyotes with a strychnine-laced steer carcass accidently poisoned Stevens's beloved hounds, Stevens vowed to never hunt grizzlies again. "I became a zealous convert to their preservation to prevent so noble an animal becoming extinct," he wrote. Stevens kept up his conservation crusade until his death in Albuquerque in 1953 at the age of ninety-four, but it was too late. In my hikes into the hills and mountains, I often wondered what it would be like to come across an eight-hundred-pound grizzly that could bash in my skull with a single swat. But there seemed to be something missing with the great bear gone.

ALDO LEOPOLD

Later, at Western New Mexico University, I read John Muir for the first time and became a ready disciple. Aldo Leopold's *A Sand County Almanac* was even more inspirational. I was so captivated that I reread the book until the covers wore off. The book had been published in 1949, shortly after Leopold's death, and it was read by millions of people interested in the growing environmental movement. I memorized what was probably the best line in the book: "A thing is right when it preserves the integrity, stability, and beauty of the biotic community. It is wrong when it tends otherwise."

In 1909, the Yale-educated Leopold was assigned to the Forest Service's Region 3 in the Apache National Forest in eastern Arizona and western New Mexico. Here Leopold came to love the "massive pines and firs" of the White Mountains. He was especially attracted to Escudilla Mountain, the third-highest mountain in Arizona, where he remembered the tassel-eared squirrels romping among the massive pines and firs.

These were the days, as Leopold remembered, when no one passed up the opportunity to kill a wolf. While eating lunch on the high rimrock near Escudilla one day, Leopold and his fellow rangers spotted a pack of wolves. Leopold was young and immature and "full of trigger-itch." In seconds, "we were pumping lead into the pack," he wrote. His rifle empty, "the old wolf was down, and a pup was dragging a leg into the impassible slide-rocks." Leopold "reached the old wolf in time to watch a fierce green fire dying in her eyes." "I realized then," he continued, "and have known ever since, that there was something new to me in those eyes—something known only to her and to the mountain." For days after reading that passage, I would lay awake at night in my dormitory in Silver City staring at the ceiling, seeing in the darkness the "fierce green fire" dying in the wolf. In those days, you grew up killing things. It was not until later that you learned that you loved what you had killed.

GREEN SCHWINN

The Christmas when I was ten proved to be the most memorable of my childhood, even more significant than when Santa brought the plastic soldiers. The front widow of the hardware store in Quemado had on display a beautiful green Schwinn bicycle. I badly wanted that bike, but I realized the thirty-five-dollar price tag was way beyond anything my family could afford. But every time my father or grandfather stopped at the store, I would rush in to stand and stare at the bicycle, dreaming of what a great joy it would be to ride it about the Mangas countryside. A week or two before Christmas, my father stopped at the store and the bicycle was gone. I was saddened, and envious of whoever had acquired the bicycle. At the same time, there was a sense of pleasure at the joy it was certain to bring to the lucky owner.

That Christmas, I arose before dawn as I always did and rushed into the front room, where my grandfather had the fire blazing, expecting to receive some underwear or socks, or perhaps an apple or orange, or even some nuts and candy in the stocking my mother always hung on the mantel. Right there in front of the Christmas tree was the big, shiny green Schwinn. My grandfather said he thought he heard Santa Claus on the rooftop during the night and that the fellow was certain to have brought the bicycle down the chimney.

I had long since stopped believing in Santa Claus, as well as the Easter Bunny and the tooth fairy. My announcing that only ignorant, superstitious children believed in Santa Claus had resulted in a fistfight at Pie Town Elementary School, one of many such fights I distinctly remember losing.

But that Christmas reaffirmed my belief in Santa. It did not matter if the jolly, old, white-bearded fellow had brought the bicycle down the chimney or pedaled it through the front door—I had to be the luckiest kid in Catron County. That bicycle gave me a mobility I had only dreamed of. It was the best Christmas ever.

"There is nothing he won't buy that kid," I overheard my father whisper to my mother later that evening, an obvious reference to my grandfather's buying the bicycle. But I professed to believe in Santa Claus for several more years, fearful that if I quit, there would be no more gifts.

RANCHO DE SAN JOSÉ

Learning to ride the bike resulted in several crashes and a lot of scratches and bruises, but I quickly mastered the art and was off on my way, exploring the Mangas Valley. I felt like the Comanche or Lipan Apache acquiring the horse for the first time, or Lewis and Clark standing at Lemhi Pass looking west toward the Pacific. I would speed off down the dirt road, pedaling as fast as I could with Rusty panting along behind. My mother would sometimes pack a bologna sandwich for me, and I would cycle to the base of a small mountain or hill and then hike to the summit.

Rancho de San José near Mangas was built only yards from one of the largest springs in the area. The ranch grew to become a small village of rock-and-adobe structures, including a store and church. Courtesy of Cristine Romero Ellis.

The Catholic church at Mangas as I knew it in the 1950s. Only a pile of weathered adobes remain of the structure today. Courtesy of the author.

I frequently stopped at the old adobe church at Mangas or made my way south to the Rancho de San José, the most magical of all places—the abandoned, two-story whitewashed headquarters of the José Ygnacio Aragon sheep dynasty. On the edge of a large vega, the crumbling ruins were only a shell of what the property had once been. The sturdy adobe walls were largely intact, as were the stairs to the second-story hallway and eight small bedrooms. Graffiti scarred the soft adobe, but you could still envision the dignity and grandeur of what had once been the epicenter of a ranching empire. Because of its whitewashed walls, everyone called the place the White House.

Nearby were several smaller buildings constructed of stone, the homes of the employees, whose roofs and doors having long since collapsed. Walking through the grove of stately cottonwood trees shading the ruins, it was evident that the Aragons had led a life radically different from the men who herded their sheep.

Also nearby was an old Catholic church constructed of rock and adobe. It seemed much sturdier than Mangas's adobe church, which seemed to always be melting away. Behind the church was a cemetery with wooden crosses and headstones. Some of the crosses lay rotting and splintered on the ground. There were several small graves, outlined by rocks, the last resting place of infants. For many years after World War I, the two churches in the Mangas Valley were serviced by Father Albert Canova, a Swiss-born priest, who, with great energy and joy, drove his Model T over wagon tracks and goat trails through the cold and snow in winter and the rains, heat, and dust in summer, all the way from Monticello in Sierra County.

A fence had once enclosed the church and the cemetery, but it had fallen down and cattle had grazed and trampled on the graves, and the crosses and the names of many of the dead had long since disappeared. It all seemed so very sad. I often wondered about these people—who they were, how they had died, what they looked like, who their families were, their joys and sorrows. The graves of the children were particularly saddening, some of their deaths likely dating back to the Spanish flu of 1918. If God existed in Mangas Valley, he seemed merciless. Grandmother said God always acted in mysterious ways and for a reason. But I could never think of a reason for why these children had to die, and I thought about it for a long time.

Not far from the main house was a dipping vat where thousands of sheep were once immersed in chemical solutions to prevent parasites. There was also a freshwater spring nearby, enclosed by a concrete wall. Lily pads grew in the crystal-clear waters of the spring, and you could look down and see tiny minnows darting about and water bubbling up out of the sand. Long-legged water striders raced about on the water between the lily pads.

The spring emptied into a small acequia that circled around the meadow through the rabbitbrush into what had once been a large garden and the gnarled remains of a small orchard. Two of the old trees still clung to life, and I once picked their small, dark-colored fruit. I could

The abandoned church at Rancho de San José. The structure still stands, but it is badly in need of restoration. Courtesy of the author.

not resist eating one or two but carried the rest home, not knowing what they were. My mother said they were plums and it was rare that such trees bore fruit in the valley. At such a high altitude, the trees would bloom in the spring, she said, but a frost always nipped the buds.

I would often sit here for hours under the tall cottonwoods, taking in the view, amazed at the profusion of summer flowers, but sometimes just watching the white-faced cows in the meadow below. Rusty would scamper among the ruins chasing rabbits or just lie nearby under the trees, resting up for the long trek home. The views from old Rancho de San José were wonderful in all directions. To the south, across the large meadow, rose the top of the Mangas Mountains and the lookout tower on the western summit where my grandfather frequently worked in the summer. Immediately behind the springs, the rocky south face of Cat Mountain and the eastern rimrock of Slaughter Mesa rose abruptly out of the valley.

In the fall, when it was sharp and cold and beautiful, the leaves of the cottonwoods turned golden, and by winter they lay on the ground and gave off an aroma that was both intoxicating and exhilarating, similar to the fragrance of quaking aspens on the summit of the mountains. The yellow bark of mature ponderosa pines had an equally intoxicating vanilla smell following a monsoon shower.

ALONG MANGAS CREEK

Up Mangas Creek a short distance south of the White House, the Frank Castillo family still lived in a big, two-story house in another grove of cottonwood trees. A half mile farther up, the Gabaldon family had also once lived in a grove of cottonwoods, and farther yet, the Gallegos family had lived in several small, rundown adobes that had been another Aragon ranch. A tall, flat, volcanic-topped peak overlooked the valley. One summer day, Rusty and I made it to the top of the peak, where we discovered circular ruins built by a people who had long since abandoned the valley. The ruins were identical in size and height to those on the peak at El Caso Spring.

Just up the creek from the Gabaldon Ranch was the forest boundary and the Mangas ranger station. At least, everyone called it a ranger station, but it was really a work center for the main Jewett Ranger Station across Slaughter Mesa to the southwest. When my grandfather worked here, whenever he was not on lookout duty on Mangas Mountain or El Caso, he lived with my grandmother and me in the modest, two-room structure. The building was set among some ponderosa pines on a small rise only steps from the headwaters of Mangas Creek. Along the creek grew a dense thicket of willows. A band of busy beavers once made their home there, building a lodge and a large dam, but for some unexplained reason, the Department of Game and Fish gave someone permission to trap the beavers.

My grandmother said the volcanic soil along the creek was better than where we lived at Mangas, and she always planted a small garden down by the creek. For water, there was a well and hand pump, and the cabin was connected to the Mangas lookout and Jewett Ranger Station by an old crank telephone. Two long rings and one short ring meant someone was trying to contact my grandfather. When the on-duty lookout spotted a fire, the ranger would call, and Winfield would pull down a map from the wall, spot the exact location of the fire, saddle Shorty, his black-and-white horse, gather some tools from the toolshed, pack some rations in a couple of saddlebags, and ride away. While he was gone, I lived alone with my grandmother for as much as a week or ten days at a time. We would not have a single visitor; we were isolated from the outside world, sleeping in one room and cooking in the other, and eating at a small folding table.

I helped Quata tend her small garden, bring in juniper wood for the cookstove, and raise the American flag every morning and lower it at sunset (and she taught me how to properly fold the flag). We would sometimes venture off to search for pottery and arrowheads beneath the sandstone bluffs on the east side of the creek.

In the brisk early mornings or in the late evenings, we could see mule deer watering in the creek or grazing on nearby hillsides. Flocks of turkey also came to the creek for water. A beautiful, shiny tom with gray, black, and reddish feathers would lead the way with the hens and chicks following behind. The toms would make a loud gobbling noise heard up and down the creek. The hens made a less noisy clicking sound. My grandmother said a hen was called a jenny and a tom was called a jake. There in the small cabin, I remember sleeping on an old army cot and listening to the coyotes howling in the night or, after a summer rain, the frogs croaking in the meadow. For a small boy, it was all very exciting.

SOCIAL LIFE

From 1929 to 1942, Pie Town boomed. There was a homesteader on almost every section of land. But World War II changed everything. In September 1940, the first peacetime conscription in United States history required men ages twenty-one to thirty-five to register for the draft. Although for Americans the war was an ocean away, in Catron County, 681 young men signed up. On October 29, 1940, in Washington, DC, a blindfolded Henry Stimson, secretary of war, reached into a glass bowl and pulled out the first capsule. From a nearby podium, President Franklin D. Roosevelt announced the number drawn: 158. Across the country, 6,175 young men held that number, including twenty-seven-year-old Harvey G. Staggs of Pie Town. The Oklahoma-born Staggs worked for Joe Keele at the grocery store and helped his wife, eighteen-year-old Lois, with the Pie Town Café. With number 192, Lorenzo Montoya Garcia of Glenwood was the second man drafted in the county.

The thread that held Pie Town together in the years before the war was the community's rich social and religious life. The small village even had a literary society that met regularly. The Baptist church in Pie Town was well attended, and several of the small satellite communities had itinerant preachers. Members of the Church of Christ met at the Farm Bureau building. Quemado, Mangas, and Aragon had Catholic churches, all served by the same priest.

At Pie Town in December 1940, with the drums of war beating in Europe and FDR elected to an unprecedented third term, the Girl Scouts put on a drama production combined with a pie supper, the proceeds going to purchase a piano for the community. The scouts were able to raise $11.50 and, combined with the pie supper, proceeds amounted to $36.45.

Led by President Joe Keele and Vice President Harmon L. Craig, the Catron County Farm Bureau had as many as 176 members that met once a month to discuss everything from prairie dog eradication and soil conservation to state and national politics. In January 1939, eighty home-steaders gathered at the Farm Bureau building to hear presentations by both Keele and Craig. Women met separately for quilting bees or fur-niture repair demonstrations. Pie suppers, house-raising parties, all-day community singing contests, and bingo parties were common. Mother's Day in May always drew a crowd, as did a Halloween party in October.

Forty-two (a type of dominoes common in Texas) parties and summer picnics in the nearby mountains were all common. In the cold winter months, there were all-night square dances. Following the directions of a caller, four couples would dance to the lyrics "Chase the rabbit, chase the squirrel, chase that pretty girl 'round the world." Such gatherings not only provided recreation but strengthened community bonds and helped alleviate the terrible loneliness that was so common in a community settled by refugees. In the summer, there were softball and baseball games. After their fields had been harvested in September, entire families caravanned to Farmington and Aztec in the northwest-ern part of the state, where they purchased and picked fruit for canning. The entire trip, Russell Lee recorded, was "a festive occasion."

Then came the drought of the 1950s, the dry years, the late freezes in the spring and early frosts in the fall that frequently ruined the bean crops. People began to drift away. Even before many of the young men in the community went off to war, attendance at Farm Bureau events had started to decline. In time, the organization ceased to exist. The small building that had served for several years as the community center and school is one of the few original structures that stands today.

The Pie Town I came to know in the 1940s and '50s was only a relic of its former self. "The Iris, the Bouncing Betts, the Holly Hawks so lovingly tended, came up for a few years, and then they were no more. All our dreams vanished," a homesteader remembered. "For less than half a century the land provided homes, piñon and cedar wood for our fuel, pine logs for our houses, lumber for many small sawmills, jobs for a few at small pay. Then 'poof!' it was all gone. Our mountain lives were no more. We left because the summer rains and winter snows failed to come for a number of years and we could no longer stay. So we moved away."

The December 7, 1941, attack on Pearl Harbor changed Pie Town and the country forever. Many of the homesteaders either went off to war or found employment in the growing Sunbelt cities of El Paso, Albuquerque, and Phoenix, or in the defense industry on the West Coast. During the war, New Mexico attracted a multitude of military instillations that offered jobs, especially at the numerous air bases, many of which remained during the Cold War.

During this time, many of the homesteaders also sold their meager plots of land to the larger ranchers for as little as a dollar an acre. Some refused to sell their land but burned their cabins and dugouts to avoid taxes. Some of the bean farmers hung on following a terrible drought in 1945, the driest year since the Dust Bowl, but were finished off by the prolonged drought of the 1950s. Bob Magee, son of Guy Magee, who said he got his PhD in "Post Hole Digging," remembered how "it just kept getting drier and drier." Farming became a thing of the past, and the last of the bean farmers drifted away, never to return.

For Doris and Faro Caudill, the Thoreauvian ideal of self-reliance that had been at the very center of Russell Lee's epic photographs of the couple became a nightmare. Only two years after Lee's photographs began to appear in print, Faro became ill and the couple and ten-year-old Josie left their homestead. As the family departed for the last time, Faro scrawled a melancholy message on the gate: "Farewell, old homestead. I bid you adieu. I may go to hell but I'll never come back to you."

A deathblow to the original townsite came in 1942, the year I was born, when a new asphalt highway bypassed Pie Town to the north. The town moved northward too. Several new businesses sprang up by the new highway, including three gas stations and adjacent garages. F. E. Younger built a general merchandise store. Wayne Hickey, who ran the store and post office at Omega for a time, built a new structure on the north side of the highway, where he sold groceries, dry goods, and hardware. My father and grandfather always stopped there, often only to purchase a loaf of bread or a few nails. Frank Wilson ran a bar. Estelle Duggins had a confectionary. For a while at the old townsite, Bill Perry operated a skating rink at the old beanery, and Marvin Few showed movies on Saturday nights at the Farm Bureau building.

Before the interstate highway system was constructed, traffic through Pie Town in the 1950s was still brisk, although Route 60 was overshadowed by the legendary Route 66 to the north. Many of those who drove across the Continental Divide and past the few businesses in the new town did not know there had once been another Pie Town.

After the war, Pie Town declined rapidly. In 1947, with his health failing and the mercantile business on the verge of collapse, Craig, who had been the very heartbeat of the community for two decades, sold his interest in the general store business to Keele, and moved with Theora to Socorro, where he bought a small farm. He died there from a heart attack in June 1958 but was returned to Pie Town for burial. Keele built a new cinder block store only a few yards east of the old store and tried to hold on.

DRY YEARS

In 1947, Quemado's *Catron County News* (actually published in Magdalena) featured a Pie Town gossip column entitled Pie Town Crusts by Lillian Cobb, along with other columns entitled Frisco River Road, Apache Creek Flood, Datil Doings, and Luna Beams. By 1941, there was not enough advertising to sustain the newspaper, and it ceased to exist.

By the early 1950s, the climate changed, much as it had during the Dust Bowl years. There was less snow in the winter and little moisture for the spring planting. The drought seemed to go on forever and, in time, engulfed the entire Southwest. It was the time it never rained. The Pie Town corn and pinto bean fields, after two decades of rich harvests, were left abandoned.

The farming and ranching economy went into decline, and Pie Town became a shell of its former self. Most of the small stores and businesses closed, their boarded-up windows and crumbling roofs rotting relics of a bygone past. Within a decade, Keele, too, closed his doors. On Route 60, only a single gas station remained open. Fewer people got their mail at the post office. The Baptist church still held a Sunday service but there were few in attendance.

ACROSS THE CONTINENTAL DIVIDE

As a young boy, I was unaware of how little was left of Pie Town and how it had changed. I was caught up in the busyness of living life with my family—running errands, watching baseball, tuning in to my favorite radio programs. Some of my earliest childhood memories were of going with my grandfather on his mail route to Datil. At one time, horses and mules were used to carry the mail to Mangas, the starting point for the route. Winfield was first awarded the contract to carry the mail during World War II, and was given a special ration of gas and tires as a result.

Why we always got our mail at Datil instead of Pie Town or Omega, much closer to where we lived, I never understood. I suspect it was because the post office at Greens Gap, halfway to Datil, had closed, and there were still a few homesteaders along the route.

In the early morning hours every Monday and Friday, we would drive south in the old family pickup toward Mangas Mountain, cross a cattle guard where there were several mail boxes, and turn east through a piñon and pine forest to the Continental Divide between Big and Little Alegres Mountains. Here the snow piled up during the winter and it would sometimes be weeks before the mail could get through. Before the war, the mail carrier had used a horse-drawn buggy to get through the deep snow. Once when the snow was deep, my grandfather carried the mail on horseback, riding one horse and leading a second. He spent the night in Datil before returning late the next day.

Just east of the Continental Divide, the road cut through a narrow canyon beside a deep arroyo to Oak Springs and the ruins of a Hubbell Company sheep camp. There, beneath a large grove of tall gamble

In the winter of 1937, one mile east of the Continental Divide, Snooks Whinery (*left*), Bill McNeal, and sixteen-year-old Jerry Thompson Jr. (looking on from behind Whinery), are trying to get the mail through from Mangas to Datil in a 1936 Chevrolet pickup. When a post office was first established at Mangas in 1909, the mail was carried by mules. Courtesy of the author.

oaks, my grandfather would frequently stop in the afternoon on the return trip to rest. Beneath the giant oaks, I scampered about gathering acorns, pretending they were gold nuggets, and placing them in the small tobacco sacks my grandfather always saved.

Going east from Oak Springs, we would rattle along past the old Greens Gap schoolhouse, through scrubby juniper and piñons to State Road 12, where we turned east to Datil. Along the route, farmers and ranchers would place a bag with letters and any packages they might be mailing in their mailboxes, along with a small coin purse. Grandfather would collect the coin purses, which contained change for purchasing stamps, and the bags of letters and packages. People would often ask for a ride to Datil, where they could catch the afternoon mail bus to Socorro. I never remember my grandfather asking for any money from these passengers; it was understood you could always catch a ride.

DATIL

The little crossroads town of Datil was a delightful place and seemed to always be busier than Pie Town. Unlike Pie Town or Mangas, there was little agriculture in the vicinity, and most of the people who frequented the village were ranchers—Datil would always be a cow town. There were four gas stations, a hardware store, two restaurants, and a small office where my grandfather renewed his driver's license. There was even an ice cream parlor.

My grandfather always yearned for the latest news. But the ranchers discussed little more than the weather, their pickup trucks, and their cows, while always cursing the federal government. They complained when there was no rain and then grumbled when the rains came and the roads were muddy. Everyone carried a set of mud chains. Although my grandfather was always friendly and seemed to know everyone by first name, in private, he frequently referred to the ranchers as welfare cowboys and seemed envious, like most homesteaders, that he could not graze his cows on government land.

Almost every week, we visited the hardware store, filled up with gas, and bought a loaf of bread. For lunch we feasted on a bologna or egg sandwich my grandmother had prepared, or on rare occasions when my grandfather had some money, on a seventy-five-cent hamburger at the Eagle Guest Ranch.

Most of the time, we just sat in front of the post office, waiting for the trusty postmaster, Kentucky-born Claude Reeves Graham, or his wife, Ruth, who alternated as village postmaster, to have the mail ready for the return trip back to Mangas. Graham would dig into the mailbags we had picked up along the way, each with a family name, place stamps on all the letters, make change, and deposit coins back into the little leather purses.

The center of the small village was the Eagle Guest Ranch, built in the 1920s by Tom Reynolds, one of the first ranchers in the county. The establishment started out as a small store and post office, but when Oklahoma transplant Russell Parrott bought the store and post office in 1933, he added a café, lounge, cabins, and dance hall, and turned it into a dude ranch.

The Eagle Guest Ranch stood at the fork of the road where one highway led west to Pie Town and Springerville, Arizona, and another

The Navajo Lodge at Datil was one of the best hotels on the Ocean-to-Ocean Highway and was thought to be one of the finest hand-hewn structures in the country. In 1920, Ray Morley moved the structure, log by log, from its original location in Datil Canyon west of the village. On January 10, 1944, while carrying the mail from Mangas to Datil, my grandfather watched the structure burn to the ground. With no fire department, there was little local residents could do. Photograph by Russell Lee. Courtesy of the Library of Congress, Prints & Photographs Division, Farm Security Administration / Office of War Information Black-and-White Negatives; call number USF34-035886-D.

highway headed southwest to Horse Springs, the Tularosa River Valley, and the county seat of Reserve. At one time in the 1930s, Parrott's establishment boasted cabins decorated with animal trophies, including a 720-pound stuffed grizzly bear, and a small zoo that included a mountain lion, coyotes, a bald eagle, prairie dogs, a baboon, and a talking parrot. Seventeen hounds and fifteen saddle horses were kept for guests. By the time I came to know Datil, the Eagle Guest Ranch was no longer catering to dudes but was still a restaurant, store, motel, and gas station. Weldon and Elizabeth Burns bought the Eagle Guest Ranch from Parrott and then sold it to Lee and Loraine Coker in 1952, the sale confirmed on a brown paper bag.

One of the more picturesque hotels in the entire state was the two-story Navajo Lodge. Built in 1886 in White House Canyon, six miles northwest of Datil, and moved log by log to the town by Ray

Morley in 1926, the structure was one of the finest hand-hewn buildings in the country. It was so quaint and striking that Russell Lee stayed there in 1940, and made a number of photographs of the interior and exterior of the dwelling. Postcards of Navajo women posed in front of the hotel with their colorful, neatly woven blankets were commonly displayed. Other postcards of cowboys with carcasses of mule deer hanging from the front porch of the lodge were also common.

During the war, on January 10, 1944, while my grandfather was in town, the Navajo Lodge caught fire and burned to the ground. With no fire department and no means of putting out the blaze, citizens stood by helplessly as the building was consumed. Winfield watched people frantically throwing and dragging as many belongings out of the building as possible, including beautiful Navajo rugs that had hung on the walls.

After an hour or more in Datil, we would head down State Road 12 and catch the dirt road back through the mountains to Mangas. When a mailbox was on my side of the road, I would lean out the window as my grandfather screeched to a stop, quickly open the mailbox and throw in the mailbag before my grandfather sped off to the next mailbox. Sometimes there were packages too large for the bags and we would just set them on the ground. At times, families would be waiting for us by the roadside.

Years before elk descended on the land, we played a game as to who could see the most animals. There were always mule deer, antelope, prairie dogs, skunks, and porcupines, as well as coyotes and rabbits. Once my grandfather claimed he saw a dinosaur, but I knew he was only joking. Somehow I thought jackrabbits and cottontails were the same species, that the bigger, long-eared jackrabbits were males and the smaller, fluffy cottontails were females. A rabbit was a rabbit, grandfather insisted.

He should have known. The family had eaten a lot of rabbits during the Depression. Cottontails would be shot, skinned, and, in the winter, hung high on the north side of the Martin Canyon cabin, where they would freeze. Many days the diet was little more than cottontail, gravy, and biscuits, Winfield said. When you are hungry, they taste really good, he insisted. Back in Texas, he had once eaten some possum by mistake and thought it was quite good until he learned what it was the next day and became nauseated for two days.

Once we spotted a badger that Winfield said was becoming exceedingly rare. They had been pretty well "trapped out" during the Depression, he said. Many homesteaders had survived by running a trapline and selling the skins of the animals they caught. Despite their deer poaching, it was hard for me to envision my father and grandfather trapping animals. They seemed to love dogs and cats and the menagerie we always had around the house. Yet at least a dozen traps with rusting, jagged teeth hung in the work shed as evidence of this grisly endeavor. The *Catron County News* frequently made mention of my father maintaining his trapline and that he had once trapped a badger. The skin of a large black bear my grandfather had killed on Mangas Mountain was nailed high on the front-room wall opposite the fireplace, along with deer and antelope heads, all trophies celebrating the family's hunting prowess. Although I sometimes thought the souls of the dead animals were looking down on me, they were never as frightening as those god-awful traps in the work shed.

WINTER DIFFICULTIES

Snowfall in the winter averaged about three or four feet, but it was unpredictable. Most of the time, it would only snow a few inches and melt within days. There were two winters that were particularly memorable for me, though. I was four in January 1947 when a blizzard rolled out of the northwest that caused misery for everyone, particularly the Diné on the reservation, where there were massive livestock losses and great human suffering. At Mangas, it snowed and kept snowing, and the wind whipped the snow into six-foot drifts in front of the house. My grandfather and father worked to shovel out paths to the work shed, the well house, and the privy. My grandfather chopped the thick ice in the tank behind the house for the cows and horses to drink and he began feeding the animals alfalfa he stored up every summer in the barn. Vehicular traffic on the dirt road in front of the house stopped, as did mail and the school bus. News on the radio said the northwestern part of the state was paralyzed.

That winter, two men from the Albuquerque Sawmill in Killion Canyon, eight miles up the road at the foot of Mangas Mountain, arrived in a red, four-wheel-drive Dodge Power Wagon. They were the caretakers of the sawmill and had shoveled their way out of the mountains. The men seemed exhausted and asked if they could stay overnight. As was our family custom, they were welcomed and given the upstairs bedroom.

It was cold and the snow did not melt; the drifts became hard and crusted, so the men stayed for more than a week. One day they tried to break through one of the drifts on the nearby hillside. After an hour or two, they gave up and returned to the house. The family was growing short of food, and one morning all we had to eat were biscuits and gravy. The same was true that evening and the next morning.

Being a growing boy and accustomed to having more to eat, especially canned fruits and vegetables, I began whining and complaining. After several of my complaints, one of the bearded sawmillers turned to me. "Young man," he said quietly, "had you been over there with me on Bataan and got caught by those goddamned Japs and forced to eat those goddamned grasshoppers for three years in that goddamned heat in that goddamned prison camp, you would not be complaining." The room fell silent. I had no idea where Bataan was, much less the Philippines, but the idea of eating grasshoppers was repulsive.

The man went on to explain that the American POWs would catch the grasshoppers in the rice paddies on Luzon in the Philippines, put them in their pockets, and with the little rice they were given, make the grasshoppers into a ball or put them into their soup. They were an excellent source of protein, the man said, and when you are starving, you will eat anything. "Why, some of the sailors stranded for months on lifeboats in the Pacific ate their shoes," he said. "You are damned lucky to have anything to eat." For years to come while sitting at the dinner table, I frequently thought of that grizzled veteran eating grasshoppers or those sailors eating their shoes, and I never complained about the lack of food again.

A few days later, there was a loud clattering coming from the road to the north. A giant yellow monster with "CAT" written on the side came down the road, puffing black smoke into the cold winter air and slowly pushing the snow off. The snow was too deep for road graders, and the county had been forced to contract for bulldozers. With a grateful "thank you," the sawmillers left for their homes in Albuquerque. Once the road had been cleared, I jumped in the old pickup with my father and grandfather and we sped off to Pie Town for groceries.

RADIO

At the time, we did not have electricity, and in the evening, after carefully trimming the wicks, my mother or grandmother would light two kerosene lamps. Despite their care, every morning they had to wash the glass chimneys because the wick had been too high and the chimney had become blackened with soot. Frequently in the summer, the light of the lamps would attract scores of irritating moths. In the winter, there was something special about sitting near the light of the lamps and reading while the fire from the fireplace warmed the room.

In winter months, which seemed to be half the year, everyone gathered around the fireplace in the evening in what seemed to be assigned seating. My father sat on one side of the fireplace in a big, old tattered chair, my grandfather on the other side in a big wooden rocking chair, and my mother and grandmother on the couch, usually crocheting or knitting. My grandfather had a bulky Zenith radio that was plugged into a large Delco battery, and it was the center of family entertainment. There was a racist comedy set in the Black community, *Amos 'n' Andy*, the very funny *Fibber McGee and Molly*, and my mother's favorite, *The Bob Hope Show*. I liked the drama and sound effects on *Dragnet*, with Joe Friday rattling off his catchphrase, "All we want are the facts, ma'am," while solving crimes in Los Angeles. Marshal Matt Dillon and his attempts to enforce law and order in rowdy Dodge City was also entertaining in *Gunsmoke*.

A long aerial attached to the radio ran out of the house and up a long ponderosa pine pole anchored to the chimney. Disaster struck one summer evening when a lightning bolt splintered the pole into countless pieces and fried the aerial. Somehow the radio was not damaged, and within forty-eight hours, my grandfather had another long pole and a new aerial, and we were back in business. The battery-powered radio became the light of my life, a connection to the outside world and dramatic events that could only be imagined.

PAIN AND TRAGEDY

When I was just a boy, I came to know my great-grandmother, Phenie Caroline Cobb, a bespectacled, no-nonsense, dictatorial little woman whom my mother absolutely adored. My mother was also close to Phenie's son, a jovial, skinny, part-Cherokee man named John William (Johnny) Cobb, who had come from Oklahoma in the waning years of the Depression and purchased a ranch just north of us.

Back in Osage County, Oklahoma, Johnny Cobb had married Mollie Burkhart, a full-blooded Osage who had been at the very center of the tragic Reign of Terror that swept over the Osage Nation in the early 1920s. From 1921 to 1925, as many as fifty wealthy Osages were shot, poisoned, or even bombed by greedy white "squaw men" who were determined to gain control of Osage headrights and lucrative oil royalties. As it turned out, Mollie's second husband, Ernest Burkhart, had even tried to poison her, but unlike her sisters and her first husband, she had survived the terror.

After Mollie's divorce from her murderous second husband, Johnny Cobb became her personal chauffeur. Despite a twenty-year age difference, the two were married. There is little doubt that my uncle was attracted to Mollie's money, but she found safety and security in their relationship, one of the first meaningful ones of her life. By all accounts, their marriage was a happy one, and it brought Mollie a degree of contentment she had never known before.

Mollie Burkhart and the Osages were heirs to a wealth that was unimaginable to most Americans. Even during the depths of the Depression, when most people in the country were lucky to own one car, Osages could afford ten. Cobb told my father how he and Mollie would fill a suitcase with money, board the train at Pawhuska, and travel to distant places and stay at fancy hotels until the money ran out, before returning home to the Osage settlement town of Gray Horse, on the prairie in southwest Osage County.

Just west of Gray Horse, in the boomtown of Fairfax, in the midst of the Reign of Terror, my mother came of age and graduated from high school in 1937. A month later, Mollie died unexpectedly at the age of fifty, and Cobb moved on, marrying a part-Choctaw woman, Lillian, whom he met while pheasant hunting in a cornfield near Pawhuska. Cobb eventually headed west with Lillian for a new life, and settled near Mangas, where he purchased a cattle ranch from Bill Dahl.

Phenie Cobb (or Grandma Cobb, as she was known to everyone), along with my mother, "followed along like bugs," as John Steinbeck wrote in his classic *Grapes of Wrath*. They were part of the seemingly never-ending, poverty-plagued Okie exodus to the West. It was at Mangas that my father and mother met and married in 1941, two years before my father went off to war.

Two years before the war, Johnny Cobb hired my father and grandfather to help him build a ranch house on a piñon-covered plateau overlooking Mangas Creek. Nearby, they renovated a two-room adobe cottage, where Grandma Cobb lived and tended a small garden. The cottage was within easy walking distance of where we lived, down the road to the south. I still remember walking there hand in hand with my mother in the late afternoons, sometimes in knee-deep snow, along a path through a grove of piñon trees, across a dry arroyo, and up a small hill. The visits were always exciting since Lillian and Johnny Cobb's young daughters, Anna and Boodie, were always there. In the winter, we built snowmen and had snowball fights. In the summer, we romped through the piñon trees, playing games and pausing to help Grandma Cobb harvest vegetables from her garden.

To escape the blistering Oklahoma heat in late summer, Mollie's children from her disastrous former marriage, Elizabeth Burkhart and James "Cowboy" Burkhart, frequently visited the Cobb Ranch. They would sometimes stay through the hunting season in early November. The Cobbs "had lots of friends from Oklahoma, all during the hunting season," the local newspaper reported. "Some were lucky and got their bucks, others were not."

Both Elizabeth and Cowboy had witnessed the Osage Reign of Terror firsthand and were ostracized by many Osage people because of their mixed blood and their father's hideous crimes. Despite declining oil revenues during the Depression, Elizabeth and Cowboy always had big, shiny new cars, of which my father seemed envious. Lillian's sons by a former marriage, Don and James, were also frequent visitors to the Cobb Ranch. There was great excitement one day during hunting season when Don Brim accidentally shot himself in the foot.

Much of the social life at the Cobb Ranch centered around

fried-chicken dinners, traveling to Pie Town for the movies, and cheering on the Pie Town baseball team. There were bone-rattling trips to the summit of Mangas Mountain, where my grandfather worked for the ranger Bob Diggs at the lookout tower during the fire season, picnic excursions in the pine-shrouded mountains in the warming days of summer, and all-night, smoke-filled poker games.

Not realizing that Johnny Cobb was related to Elizabeth and James by marriage and not by blood, I somehow thought that my mother—since she was a Cobb—had to be part Osage. There was little doubt that Oklahoma had been a large part of my mother's early life. To this day, I can still hear her quietly humming an old Woody Guthrie ballad as we walked through the woods:

> Many a month has come and gone
> Since I wandered from my home
> In those Oklahoma hills where I was born.
> . . . .
> Way down yonder in the Indian Nation
> Ridin' my pony on the reservation
> In those Oklahoma hills where I was born.

When I was young, I often wondered why my mother never mentioned her parents. The maternal side of her family, the Cobbs, were always present, but the other side of the family was missing. At the time, I was too young and immature to question my mother about my missing grandparents. But there were hints. I have a hazy memory of riding in the back of Johnny Cobb's car when I was five or six and hearing him tell my father about a fellow named Joe and his girlfriend, Lula. Everything would have been different, Cobb insisted, had "Joe not spent so much time in the pen at Leavenworth." Since my grandfather and Cobb owned some livestock, I thought they were talking about a cattle pen somewhere. I thought the pen had to be somewhere beyond the Continental Divide and Pie Town, the edge of my world at the time. There was also confusion in my mind since my mother's name was Jo.

In 1982, following my mother's painful death from emphysema, I found seventeen letters, a telegram, and five hand-colored greeting cards in a shoebox in the bottom drawer of an old dresser. Little did I know at the time that the letters would unravel a long-lost family history of passion, pain, and murder. The letters helped expose the life of my grandfather, a mixed-blood Cherokee cowboy from Oklahoma named Joe Lynch Davis, after whom my mother was named. Although Davis came from a wealthy ranching family in east-central Oklahoma, he spent much of his young life on the outlaw trail, robbing at least sixteen banks and five trains and winding up in Leavenworth Federal Penitentiary for fourteen years.

Despite strong objections from his family, Davis fell in love with and married Lula May Cobb, my grandmother. Although the two later claimed they were married on the Choctaw Nation, there is no written record of such a marriage. When Davis wound up in Leavenworth following a train heist in Arizona, Lula moved to Colorado Springs, Colorado, where she met and married a man named Thomas T. Nelson, who physically abused her. When she left Nelson, he began stalking her. After she refused his advances, he walked into the laundry where she was working, pulled out an automatic pistol, and shot Lula in the head, after which he fatally shot himself. My mother, who was only six at the time, was traumatized, unable to comprehend the tragedy, refusing to believe her mother was really dead. "I'm glad he shot himself," she told a Colorado Springs newspaper.

While my grandfather was in Leavenworth, my mother lived with Grandma Cobb until she married my father in 1941. Researching her life after her death, I came to realize why at times she seemed so sad and withdrawn, and why she found joy in the simplest of things. I remember her being depressed for days when Grandma Cobb moved with her son and his family to California in 1948.

PIE TOWN ELEMENTARY SCHOOL

In the spring of 1939, a group of Pie Town citizens led by Joe Keele sent a petition to the county school superintendent asking that a public school be established at Pie Town. The county already had twenty-three elementary schools, including, in the northern part of the county, those at Dyke, Mesa, Mountain View, Divide, Adams Diggings, Salt Lake, Sierra Mujeres, Sunnyside, Tres Lagunas, Greer, Greens Gap, and Mangas. Keele argued there were nineteen students attending a private school at the Farm Bureau building and more students were expected. When the petition was denied, the citizens appealed again the next year, and in May 1940, the Catron County Board of Education finally agreed. Grace Lucas, forty-four years old and single, with three years of college, was hired at $500 a year. Originally from East Owen, Ohio, where she was again residing, Grace had previously taught at the Dyke school.

It was agreed that the Farm Bureau building, the only suitable structure in town, would be renovated into a proper schoolhouse. On the east side of the building, a small stage was constructed and a large curtain was installed that could be rolled up during classes and performances. The curtain featured scenes of picturesque waterfalls, green meadows, and tall conifer trees with advertising along the edges by Craig and Keele and businesses in Magdalena and Socorro.

Lucas arrived on the mail bus from Ohio in August, only to be told there would be no school after all. The county had not come up with the promised funds. Community members felt deceived; some were furious. Families would have to send their children to school in Quemado. Pie Town community leaders wondered where the money to bus the students

The Farm Bureau building at Pie Town was used as a private and then public school before a new school was constructed in 1948. Photograph by Russell Lee. Courtesy of the Library of Congress, Prints & Photographs Division, Farm Security Administration / Office of War Information Color Photographs; call number LC-USF35-325.

to Quemado was to come from. The county school board blamed the lack of funds on the bureaucracy in Santa Fe, but when Keele made inquiries at the capital, he found the fault was with the school board.

Refusing to give up, Pie Town leaders banded together and agreed to pay Lucas themselves, if she would agree to stay. Several times in the ensuing year, parents were unable to pay their share of Lucas's meager salary, and they sent milk, butter, eggs, chickens, piñons, and pinto beans to her instead.

FESSOR MAGEE

In 1941, the county finally came through with the funds and Lucas was officially employed. When she left the following year, a Ms. Pigg arrived on the mail bus from the East Coast to replace Lucas, but Ms. Pigg took one look at the isolated community and all its outdoor privies and got back on the bus and left. Billie Black taught school for a few months before Guy E. Magee agreed to come in from Adams Diggings. Magee lived in the teacherage, a log cabin across the street from Craig and Keele's general store. Every summer, Magee and his wife, Daisy, returned to their homestead at Adams Diggings, where for several years he taught school, operated a small store, and ran the post office.

"Professor Magee," or simply "Fessor," was a competent, strict, skilled professional of the "old school" who tolerated little nonsense. He remained as principal of Pie Town Elementary for eight years, often teaching all eight grades. The bespectacled Magee had a fiery temper, rarely smiled, and always dressed in a white shirt with a tie, a neat vest, and a starched pair of slacks. To ease the pains of an ulcer, he consumed Tums as if they were candy. Respected but feared, he was a firm believer in corporal punishment, but instead of being a "paddler," he was a teeth-rattling "shaker." Any perceived misbehavior resulted in the transgressor being grabbed by the collar and violently shaken. The result was both tears and terror. Anyone who received one of Magee's shakings became the talk of the school and they never forget the experience. I was deathly afraid of him.

Enrollment at Pie Town Elementary School continued to grow, and in 1944, Ruth Ayers was hired to teach the lower grades. A partition was added that divided the Farm Bureau building into two classrooms and could be raised to the ceiling for community events such as dances, movies, and box suppers. In the fall of 1946, Ayers was replaced by Texas-born, forty-eight-year-old Carrie Belle Scoggins, who homesteaded near Mangas with her husband, Allen. Short and stocky, with glasses and only a seventh-grade education herself, Scoggins drove an old pickup to school, wore a long dress, and always had her hair tucked in a net. Scoggins was always patient and the students loved her. When not teaching, she collected antiques, especially old telephones.

A NEW SCHOOL

In the late summer of 1947, when I was five, my mother took me to enroll in the first grade at Pie Town Elementary. My insecurities reached new heights when my mother's uncle, Johnny Cobb, told me no one enrolled in the first grade anymore, that children began in the third grade. I was worried almost to tears until my mother explained that he was joking.

The year before, after more than a decade at the Farm Bureau building, the county had agreed to construct a new four-room school in the woods two hundred yards east of the Farm Bureau building on land donated by Theora and Harmon Craig. Nine hundred dollars' worth of concrete blocks arrived from Belen, and the abandoned WPA schools in the area were salvaged for materials. The new school had rows of windows on the east and west sides, electric lights, and heating from a butane furnace, but no indoor plumbing.

Students carried their desks and books from the Farm Bureau building to the new school. Every student had a cup with their name on it that hung on the wall near a large bucket of water. There was a lunch program for a minimal fee, but many parents could not afford it. I remember the Leyba children from Mangas bringing a mason jar of beans and tortillas and sitting on the floor in the hall to eat while other students sat at tables in the lunchroom. I never knew whether they willingly segregated themselves out of embarrassment or it was forced upon them. Regardless, it seemed unfair and racist.

After the war, Pie Town entered into a long decline, although the elementary school seemed as vibrant as ever. What little commerce there was centered on the few businesses along Route 60. Except for Keele's store, the old business district on the Ocean-to-Ocean dirt track was boarded up and abandoned. There were about seventy students in the school and three teachers. The feeder bus I rode brought students from Pipe Springs and Mangas, while a second bus carried students from Tres Lagunas, Hickman, and the ranches and homesteads north of town. A third route south of town brought students from Greens Gap and the area around Big Alegre.

Every year, several students missed the beginning of school due to the bean harvest. Other students were absent in October and November picking piñons, and some skipped school during hunting season. I would later calculate I rode a school bus more than 130,000 miles during the eight years I attended school at Pie Town.

In the mornings, my grandfather hovered near the fireplace and had the task of watching for the arrival of the school bus. He would tell me when he spotted the bus coming over a small rise south of the house, sometimes in a cloud of dust, and I would grab my book bag and dash out to the mailbox to await the bus. The Reid, Gallegos, Parker, and Castillo children were already on board, some half-asleep.

Several children never seemed to have shoes, and yet they would stand by the roadside, even in winter. At the time, no one paid any attention to what decades later would be considered child abuse. That is just the way things were at the time. In Russell Lee's 1940 photograph of children singing on the stage at the Farm Bureau building, a majority are without shoes.

After my stop, the bus would pick up the Leyba and Baca children and we were off to Pie Town. At Route 60 on the open plains, a mile east of Omega, the Mangas bus met the Pie Town high school bus headed for Quemado. High school students would disembark and we would turn east along Route 60 for Pie Town. After a bumpy and sometimes muddy or dusty ride, the asphalt was always welcome.

One student who rode the Mangas bus had a large open sore on his head from ringworm. The county nurse visited the school once a month and she kept putting medicine on the sore, but it only seemed to get worse. Another Mangas student, Buster Reid, had Saint Vitus' dance, a neurological disorder that caused a constant rapid, uncoordinated jerking of his face, hands, and feet. It was frightening to see Buster's agony. He could hardly sit or eat without shaking violently. My mother said he was certain to have had rheumatic fever at one time. His family did not have money for a physician, but the county nurse finally got the boy to a doctor somehow, and with medication, he seemed to get better.

The problem on the bus was boredom. It was the same monotonous scenery day after day. The heater on the bus was in the front, and in the cold winter months, there was often scuffling over the front seats. Boys never sat with girls and girls never sat with boys. To do so would have caused a stir and embarrassment.

We played all kinds of games as time and space permitted. On rare occasions, there were fisticuffs over something trivial and the bus driver would be forced to stop the bus and separate the combatants and arbitrate the dispute. With the help of Reynaldo Baca, I once dangled the mud chains out one of the side windows, over the dirt road. When the

In 1948, first and second graders pose with their superbly skilled and nurturing teacher, Colita Schalbar, on the steps of the Pie Town Elementary School. I am standing in front on the left beside my mischievous buddy Donald Holley. Courtesy of the author.

---

bus driver happened to look in the rearview mirror, he almost had a heart attack. He brought the bus to a screeching halt and before his wrath had ebbed, we solemnly swore we would never do such a thing again.

One of the great joys in riding the bus was stopping at Keele's general store for candy. This was always on a Friday. My grandfather sometimes gave me a nickel, which was enough for a Baby Ruth or a Hershey's bar. Several of the students on the bus never had any money, and out of embarrassment for my "riches," I was forced to share the candy.

I never realized that being an only child and socially and geographically isolated had its consequences. I did not know this until I was forced to make my way through the real world on my own. I never learned to dance, was always shy, and did not know how to use a telephone until I was in college.

Chapter Ten

COLITA SCHALBAR

In 1946, Colita Schalbar replaced Scoggins as the first- and second-grade teacher. Over time, I became convinced she had to be the greatest elementary school teacher who ever lived. She was a stickler for penmanship and spent hours teaching us how to read and write. To this day, I still remember sitting at a crude desk with a Big Chief tablet, writing hundreds of letters over and over, making sure the letter "e" was not too tall and the letter "l" was not too short. Each letter had to be carefully drawn. Each one was judiciously judged, and if it was not perfect, you repeated the process with another hundred or two hundred letters. This new teacher was to shape my young life more than she could ever imagine.

Schalbar was in her late twenties. Slender, she donned glasses and a long skirt, and wore her hair in a bun. She seemed to always have a great moral sense about her. You always knew what was right and what was wrong. There were four of us in the first grade: Melba Jean Schalbar, the teacher's daughter; Janet Julian, who lived in town; George Reid, who rode the bus with me from Mangas; and me.

Along with three older half-brothers and a younger sister, Colita Lee Schalbar had come to the area with her family from Brownwood, Texas. They had settled near Quemado, where she attended elementary school, before her mother took her back to Texas, where she completed two years of high school. In December 1934, the family returned to New Mexico. Two years later, Colita married Oscar Schalbar and the couple raised three children, of which Melba Jean was the youngest. Colita Schalbar is depicted in one of Russell Lee's epic photographs at a Saturday-night dance. She calmly sits in the background as Ollie Magee dances a jig.

Schalbar began teaching the first four grades in Pie Town in 1946. At the time, the Schalbar family lived on their family homestead twelve miles south of town. Her husband worked in a sawmill during the week and returned home on the weekends. When Harve Hamilton was driving the school bus from Greens Gap and was absent thrashing beans or during the hunting season, Mrs. Schalbar took on the task. She would get up before dawn, cook breakfast, get the children out of bed, feed and get them ready for school, drive the school bus to Pie Town, and teach all day from nine to four, including supervising the lunchroom. She then drove the bus back to the homestead, where she milked four cows, fed a flock of chickens, slopped the pigs, nurtured several cats and dogs, prepared supper for the family, put them to bed, washed the dishes, worked on lesson plans for the next day, and went to bed after midnight, only to get up before dawn the next day. It was especially tough in the winter, when the roads were icy and the nights were long and cold. In the summer, she attended New Mexico Western College in Silver City.

These were the "good times," she remembered years later. "We were young and healthy." Nobody "got sick, because they couldn't afford it—it was too far to a doctor and we didn't have the time to be sick," she said. "Everybody was busy and everybody was happy."

In the classroom, Schalbar had a small desk in front of a small blackboard. High on the wall was a large framed image of George Washington—long hair, false teeth, and all. Washington was looking down on you, like the eyes of God or those of the oculist Dr. T. J. Eckleburg in the "valley of ashes" in F. Scott Fitzgerald's *The Great Gatsby*. No matter what the lesson was, you could look up and there was Washington watching you. Schalbar's daughter Melba Jean, or Jeannie, was an exceptional student, and she and I competed at every opportunity. She stood at least a head taller than me and I sometimes felt intimidated.

Every week, we were required to stand in front of the class and read a few pages from our Dick and Jane reader. At the end of every month, providing you did not miss any words, you were called to the front of the room and given a Baby Ruth. Receiving the candy was like winning a gold medal at the Olympics.

The Dick and Jane reader depicted a world a million miles from Pie Town. Dick, Jane, and their younger sister, Sally, led lives that no one in Pie Town could identify with. Their dad worked in an office and mowed the lawn on weekends. The reader related a simple narrative of a stereotypical white, middle-class American family who lived in the suburbs. I never saw a single lawn in Catron County. Moreover, most of the students at Pie Town came from poor families who had no concept of life in a suburb.

Schalbar was in charge of ringing the school bell, and every morning at nine fifteen, after the three feeder buses arrived, she rushed out to the front steps and promptly rang the bell. Even in rain and snow, the students lined up by grades for attendance. Schalbar rang the bell again to end a brief morning recess, a thirty-minute lunch break, and a fifteen-minute afternoon recess. I hated the sound of that bell.

The Schalbars later bought several lots in Pie Town from Craig, and Oscar Schalbar purchased a small house from the sawmill where he worked. The couple took the house apart board by board, nail by nail, and rebuilt the structure in Pie Town. "Dear God, I don't know how many nails I straightened," Colita Schalbar said years later.

In the early 1950s, the Schalbars installed the first television in Pie Town, a small black-and-white set that required a long-range antenna. In the evenings, the Schalbar living room was "littered with people," the teacher recalled. It would grow late, people would still be watching, and Mrs. Schalbar would go to bed. The last individuals out of the house would turn off the television and lock the door.

GILDA NUTT

When I advanced to the third grade, my classmates and I moved to a new classroom and a new teacher. Gilda Nutt taught grades three through five. Nutt and her husband lived in the old Pie Town Hotel on top of the dike and she walked through the woods to school every day.

She had never learned the nurturing skills Schalbar had mastered. She thought memorization and class recitation were a large part of learning; crucial was your ability to recite all fourteen stanzas of Henry Wadsworth Longfellow's "Paul Revere's Ride." At times, she seemed downright mean. Any misbehavior was met with a rapid rap on the knuckles with a ruler.

Every student seemed to struggle in Nutt's class, and I sometimes saw students break into tears of frustration. For some strange reason I never understood, you could not take a book home, and she stood by the door to enforce her rule. I once tried to smuggle a book under my coat, and when she detected the book, she took great offense and responded with the usual—and painful—rap on the knuckles. In the first and second grade, I had always looked forward to school with excitement and joy. But with Nutt it was pure dread and drudgery. I so badly wanted to return to the second grade.

PIE TOWN, 1940-1950

Ⓐ Cemetary

Ⓑ Bar (Frank Wilson)

Ⓒ Cafe and Gas Station (Bill Perry)

Ⓓ Post Office

Ⓔ General Merchandise (Vilma and Wayne C. Hickey)

Ⓕ Gas Station (Bessie and Claude Holley)

Ⓖ Claude Rhodes

Ⓗ Gas Station (Billie A. and Tom B. Weathers)

Ⓘ Baptist Church

Ⓙ Margie and Ray McKinley

Ⓚ Colita and Oscar Schalbar

Ⓛ Carrie and Joe Keele

Ⓜ Theora and Harmon Craig

Ⓝ Craig Motors

Ⓞ Rock Wall

Ⓟ Campgrounds

Ⓠ Pie Town Hotel

Ⓡ Business District (SEE DETAIL)

Ⓢ Tourist Court

Ⓣ Pump Well

Ⓤ Teacherage

Ⓥ Bean House

Ⓦ Mae and Samuel O. Burrell

Ⓧ Farm Bureau

Ⓨ New School

Ⓩ Baseball Field

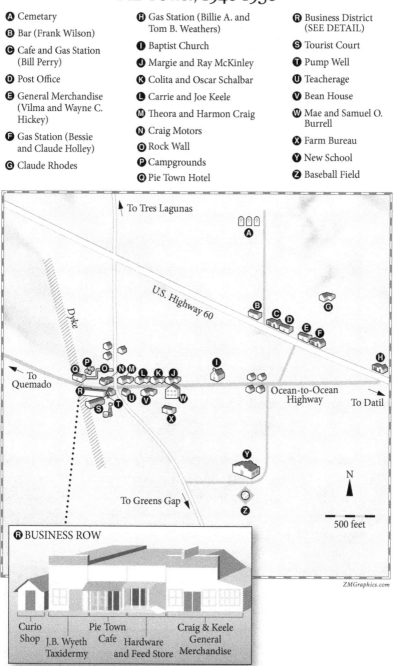

To Tres Lagunas

U.S. Highway 60

Dyke

To Quemado

Ocean-to-Ocean Highway

To Datil

To Greens Gap

N

500 feet

Ⓡ BUSINESS ROW

Curio Shop

J.B. Wyeth Taxidermy

Pie Town Cafe

Hardware and Feed Store

Craig & Keele General Merchandise

ZMGraphics.com

Tough and demanding, Nutt seemed to care little about anything except music. Upon arriving every morning, all the grades gathered around a piano in the lunchroom, where she played and everyone sang. I can still hear the sound of Stephen Foster's old antebellum minstrel song, "Camptown Races":

> Camptown ladies sing dis song, Doo-dah! Doo-dah!
> Camptown race-track, five miles long, Oh, doo-dah day!
> . . . .
> Gwine to run all night!
> Gwine to run all day!
> I'll bet my money on the bog-tail nag,
> Somebody bet on de bay.

A classmate, Jeannie Chadwell (Schalbar), remembers singing another of Foster's parlor songs inspired by an African American servant, "Old Black Joe," a song of sorrow without bitterness that had a kind of wistful tenderness:

> Gone are the days when my heart was young and gay,
> Gone are my friends from the cotton fields away.
> Gone from the earth to a better land I know,
> I hear their gentle voices calling, "Old Black Joe."

Nutt asked every student in the fourth grade to purchase a small, black plastic tonette, a whistle-like instrument with seven finger holes. It was really a cheap flute popular in American elementary education at the time. Nutt was hoping to prepare us for the band at Quemado High School. Merle Lee Schalbar had a mandolin he got somewhere and Bobby Ray McKinley acquired a violin. The only notes I learned were those from an old English lullaby:

> Twinkle, twinkle little star
> How I wonder what you are
> Up above the world so high
> Like a diamond in the sky.

Once, a band from Quemado High School arrived in an old, yellow bus to entertain us. Everyone gathered excitedly in front of the school as the ten-member band filed out of the bus with their shiny instruments and positioned themselves on the steps. After a few lively and patriotic tunes, they took a break and went inside for Kool-Aid and cookies. While they were inside, I found a round rock that might fit perfectly in the tuba that was left leaning against the steps. My buddy Donald Holley looked at me with a sneaky grin and I knew instantly what he was thinking. After making sure no one was watching, I jammed the rock into the instrument as far as I could reach.

When the band resumed their concert a few minutes later, the tuba player appeared panic stricken, trying frantically to adjust his instrument while the band director kept motioning and looking in his direction. Donald and I tried hard not to laugh. The more the aspiring musician struggled with his tuba, the more the band director became frustrated, and the funnier the scene became. The poor kid was exasperated with his tuba, and it was evident the band director had lost all faith in his musical abilities. The entire concert came to an abrupt end, and the band and the director were soon back on the bus headed to Quemado. Donald and I often wondered how long it took the poor tuba player and his teacher to find the rock and what their thoughts must have been at the time. Every time we thought of the event, we burst out laughing. The mischievousness of two young boys seemed to know no ends.

Another time, the county game warden came to Pie Town to present a program on wildlife. After setting up a screen in front of the classroom, he was showing a series of colorful slides that depicted various animals indigenous to the county and telling a bit about each animal. When he showed a herd of mule deer, one of the young students excitedly raised his hand and was called on by the warden. "My father shot one of those last week," the boy said. The warden seemed a bit stunned but did not ask the student's name and resumed his presentation with an image of a black bear.

One year, Nutt decided her three grades should have a maypole pageant on May 1. She got a tall wooden pole from somewhere and her husband planted it squarely in front of the school. Colorful ribbons were attached to the top of the pole. Although we practiced several times, on the day of the event, two or three students became irreversibly confused. The girls in their colorful, short crepe paper skirts were to walk in a clockwise direction while the boys moved counterclockwise. A couple of boys went in the wrong direction, and this caused several of the girls to become confused, and they, too, went in the wrong direction, and all the ribbons became terribly entangled. Several of the older students in the upper grades began laughing, parents had no idea what was going on, some of the students holding the ribbons started giggling, and Nutt became furious. She rushed forward to correct everything but the more she tried to intercede, the worse things became. In the end, the ceremony was an absolute disaster. Going in circles with ribbons never made any sense anyway. Trying to untangle all those ribbons would have taken hours and it was time for everyone to get on the buses.

I don't think Nutt ever recovered from the maypole disaster. For days, you could see the disappointment in her face and in her demeanor. Such a ceremony might have worked in medieval England; it did not work at Pie Town Elementary School. There were few tears when the Nutt family moved away. When Mrs. Nutt left, a Ms. Francis Steck was hired. She was kind and encouraging, but she smoked in the classroom and never moved out from behind her desk, perhaps because she weighed well over three hundred pounds. She seemed to spend as much time with her makeup as she did with instruction. The girls liked her because she invited them to her house to make fudge. I remember learning nothing of significance. Thankfully, she only lasted a year.

CARRIE W. KEELE

In the fifth grade, I had the great fortune of having Carrie W. Keele, the wife of the town merchant, as my teacher. Small and bespectacled, she was a ball of energy and reminded me a lot of my grandmother. Like Schalbar, she was a great motivational force. Keele had taught at Mesa Elementary School, and when the school closed, she took over the fourth and fifth grades at Quemado, riding the high school bus forty-four miles every day, before coming to teach at Pie Town Elementary. Keele was organized and demanding, but gentle and encouraging. I remember drawing the digestive and skeletal system of the human body over and over. We also studied geography, my favorite subject, drawing map after map, continent after continent. Keele seemed to detect she had found a soft spot in me, and she challenged me in ways I had never known. "Someday you will be a geography teacher," she said.

After learning the location of all the states and their capitals, I took on Canada, Mexico, and the rest of the world, memorizing cities, highest mountains, longest rivers, largest islands, and all the big deserts. I learned all the countries in South America, Central America and the Caribbean, Europe, and Asia, but I could never quite master the countries in sub-Saharan Africa. One of the problems was that the globe and the books we had were decades old. There were too many countries, and in the postcolonial era, the ones in central Africa seemed to always be changing names. To impress my parents, I would quiz them as to the location of Bhutan, San Marino, Andorra, the Pitcairn Islands, Easter Island, or Saint Pierre and Miquelon.

Once, when Keele saw that I was idle and bored, she told me she had a special assignment for me. For the rest of the school year, while she was instructing other grades, I would read the *World Book Encyclopedia*. Each week, I would write a brief one-to-two-page report on what I had learned, and she would give me a grade. I skipped some of the more boring entries, but for the next seven months, I read constantly, more out of not wanting to disappoint her than anything else.

Learning was a beautiful thing that seemed to go on forever, and I could never understand why other students were not interested in what I was interested in. Any knowledgeable person should know that Mount McKinley was the highest mountain in North America, or Pico de Orizaba was the highest in Mexico; that Mount Everest was the highest in the world, or that the Andes were the longest mountain range, the Nile the longest river, or the Soviet Union the largest country. It did not matter that Carson City was a small town; it was the capital of Nevada.

I found many of the encyclopedia entries fascinating. But naughty students had thumbed through the books and added crude and inappropriate appendages to all the Greek and Roman statues, especially those of the males. I tried to erase as many as possible, fearing that Mrs. Keele would think I had defaced the books.

JONAS SALK TO THE RESCUE

From the time I entered the first grade, my mother was afraid that I would catch polio—poliomyelitis or infantile paralysis—a life-threatening disease that spread like wildfire across the country during my childhood. Shortly after World War II, polio swept through North Carolina, killing hundreds of children and disabling thousands. By the time I was in the fourth grade, as many as sixty thousand children were contracting the dreaded disease every year and three thousand were dying. One of the great leaders of the century and a family hero, Franklin D. Roosevelt, had contracted polio at the age of thirty-nine in 1921 and spent the rest of his life in a wheelchair. Few Americans were aware of his inability to walk, though FDR was seen in the old newsreel films swimming with polio survivors at his resort at Warm Springs, Georgia.

Even those who lived through polio, like FDR, were scarred for life. Hospitals set up special iron-lung machines to accommodate the more critically ill. New Mexico had the Carrie Tingley Hospital at Hot Springs. Devoted entirely to disabled children, the hospital was one of the best in the entire country, where those inflicted with polio had access to the hot mineral springs in the town.

I remember seeing several polio survivors who had withered arms and legs. At the time, Catron County had only one physician, no hospital, and not a single elevator for anyone who was disabled. The only ramps were for cattle.

Polio seemed to always be lurking in the shadows and was greatly feared by everyone in my family, as it was in many families. Every time I had an ache or pain, my mother became anxious. After hiking long distances or climbing mountains, I would sometimes be tired and sore, and my mother would panic, inquiring every day if my legs felt better.

But there was hope on the horizon. Each year, the teachers at Pie Town distributed little red-and-yellow cards that had places for us to fill them with dimes for the March of Dimes, which was pouring millions of dollars into an attempt to find an effective vaccine. The card featured five slots for dimes and a squirrel climbing a tree, symbolically helping you put the dimes in the slots. My grandfather helped, and in two weeks, we filled the five slots. When it came time to turn in the cards, some of them were empty and others had only a dime or two.

Jonas Edward Salk had been testing a vaccine in his laboratory at the University of Pittsburgh, down the street from where I would attend Carnegie Mellon University years later, and he came up with a vaccine that was successfully tested and released in April 1955. Polio shots were a godsend. I will never forget my mother watching with great nervousness as thirty-six children waited in line for the county nurse to administer the shots. There were a few tears among the younger children, but most everyone realized the significance of the moment. Jonas Salk brought a miracle to Pie Town, and he would always remain a great hero to my mother. I was one of more than 1.8 million schoolchildren injected with the vaccine.

CHAPTER ELEVEN

PISSING IN THE SNOW

During the fifteen-minute midmorning recess and the thirty-minute break at lunch, the older boys would gather on the basketball court to shoot hoops while the younger boys and girls played on the playground. In the early grades, we had tag games, kick the can, hide-and-seek, red rover, and London Bridge. The girls sometimes segregated themselves to play jacks, patty-cake, or hopscotch, while the boys concentrated on a more serious game of marbles.

HANGING RICHARD PARKER

One Saturday night, after watching one of the shoot-'em-up Western movies that Bill Perry hosted at the Farm Bureau building, some of the older boys got carried away. At recess on Monday, one of the boys, Richard Parker, was found guilty of being an outlaw, and it was decided the lawmen should hang him, like in the movies. A makeshift noose was fashioned and placed around Parker's neck and thrown over a sturdy juniper limb. Three boys hoisted Parker up and held him until he began to choke and his face turned red. Scared, they dropped him to the ground and fled for the schoolhouse. The lawmen came close to receiving one of Guy Magee's character-changing shakings, though one of the hangmen was Magee's grandson, and another was Colita Schalbar's son.

On the playground, it was John Wayne's Wild West all over again, more in myth than reality. We never played cowboys and Mormons, or cowboys and pilgrims. It was always cowboys and Indians, though our fantasy had nothing to do with portraying Native Americans. Despite the large number of homesteaders who settled Pie Town and the neighboring satellite communities, the small community was and always would be cowboy country. Cowboy culture dominated almost everything we did.

One of the more memorable school days was when two workmen arrived in a big truck to install some playground equipment. There was a swing set with a slide, a seesaw (or teeter-totter), a merry-go-round, and a set of monkey bars. There was instant competition to see who could swing the highest or go the fastest on the merry-go-round. It was great when Magee announced that none of the upper-grade students were allowed near the playground. There were the usual cuts and bruises from students falling out of the swings or off the seesaw or merry-go-round, but Schalbar, who acted as the school nurse, always had her iodine ready. One student bragged he went so high and so fast in one of the swings that he made a 360-degree circle over the top and came down the other side, but we all knew he was lying. This was impossible, and when challenged, he could never duplicate his feat.

In the early grades, we sometimes played red rover, which to me seemed boring and stupid. There was hide-and-seek, but there was no place to hide except behind the privy or off in the piñons, and the teachers frowned against this for fear, I guess, that we would not return. Sure enough, two older students thought they would test the system, and as soon as they got off the bus one morning, they fled west through the trees toward the dike, only to return just as the school buses were loading that afternoon. Magee was there to meet them, grabbing each by the collar, and off they went up the steps into the school. I had never seen anyone as white faced and frightened as the two boys when they emerged a few minutes later with tears running down their cheeks. They did not play hooky again, and it was weeks before they would even talk about their excursion to the dike.

BLUE RIBBONS

Once a year in late spring, usually in early May, after the snow had melted and the cold winds had eased, hundreds of elementary school children from all over the county gathered in Reserve, the county seat, for a daylong competition in everything imaginable. There was a 440-yard relay, long-jump and chin-up contests, and all kinds of academic competitions to see who could read, write, spell, compute, and even tell stories the best. There was also a drama contest, with each school presenting a one-act play.

Early in the morning, all the children, grades one through eight, along with their three teachers, piled into Harve Hamilton's old, yellow school bus and another bus, and off we went, fifty-five miles through the mountains to Horse Springs, and down the picturesque Tularosa River Valley to Reserve. It was all very exciting. At the time, there were six elementary schools in the county—Glenwood, Luna, Reserve, Datil, Pie Town, and Quemado—all competing for a coveted blue, red, or white ribbon. For each event, five points were awarded to the first-place winner, three points for second, and one point for third. The school that accumulated the most points got a big golden trophy featuring some winged goddess holding a laurel wreath.

It was decided that the lower grades at Pie Town would compete in the drama contest. For weeks, we rehearsed a simple play that featured a circus arriving in a small Midwestern town. Donald Holley was a clown and I was his trained bear that he led onto the stage with a leash. The clown performed somersaults while the bear hopped about like a rabbit and did a silly little dance. One of the more robust boys was designated an elephant. A taller, redheaded girl with skinny legs was the giraffe. Other students acted as part of a band. Grandma Quata sewed a brown bear suit for me that had a bright-red tongue hanging out.

The only problem was that unlike in Pie Town, where we rehearsed in the classroom, the old Depression-era gymnasium in Reserve had a stage on which we were to perform. Glenwood went first and all the children seemed to know their lines perfectly; their play went off without a hitch, though no one in the audience seemed overly excited. We were next. The curtain went up and out went Donald with his well-rehearsed somersaults as his bear obediently plodded along behind, barely able to see through a small peephole. After two somersaults, the clown tumbled off the stage and crashed into the audience. Students watching the play thought this was hilarious and part of the act, but Colita Schalbar rushed to the crash site, fearing that Donald had seriously injured himself. But the clown struggled to his feet and confidently climbed back onto the stage, and we finished our performance as if nothing had happened.

Before departing for home, teachers and students anxiously crowded into the gym for the awards ceremony. Pie Town Elementary School, it was announced, had won first place in the drama competition. It mattered not that the larger schools like Reserve and Quemado had won most of the ribbons and that only three schools had bothered to compete in the drama contest. For my peers and me, it was a grand and joyous day. In fact, Pie Town won several ribbons. One student won the chin-up contest, and there were third-place ribbons in spelling and storytelling. Donald Sanders received a blue ribbon for throwing a softball the farthest.

It was already dark when I jumped off the bus with my bear suit in hand and raced into the front room to give my family the wonderful news. Our blue ribbon hung in the school hallway at Pie Town for years.

BLOODY BULLY FOOTBALL

When I was in the fifth grade, some classmates and I began playing football on the south side of the schoolyard, where the summer monsoons always deposited a layer of soft sand. Not flag football, but rough, smack-in-the-face, tackle football. We had no helmets, padding, or any kind of equipment and had never played the game before.

We learned quickly, thanks to an older boy in the seventh grade. At least a head taller and forty pounds heavier than anyone else, Gunther was a real bully, if there ever was one. He rode the bus in from a small ranch near Tres Lagunas, north of town. He had transferred from Fort Sumner in the eastern part of the state, where he had learned to play football from a real football coach. He claimed to know everything there was to know about the game. Everyone grew sick of his talking about the mighty Fort Sumner High School Foxes. They were the best team in the state, he boasted. The team represented by the orange, white, and black fox could even beat the University of New Mexico, or any professional team in the country, he insisted. Everyone knew he was a braggart and that what he was saying was absurd, but no one dared challenge him.

Pie Town was "a shithole," Gunther said. He hated the school. He hated the place and he hated the people who lived there, and he was just waiting for his father to find a job somewhere else so he could move away. Importantly, though, Gunther brought his football to school with him.

In contrast to his athletic prowess, Gunther was a real dummy in the classroom. In fact, he was so dumb that it was embarrassing. I remember he once asked the teacher where Canada was on the map and, during another geography lesson, if France was part of the United States. If that was not enough, he once inquired how ships got across the equator, pointing to the big black line on the globe. He never mastered basic mathematics or how to write a simple sentence, yet in the schoolyard, it was as if he were almighty God, and he never stopped flaunting his authority. I always suspected he had failed a grade or two, but I never had the nerve to ask him.

During our matches on the playground, Gunther dictated everything. He determined who was on what side, what position you played, the stance you took on offense and defense, how to pass the football, how to run with it, how to tackle, and how to kick the ball. He was always the running back and he seemed to pick the smaller players as opposing linemen. He only played on offense and he seemed to take great joy in running over people. He never ran around us—he ran into and over us. Without any padding, it was sometimes painful. Bloody noses and bruises were common.

Several times, I was almost brought to tears as he smashed into me at full speed, knocking my breath out, before bouncing and twisting and scampering triumphantly into the end zone that was determined by a line he drew in the sand. He would raise his arms into the air to indicate a touchdown, as if he were the referee too. I came to hate him.

Gunther was so sadistic that I joined three of the smaller players in a plot to do him in. If our plans failed, we knew we were in for a beating, but we were desperate. Our playground had been a place of great joy, but Gunther had turned it into a place of dread and fear.

Our scheme reached its climax during the first play at recess the next day as Gunther, on his way into the end zone, smashed into one of the smaller players, who slammed his knee as hard as he could into Gunther's crotch. With a piercing, eerie scream, the bully collapsed into a heap in the sand and commenced a pitiful moaning. One player was certain that Gunther was dying. Several frightened players gathered around while another student ran for help. After several moments, Gunther stopped moaning and began crying and pleading for his mother as two teachers arrived on the scene to launch an investigation. With Gunther tightly holding his groin, it was obvious what had happened. The teachers carried him off to the lunchroom, where he lay prostrate and embarrassed on one of the tables for the rest of the afternoon.

A few days later, after Gunther had recovered, one of the teachers confiscated his football and told him not to bring it to school anymore. That was the end of football at Pie Town Elementary School. The bully regained his strength to bully some more until he moved away a few months later. We often joked and ridiculed him behind his back, wondering if his "family jewels" were still part of the family.

FROLICKING IN THE SNOW

During recess in the winter, we built snowmen in front of the school, lining them up like sentinels. One perverted fourth grader seemed to enjoy getting sticks from the woods and adding extra appendages. Somehow making snowmen evolved into snowball fights. Most of the time, we chose sides, with one side hiding behind the snowmen that guarded a mythical fortress where a five-minute supply of snowballs was stored.

Few things were as invigorating as receiving a well-aimed snowball to the face. Bobby Sanders, the county softball-throwing champion, was always the first to be picked for a team. He was not large in stature, but he could throw a softball twenty to thirty feet farther than anyone else, a skill that easily translated to snowball fights.

At first, the snowball fights were innocent—friendly encounters with everyone laughing and shouting and having a good time, often just joyously frolicking in the snow. There were no rules except that girls were not allowed to participate. We lined up and began throwing. Few students had mittens, and our hands quickly froze, but no one complained.

Things changed when some unprincipled students began putting chunks of ice in their snowballs. An ice snowball inflicted pain and often caused a big, black bruise on your arm or leg. Tensions escalated when someone replaced the ice inside the snowballs with rocks. These not only caused bruises but could leave you bleeding. Once in the pitch of battle, Sanders let fly a rock-snowball that hit an unfortunate student square in the forehead and knocked him senseless. When the teachers arrived on the scene and found out what had happened, that was the end of our snowball fights.

BEHIND THE OUTHOUSE

When we grew tired of making snowmen or playing cowboys and Indians and the girls were out of the way playing jacks, the boys would gather behind the old privy on the southeast corner of the schoolyard for a pissing contest. Here we were shielded from the teachers, who huddled on the steps of the school during recess. The best time for such a contest was after a light snow, when we competed to see who could write their last names in the snow the fastest. Boys with short names like Reid or Baca seemed to always finish first, while those with names like Thompson or McKinley finished last. If the winner was in dispute, there were pissing contests for distance and even for height, with the back of the privy the target. It did not matter that the girls might be only yards away, using their side of the john. Winners were proclaimed "champion pissers," at least until the next light snow, when the competition began all over again.

The sizeable wooden privy was not that old, but it looked as if it might collapse at any moment. Inside, there were eight holes, four for the boys on one side and four for the girls on the other. All that separated the sexes was a poorly constructed wooden wall. If you dared venture into the girls' side of the privy or even got close to their entrance, there was the distinct possibility of a paddling or one of Guy

Magee's frightful shakings in your future. Some of the boys had pocket-knives, and they carved small holes in the old wooden boards so they could peep at the girls. In a game that seemed to have some kind of sexual underpinnings, certainly more so than cowboys and Indians, the girls would stuff the holes full of toilet paper, but the boys would poke out the paper and carve even larger holes. Eventually, the girls got their own privy and the games ended.

At the time, I cannot recall a single home in Pie Town or the entire area having an indoor toilet, much less running water. Most had a wooden privy, or an outhouse, as they were called. Some, like the one at the Pipe Springs school, were made of logs. The one at the Mangas school was constructed of sturdy adobe. Most were made of wooden planks. The size of the family and their economic status seemed to dictate the size of the privy. The Thompson family had a two-holer, but some families had three holes, even four, while others had only one. The pages of Sears and Roebuck catalogs were used as toilet paper. The thinner, softer yellow pages in the back of the catalog always disappeared first. When all the pages were gone, my grandfather gathered up a sack of corn cobs to take their place.

MIGHTY CHICKEN HAWKS

After the demise of Gunther's football team, I began playing basketball with the older boys, mostly seventh and eighth graders. We had two forlorn-looking basketball hoops on the east side of the school, not far from the privy, the nets having long since blown away. The older boys were taller and could jump higher, but in time, I learned to dribble, pass, and shoot better than almost everyone else. Basketball was played outside in the late fall, winter, and early spring, and the problem at Pie Town was that it seemed to snow all the time, sometimes as late as May. When the snow melted, the court became a quagmire. At night, after the snow had melted, the ground froze and the next morning the court resembled a World War I battlefield. The frozen puddles of water along with the footprints and ruts made dribbling impossible.

When it snowed in Pie Town during the day, the other players and I would rush out at recess with a broom and sweep as much of the snow away as possible. At times, it was so frigid that we could hardly bear it, but we always continued. We only had one rubber basketball, and it was worn out. The ball became easily deflated in the cold and we had to constantly pump more air into it. But that didn't stop us—and that the ball was splattered with mud or the court was frequently frozen solid and uneven didn't matter, either. We sometimes chose sides and played half-court. But most of the time we just shot baskets or played H-O-R-S-E.

In the summer when there was little to do, I began devoting several hours a day to practicing. Somehow, someway, I could excel in basketball but not in other sports. Fellow students seemed to care less if you made good grades, but if you were a good athlete, you were popular with the girls. When my father sensed my interest in basketball, he welded a hoop out of scrap iron and bolted it to a wooden backboard, which he nailed to a tall juniper post in the backyard just beyond a large lilac bush. The circumference of the goal was too small, and it was too close to the backboard, but that mattered little. I spent entire weekends practicing, playing H-O-R-S-E with an imaginary partner, shooting two-hand set shots, jump shots, hook shots, layups, or any other shot I could invent. I even mastered passing behind my back and making layups by first bringing the ball under a leg. I would sometimes shoot as many as fifty consecutive free throws and managed to get my free-throw success percentage over 80 percent, which was not bad for an elementary school kid.

By the time I was in the seventh grade, John T. Moore had become the principal and taught the upper grades. Moore had coached basketball at Quemado High School and he organized our practices. We learned how to play zone defense (mostly a 2-1-2 or a box-and-one, and Moore's version of a full-court press), how to trap the dribbler at midcourt, and how to play an in-your-face man-to-man. When I was in the eighth grade, there was great excitement when Coach Moore announced he had scheduled games with Datil Elementary School. They would be coming to Pie Town and we would travel to Datil two weeks later.

BEATING DATIL

With much anticipation and a heightened sense of purpose, we practiced hard. Pie Town had no uniforms, so my mother sewed "PT" in bright-red letters on a white T-shirt. Other players had similar T-shirts with red letters—and some even had numbers—but two or three players just wore their regular shirts. No one had shorts, so we always played in jeans.

Another problem was that we did not have a mascot. Quemado had the Eagles, Springerville claimed the Elks, and Reserve played as the Cactus Jumpers before someone thought the name unbecoming and they became the Mountaineers. At the end of the Livestock Driveway, Magdalena claimed the Steers, Horse Springs—appropriately—the Prairie Dogs, and Mountain View the Busy Beavers. After considerable discussion, we concluded we should be the Chicken Hawks. Hawks were common around Pie Town, and everyone liked the idea of being a predator and flying high in the air. Coach Moore said he did not care what we called ourselves as long it was not something nasty.

At the time, Quemado and Reserve were the only high schools in the county, high schools at Pipe Springs, Mogollon, and Datil having long since disappeared. Although they lived in Catron County, high school students from Datil were bused to Magdalena in Socorro County, which somehow meant they could not be trusted.

When Datil arrived for the first game, several Pie Town parents showed up and parked their cars along the east side of the dirt court, as if it were a rodeo arena. No sooner had the game started than it was evident that the players from Datil had no idea what they were doing. They ran this way and that in haphazard chaos. Once, one of their players stole the ball from his teammate. More than once, they shot at the wrong basket, and they had no idea what a jump ball was or even a foul, for that matter. When I was dribbling the ball at one point, one of the Datil players tackled me as if Gunther had taught him basketball. I would dribble downcourt, and rather than guard me, the Datil players all gathered under the backboard waiting for the rebound.

Our pressing 2-1-2 zone defense was stifling. Most of the time, Datil never got the ball past half-court. When the final whistle sounded, the score was Pie Town 26, Datil 4. The shy, skinny kid from Mangas, who had been badly bullied playing football, had scored 22 of Pie Town's 26 points. My whole attitude on life changed. My shyness never went away, but a greater self-confidence and assertiveness emerged.

Two weeks later, we arrived in Datil cocky and sure of ourselves. Their court was more rutted and uneven than ours and at least twenty feet shorter; their backboards were a peculiar shape, and their hoops seemed to be at a different height. More importantly, since their crushing defeat two weeks earlier, they had now learned the basics of how to play defense. I noticed that after the drubbing they received in Pie Town, Coach Moore gave their coach a book on the principles of coaching basketball. Nevertheless, the mighty Hawks prevailed 16–8.

BITTER DEFEAT ON THE HARD COURT

Two weeks later, Coach Moore announced to everyone's great delight that the Chicken Hawks had received an invitation to an elementary school tournament in Magdalena, and the school superintendent said we could go. During the Depression, an annual elementary school tournament was held at Reserve, but when so many people moved away after the war, and the county lost a big chunk of its population, many of the schools closed, and the tournament became a thing of the past.

Six teams would compete: Pie Town, Quemado, Datil, an A team and B team from Magdalena, and Mount Carmel, a Catholic school in Socorro. Quemado and the Magdalena A team, since they were the larger schools, would receive a bye in the first round. Pie Town would play the Magdalena B team and Datil would take on Mount Carmel.

As soon as the feeder buses arrived the morning of the tournament, we set out with Coach Moore east along Route 60, across the Continental Divide, through Datil Canyon, and across the vast Plains of San Agustin. Part of our excitement was that we would be playing indoors for the first time. In fact, few players on our team had ever seen an indoor court before. We arrived at the gym on the southeast side of Magdalena, on the road to Kelly, in time for the second half of the Mount Carmel–Datil game.

We stared at a magnificent gym. Not only did they have lines painted on the court, but the baskets had nets, there were bleachers on both sides of the court, and a scoreboard lit up one end of the court opposite a spacious stage on the other end. There were also two officials in striped shirts with loud whistles.

The game itself was pitiful. Mount Carmel had fancy uniforms, ran all kinds of intricate offensive plays, including some kind of a weave, and played tough defense. At halftime, the score was so embarrassing that at the beginning of the second half, the Mount Carmel coach put all his substitutes into the game.

I noticed the Mount Carmel players made the sign of the cross before every free throw. Although I was not Catholic, I thought this might be a good idea. After all, there was nothing to lose. I could be Catholic, at least for a day. But when I missed three free throws in a row in the first game, I realized that perhaps God was not on my side after all.

Before the game with the Magdalena B team, we gathered in a dressing room for a pep talk. Then we raced onto the court as if we were the Harlem Globetrotters come to conquer the world. Playing on a wooden floor for the first time was exhilarating. Somehow the ball dribbled evenly.

I noticed the Magdalena team, like Mount Carmel, had nice uniforms and an organized warm-up. We just ran out and shot hoops. At the end of the first quarter, I had made a couple of layups and we were leading 6–4. In the second quarter, we could only manage two free throws, and at halftime, the score was tied 8–8. At the beginning of the third period, I quickly hit two shots from the top of the key, but the Steers quickly responded, and going into the fourth quarter, the score was tied again, this time 14–14. In the fourth quarter, the Steers managed to get past our zone to score four quick points. I responded with a layup and a free throw, but the Steers managed to stall for the remainder of the game and the mighty Hawks went down in defeat, 18–17.

There would be a consolation game the next day, Coach Moore said, and the winner would get a trophy. We would be playing Datil and we were certain to win. On the bus ride home across the plains and through the mountains, we slept and said little. There was no doubt we could beat Datil and bring the trophy to Pie Town. After all, we had beaten them twice already.

When the game started the next day, it seemed as if we were playing a different team. They had learned even more about defense, and every time I went to shoot, a player that was on their team for the first time had his hands in my face. When I dribbled to the side of the key, another player magically appeared, and he, too, put his hands up.

In the second half, Datil switched to a box-and-one defense; four players remained in a zone, but the new player guarded me man-to-man. Somehow they had learned this defense from the book Coach Moore gave their coach. Wherever I went, the new player went too. Not only could I not drive past him into the key for a layup, but I couldn't even get a shot off. He was also taunting and trash-talking, just loud enough for me to hear him, but not the officials. It was the first time I had experienced anything like that before. "The best part of you," he said, "ran down your father's leg." I wasn't exactly sure what he meant, but I knew it wasn't complimentary. He kept calling me "shit for brains," a gringo, an asshole, and a *cabrón*, which I had no trouble understanding.

Going into the fourth quarter, Datil was ahead by a point and I began to worry. Twice Coach Moore called time-out to encourage us to be more aggressive. One of the Pie Town players asked him what aggressive meant. I was in the corner with about four minutes to go, trying to maneuver for a shot, when the potty-mouthed player, guarding me forcefully as he had done for much of the game, went into another insulting tirade, saying something about my mother. I was already frustrated, and this time I lost any sense of composure. I bounced the ball to a teammate and proceeded to kick the nasty kid as hard as I could. He screamed out and one of the referees blew his whistle, shaped his hands into a "T," pointed at me, and in a sweeping motion like he was hitchhiking somewhere, threw his thumb into the air and pointed toward our bench. Not knowing what was happening, I just stood there until the official came up and said, "Son, you are out of the game. You can't do that."

I was already in tears when Coach Moore said I had received a "technical," something I had never heard of before. It was the first one in the entire tournament, something unheard of in elementary school, and I was indeed out of the game. "Why in the hell did you do that?" Moore kept asking. "You're going to lose the game for us. Damn!" I sat at the end of the bench in tears and disbelief as the clock ran out with Datil ahead 14–12. The mighty Chicken Hawks had gone down in defeat a second time. The loss was devastating. In the six-team tournament, Pie Town finished last; Datil received the consolation trophy. I was still pouting when we boarded the bus for the long ride home. Coach Moore was mad at me for weeks, but I always blamed him for giving that basketball book to the Datil coach.

OVER THE COW PASTURES AND THROUGH THE TREES

$\mathcal{W}$hen I first arrived at Pie Town Elementary School, I made friends with a second-grade student named Donald Holley. Claude and Bessie Holley, Donald's parents, ran a gas station and garage where my father frequently filled up with gas. For a time, the Holleys took turns driving the school bus from Pie Town to Quemado. One day, Donald announced he was bringing me something special. I had no idea what the gift might be or why he would be bringing me something special except that we were best friends and that is what best friends do.

RUSTY

I waited with great expectation. Just receiving a gift was exciting for a six-year-old. No sooner had the school bus arrived the next morning than Donald rushed out, carrying a red, curly-haired, long-eared, mixed cocker spaniel puppy. I was so excited I could hardly control myself. Colita Schalbar said I could keep the puppy in the classroom providing he did not "go to the bathroom." If this happened, she warned, I had to clean up the mess, and the dog would have to stay outside.

Just before boarding the bus that afternoon, I carefully zipped the puppy into my small backpack. All that stuck out was his curly red head and his long floppy ears. At home, I rushed into the kitchen where my mother and grandmother were preparing dinner and excitedly dumped the puppy out onto the floor, much to my mother's chagrin. It did not help when the puppy promptly urinated on the linoleum.

"Where did you get that dog?" my mother angrily asked.

"At school. Donald gave him to me," was my meek response.

"I don't think you can keep him," she replied as tears welled up in my eyes.

That evening, my father passed the decision of keeping the dog back to my mother, who said she did not know how we could take care of another dog. It was then that my grandfather calmly intervened, saying there was no reason not to keep the puppy. We already had Sweet Pea, and another dog would not be that much trouble. We always had enough scraps, and the new dog might make a good companion for Sweet Pea.

Sweet Pea was an old, black-and-white mongrel that hobbled around on three legs. During the Depression when my father and grandfather ran a trapline, Sweet Pea had been caught in one of the traps and the lower part of his right hind leg was severed. He was a gentle dog who loved affection, never growled at anything, and never strayed far from the house.

When my mother started calling the puppy Rusty, gave him a bath, and began feeding him, I knew the dog was there to stay. Being able to keep the dog was one of my fondest memories. He was truly my best friend. For well over a decade, Rusty was a constant companion on many a grand adventure, a substitute for a brother or sister. He would live well into old age, and when he died at the age of seventeen while I was home from college one wintry day in 1965, I gently wrapped him in his favorite blanket and buried him under a big juniper tree.

A JUVENILE DATING RITUAL

The most popular game at Pie Town Elementary School, as noted before, was cowboys and Indians. But the game really should have been called cowboys and horses, or cowboys and heifers. We worked hard to construct cattle corrals from the piñon and juniper branches in the woods near the school. The bigger, more assertive boys were always the cowboys, and the smaller boys became their horses. Usually there were too many cowboys and not enough horses, and there was pushing and shoving and, on occasion, fisticuffs.

The cowboys would attach their belts to the pants of the horses and, with plenty of "whoas" and "giddyups," hold on to the horses and whip them around the woods. The girls were the heifers; the objective of the game was to herd the heifers into the corral. This was an unwritten rule that no one questioned. It was the only way the girls could participate.

The problem was that the heifers kept escaping and the brave cowboys were forced to gallop off after them and drive them back into the corral, only to have them escape again, whereupon the process began all over again. Only Schalbar's ringing the school bell ended the juvenile dating ritual.

ABNER WHYTE AND BRER RABBIT

Children in the lower grades always cheered the arrival of Arkansas-born storyteller Abner A. Whyte to Pie Town. Whyte was beloved for his renditions of the all-American folktales about Brer Rabbit and the rabbit's friends Brer Fox, Brer Bear, Brer Coon, and other animals. Brer Rabbit, the heroic central figure in the Uncle Remus stories of the Old South, and his adventures in the briar patch, were mesmerizing to my peers. Brer Rabbit always succeeded by virtue of his wits rather than his brawn, bending social mores as he saw fit. Popularized by Walt Disney, the tales could be traced back to Africa; Brer Rabbit is thought to represent enslaved Africans who also used their wits to overcome hardships and horrors and exact revenge on their adversaries, the white slave owners.

I was more interested in Whyte himself than in Brer Rabbit. Whyte was born with spina bifida, but the congenital birth defect was not correctly diagnosed until he was twenty-four years old. Although he was able to walk for a time as an infant, his legs never fully developed. He became permanently disabled, only able to get around by using his arms as legs and swinging his body forcefully from one side to the other. Although his arms and shoulders were abnormally strong, his legs were those of a two-year-old. He wore strange-looking shoes with thick leather soles. Whyte was one of eleven children in his family, born in a log cabin in Arkansas in 1882.

When I first saw him, Whyte was approaching seventy. Before coming to Pie Town, he had attended Sam Houston Normal Institute in East Texas for two years and taught school in Lamb County in the

Lone Star State. In Catron County, Whyte taught at Greens Gap and other one-room schools. Most of the time, he lived with a cousin, Mabel Phipps, and her husband, Wallace, in Greens Gap; the 1940 census there enumerated him as a "private teacher." After retiring, he moved to Pie Town and traveled all over the county telling his stories.

Whyte would always arrive at the school in a beat-up, rusty pickup truck with a tarp over the back, where he sometimes slept when he was traveling. He guided the truck with the help of three long wooden sticks that served as the accelerator, clutch, and brake.

Why Whyte didn't use crutches I never understood, but watching him scurry out of his old pickup and up the steep steps to the school and then scoot down the hall into a classroom was captivating. After finishing his stories, he always encouraged questions about Brer Rabbit or the Bible, but I never had the nerve to ask about his disabling illness. Decades before disability accommodations, his life must have been incredibly difficult and I felt so very sorry for him. On the long bus ride home after Whyte had been at school, I would often ponder what his life must have been like, and I would recall one of my grandfather's favorite sayings: "It doesn't matter how bad off you are, there is always someone worse." Whyte died in a Socorro hospital in 1967 at the age of eighty-five and was buried at Pie Town.

GREAT EASTER EGG HUNT

An exciting event at Pie Town was the annual Easter egg hunt. Each child brought a dozen colored Easter eggs to school and the parents would hide them in the woods around the building. Even the poorer children managed to arrive with a few eggs. Most were colored with crayons, although some were dyed. Since the first- and second-grade classroom was on the west side of the building, if you stood by a window and jumped high enough, you could see where the eggs were being hidden. You only had a second for a quick glimpse before having to jump again. Once, we pulled our desks to the windows and were looking out when Schalbar arrived and threatened to cancel the entire event if we were caught cheating again. We also had to endure a short lecture on morality and fairness.

There were prizes for finding the most eggs and for finding a special "prize egg." Students would line up along the edge of the woods and, with our baskets or hats in hand, go charging off into the woods and rabbitbrush after the eggs. The eggs could be hidden in the grass, behind rocks, or even up in trees. Often there were serious confrontations when students ran over one another or spotted an egg at the same time. I think I was in the second grade when George Reid found twenty-five eggs, but an unfortunate first grader found none. Scampering around with an empty basket, she was in tears before Schalbar arrived on the scene to assist her, and, as if by magic, she found two eggs behind a tree—eggs I was certain were not there seconds earlier.

But Easter could be confusing. As everyone anxiously awaited the day of the Great Easter Egg Hunt, we colored cute little Easter bunnies that Schalbar pinned above the blackboard. I knew the bunnies did not lay eggs because I sometimes helped my grandmother gather eggs from the chicken house; I was certain eggs came from chickens. It wasn't until years later that I was able to figure things out.

RUMPELSTILTSKIN

The school at Pie Town was one of the few in the area that survived the exodus of homesteaders during and after World War II, and it was the center of social life in the small community. To raise money, the parent-teacher association, of which my mother was president for several years, held bingo games several times a year. The prizes were not much, but the social interaction lured as many as thirty people.

From the time I was very young, my mother seemed determined that I receive the best possible education. Her son would somehow achieve in life what she had not. Although Schalbar taught me how to read and write, my mother gave me the enduring joy of it all. Story time, just before bedtime, was a delight. Here a creative imagination knew no bounds. It all started with a colorfully illustrated, blue-covered Catholic reader my mother obtained somewhere. It did not matter that it had several other students' names in the front, or that it was worn and tattered.

She would sit by the small cot where I slept, reading by the light of a coal oil lamp for as long as I remained awake. To this day, late at night, decades later, I can still see the slight flickering of the wick in the lamp, and hear the gentle pat of the falling rain on the rooftop, the haunting, not-so-distant, call of a family of coyotes, and my mother patiently reading.

Of all the stories in the book, I liked the old English fairy tale of Jack and his beanstalk best and always hoped that somehow one of my grandmother's beans would magically sprout and grow into the sky. Jack seemed like the brother I never had. He helped his mother chop wood, weed the garden, and milk the family cow. I even began calling one of my grandmother's milk cows Old Bess.

That damnable giant with one eye in the center of his head haunted me for years with his "Fee-fi-fo-fum, I smell the blood of an Englishman." Every time my mother read the story, I was fearful it would somehow end differently and the giant would eat Jack for breakfast. I was ready to solicit my grandfather, if necessary, to help me chop down the beanstalk. I sometimes hoped we might have a hen that could lay golden eggs, but I realized this might be difficult.

I also identified with the brave, chivalrous, yellow-haired Christian warrior Roland, who after fighting seven years with Charlemagne against the Moors in Spain, was making his way home when he fell dead at the hands of the Basques while traversing a pass in the Pyrenees.

Rumpelstiltskin, a Brothers Grimm tale of a miller who tells the king his daughter can spin straw into gold, was always a favorite, and my mother must have recited it fifty times. Of course, when the daughter married the king, I knew it was wrong for Rumpelstiltskin to demand her firstborn child. But when the queen goes into the woods and watches the little imp dancing around a fire singing, "The queen will never win the game, for Rumpelstiltskin is my name," the tale became captivating. I named one of the family's tabby cats Rumpelstiltskin, but my grandfather said the name was too long, and he shortened it to Rumpel. Acquiescing to my demands, my mother never seemed to tire of reading the story—if I seemed to enjoy a story, she enjoyed it too.

Although we never had more than three or four books, including a Bible my grandmother inherited, I knew that books mattered. Books opened a magical world that went way beyond the Mangas Valley and Pie Town.

THAT OLD-TIME RELIGION

For reasons I never understood, I was petrified of the dark. Perhaps it was the terribly insecurity I suffered for most of my life. Being an only child did not help.

My grandmother frequently corresponded with relatives back in Texas and she would sometimes write late into the evening. After Winfield lost the mail route to Prospero Leyba (son of Procopio), it was my duty to deposit our mailbag in the mailbox, a good hundred yards from the house, every Sunday and Thursday evening after Quata had finished her letters. I would carefully walk out the front door into the darkness, stumbling along, imagining there were monsters—some mythical, androgynous creature or the boogeyman behind every bush, rock, and tree, waiting to grab me and perhaps eat me. Reaching the mailbox, I would throw the bag in, slam the door, and race back to the house as fast as I could.

There was a small, narrow hallway between my parents' and grandparent's bedrooms, and it was there I slept on a small army cot. There was no heat in the hallway, and in the winter, it was very cold. I would sometimes wake up in the middle of the night and listen to the wind whistling around the corner of the house. More memorable was the howling and barking of the coyotes at night and the chatter of the blue piñon jays in the early morning. One night, I awoke to strange popping noises I had never heard before. After I rushed to the warmth of the fireplace in the morning, Winfield told me to look outside at the white wintry landscape. The storm was gone, the sun was out, and the snow, two feet deep, was glistening in the morning sun.

The snow was heavy and wet and all the lower limbs on the piñon trees were broken and twisted. Some of the limbs clung to the trees as if for dear life, others had fallen to the ground, and everywhere there were yellow scars on the trunks of the trees. I always imagined the trees felt pain just like people and animals and fish, and that they had spirits.

All broken and scarred, they had to be in great pain. My grandfather said he had never seen anything like it. For two weeks after the snow melted, my father and grandfather dragged and hauled all the broken limbs into the dry arroyos near the house. For years to come, you could still see the big, ugly scars on the trees, sap running down their trunks almost to the ground. Mother Nature could be cruel and unforgiving.

It was about this time that my mother decided I needed some religion. Although my family was Christian, we never prayed before meals, and no one went to church. Perhaps it was too far to go from Pie Town, or they just didn't care to go. I know there had been religious services at Pipe Springs, and there were Catholic churches at the old Aragon hacienda and at Mangas, but Catholics burned candles, had too many saints, played with beads, and did strange things, from the family's perspective. I think my grandparents were Methodist, but I was never sure and I never asked. I suspect my mother attended the Assemblies of God church back in Oklahoma when she was a teenager, since she was a Cobb.

My religion began one summer after I finished the fourth grade. A tall, old, grizzled itinerant preacher, who looked like he had stumbled out of a Great Depression bean field or emerged from the Old Testament, came to the house announcing that he would be holding Sunday school at Mangas Ranch, a few miles down the road, for the next three weeks. All good Christian children were invited, he said. In fact, he could pick me up next Sunday. My mother assured him that I was a good Christian boy and I would be waiting.

Sure enough, the next Sunday, promptly at 9:45 a.m. on a warm summer day, the preacher knocked on the front door. After my mother carefully combed my hair, I anxiously crowded into the back seat of his banged-up, rusty, old car, along with six other students of various ages. Two other recruits sat in the front seat. After he stopped for another good Christian, we arrived at Mangas Ranch.

Everyone seemed excited as we filed into a small, unlit, dirty work shed, rife with the smell of cow manure. Among the rusting shovels, rakes, and carpenter tools, we sat on rough wooden benches. After we all bowed our heads for a brief prayer, the old preacher in the torn brown shirt began to preach. I quickly realized we would not be coloring Christmas scenes of Bethlehem or drinking Kool-Aid or eating Jell-O, as I had hoped.

The man had not been preaching for three minutes when he began to rave in a loud voice that seemed to reverberate beyond the toolshed and the cattle corrals, into the woods. Looking skyward and holding a Bible high in the air, he screamed out something about everyone going to hell and being burned alive unless they were saved. "You must not, you will not, forsake Jesus for Satan," he thundered. Suddenly the old preacher paused. The room became ghostly quiet. "How many of you have been saved?" he asked. Scared and insecure, I glanced around to see several hands reach for the ceiling.

My problem was that I did not know exactly what the preacher meant by "being saved," and I certainly did not want to tell a falsehood. Telling a lie would *cause* you to burn in hell. I had learned that from my parents. With the help of my grandfather, I had been saving pennies in a small glass piggy bank for over a year and I had well over a hundred. Perhaps this was what he was talking about, but I was not sure.

Anyone who lied would betray the Lord and would be doing the work of the devil, the preacher said. I sat silently. The last thing I wanted to do was betray the Lord. Suddenly he spotted the one student who had not raised his hand and my fear turned into terror. "You have not been saved!" he thundered at me. I was so scared that I could not even nod yes or no. I was petrified and trembling when he placed his hand on my head and asked that I pray with him, still holding the Bible high in the air in the other hand. Not to worry, he said. With the help of Jesus, he would save me. Although I had gone astray, there was hope for all sinners. Frightened and almost in tears, but not wanting to embarrass myself in front of the other students, all of whom went to school at Pie Town and were certain to tell their friends and everyone on the school bus how the Thompson kid had become so scared in Sunday school, I just sat there as the preacher cried out.

Worried and embarrassed even after the incident, I never told my family what happened. Thompsons were brave. They were never scared. Not of anything or anybody, my grandfather said. If the Thompsons could fight in two world wars, survive the Dust Bowl, and live on beans, corn bread, and cottontail rabbits, we could survive anything, even if we had to "eat damned grass," he insisted.

The next Sunday, when the preacher arrived on schedule, I was hiding under my grandparents' bed, and although my mother tried in vain to find me, no one seemed to know where I was. Embarrassed, my mother told the preacher I was ill, a bold-faced lie I worried would send her down the road to perdition. When I hid behind the toolshed the next Sunday and my mother again proclaimed I was ill, I think the preacher got the message, and I think my mother did too. My religious days were over. From that point on, I would do my own praying.

MATTHEW 5:30

My father related an even more harrowing brush with religion that occurred a few years before I was born. Down the road on the west side of Mangas Creek, a few miles north toward Pie Town, lived a homestead family by the name of Webb. On a slight rise above the creek, they built a nice log cabin with a porch and a swing, and they seemed happy and content.

The Webbs had a son who was caught in the religious fervor sparked by the Great Depression, when millions of Americans tried to push aside their poverty and find happiness and security in their faith. He attended the Baptist church in Pie Town, read the Bible daily, and prayed for hours at a time. One day in early spring, the father came speeding in his car to the Thompson house through a dust storm, blaring his horn as he screeched to a halt. He badly needed help, he said. His son had been reading the Bible and fell into a trance when he came to Matthew 5:30: "And if your right hand causes you to stumble, cut if off and cast it from you. It is better for you to lose one part of your body than for your whole body to go into hell." The young man had gone to the woodpile behind the house, placed his hand on a chopping block, taken a hatchet, and after several whacks, completely severed his right hand.

When my father arrived, the young man was sitting calmly at the kitchen table, the bloody stub of his wrist wrapped in a towel and his mother sobbing inconsolably. A bloodstained trail led out the back door to where the young man's hand lay on the chopping block.

To stop the bleeding, my father tied a leather strap around the stub, and then raced the young man to the doctor, more than two hours away in Magdalena. At first, the man was still in a daze, preaching loudly, and seemed to have little pain, holding his bloodied arm with his good hand. After an hour of the journey, just as they were approaching Datil, he began to moan and complain loudly as my father sped across the Plains of San Agustin. After leaving him with the physician in Magdalena, my father never learned what happened to the young man.

GOLDEN AGE OF COMIC BOOKS

When I was in the sixth grade, my mother began purchasing *Classics Illustrated* comic books that featured "stories by the world's greatest authors." Others my age, if they had comic books at all, were reading *Superman*, *Captain America*, or *Wonder Woman*, but once a month my mother bought a new fifteen-cent *Classics Illustrated* comic. My favorite was Herman Melville's *Moby Dick*, with a harpoon-yielding protagonist, Captain Ahab, on the jacket. I read Mark Twain's great classics *The Adventures of Huckleberry Finn* and *The Adventures of Tom Sawyer* so many times that the covers frayed and fell off. Equally captivating was Robert Louis Stevenson's *Treasure Island* and Homer's ancient Greek epic poems, the *Iliad* and the *Odyssey*. Many nights I went to sleep with Odysseus, king of Ithaca, and his ten-year journey home after the Trojan War firmly embedded in my head.

I went several times with Jules Verne's *From the Earth to the Moon*, *Around the World in Eighty Days*, and *Twenty Thousand Leagues under the Sea*. For some reason, I could never identify with Mary Shelley's *Frankenstein*, and I never understood what William Shakespeare's *A Midsummer Night's Dream* was all about. Charlotte Brontë's *Jane Eyre* and her sister Emily's *Wuthering Heights* were not particularly enthralling either.

I did go to Tenochtitlán with Hernán Cortés and Bernal Díaz del Castillo, to the Orient with Marco Polo, and all the way to the frigid Yukon during the Klondike Gold Rush with Jack London in *The Call of the Wild* and *White Fang*. I cried after reading Harriet Beecher Stowe's *Uncle Tom's Cabin*. I have no doubt the gripping story later helped shape my civil rights activism, just as it had helped to inspire the abolitionist movement a century earlier. I could not believe the injustice portrayed in *The Ox-Bow Incident* by Walter Van Tilburg

Clark. No classic was as fascinating as Erich Maria Remarque's great war story, *All Quiet on the Western Front,* or the epic adventure of poor Lieutenant Bligh in *Mutiny on the Bounty.*

WITH HILLARY AND NORGAY

When I was ten, my father brought home a *Life* magazine he purchased at Wayne Hickey's general store in Pie Town. The magazine featured the conquest of Mount Everest by a New Zealand beekeeper, Edmund Hillary, and a Himalayan Sherpa, Tenzing Norgay. Several days earlier in May 1953, I remember getting up one morning and hearing my mother excitedly saying she heard on the radio that Mount Everest, the highest mountain in the world, had been climbed for the first time. I had no idea where Everest was, but the tone in my mother's voice indicated the feat was significant.

The magazine had photograph after photograph of the two climbers, many in color. Other images showed the mountain from different angles and elevations. To me, the two climbers in their oxygen masks and thick, heavy coats seemed like men from outer space. One epic image showed Norgay on the summit of Everest with several small flags attached to his ice axe and whipping in the wind. There was even a personal account by Hillary of the epic ascent, complete with a map of the camps the climbers used on their way to the summit.

In the days and weeks that followed, I devoured the magazine. I must have read every page at least ten times and carefully examined every image. There was something about this grand adventure that eclipsed even anything I had read in the comics. This was better than being on the *Bounty* with Lieutenant Bligh, going to Cathay with Marco Polo, or exploring the Rocky Mountains with Kit Carson. Every time I looked at the magazine, I became mesmerized, envisioning myself standing on the summit with Hillary and Norgay and holding an ice axe in the wind.

CAT MOUNTAIN

My Mount Everest became Cat Mountain, a small, rounded hill that rose some five hundred feet above the Mangas Valley. On the edge of the Apache National Forest, the mountain was detached from the much larger Slaughter Mesa to the west. The name of the mountain came from a mountain lion, of course, but no one seemed to know who gave it that name, when, and under what circumstance. After I announced that I intended to "conquer" the mountain, my mother made her only request: that I be careful and begin the descent no later than noon when the sun was high in the sky. The monsoon thunderheads and lightning storms that crossed the sky were common in the afternoons.

Young and full of life and with my faithful dog, Rusty, a canteen of water, and a walking stick I fashioned from an elm tree, I started out. The walk through the rabbitbrush to Mangas Creek and the piñon forest beyond was easy. The rocky soil was dotted with colorful red-and-orange-tinted Indian paintbrush, their cuplike bracts bright in the morning sun. Furiously fluttering on dark wings against a vast blue sky, there was always a blue-feathered flock of twenty to thirty piñon jays chattering noisily as they flew along from treetop to the ground and back into the trees. For some reason, the jays seemed to always be in a great hurry, ranting and squawking endlessly.

In my imagination, the walk was equivalent to Norgay and Hillary's trek through the Nepalese lowlands, minus the leeches, of course. Then came the steep climb up the east face of the hill, following deer trails that spiderwebbed ever upward. After an hour and resting several times with Rusty, panting along and always in front, I was through the piñons and within fifty yards of the rocky summit. It was then that the pretense really began. I struggled onward, gasping the fresh mountain air, wielding my stick like an ice axe, pretending that I, too, was gulping oxygen in knee-deep snow, and hoping that a photographer from *Life* magazine was along to record the moment. After another ten minutes of make-believe and struggle, I was on the summit and the view was spectacular.

Here stood a small, lichen-covered rock cairn, indicating that a lonely sheepherder, lost prospector, or perhaps an Aboriginal hunter, had been there decades or centuries before. Here the air was fresher, the sun seemed brighter, the trees seemed taller and greener, the sky a turquoise blue, the wild animals wilder, and the world a lot wider. It was magical to sit there in the warmth of the summer sun, with my loyal climbing partner resting by my side. He, too, seeming to enjoy the solitude, in which the mountain spirits dominated every thought. There was something special in the air. It was almost hypnotic.

To the east, I could spot where the homesteaders had cleared the piñon trees and grown their corn and pinto beans. The hills were timbered, but the small valleys were covered with rabbitbrush. In the lower elevations along the dark-green vega at Mangas Creek, you could see the yellowish tint of the chamisa, another form of rabbitbrush. There was something very special about this wide-open, primitive country.

In the weeks and months that followed, Rusty and I would make our way to this very spot several times. We would sit and share a bologna sandwich and listen to the squawk of the piñon jays and the whirr of grasshoppers in the air, feel the cooling breeze in the trees, and gaze out over a landscape that had changed little since ancient peoples had hunted here. The Diné and Apache had roamed these hills searching for game, or fleeing Spanish and Mexican slaving expeditions and the long arm of the US Army.

During the Civil War, Hispanos under the legendary colonel Christopher "Kit" Carson not only chased the hated Texans out of the territory, but they also made war on both the Navajo and Mescalero and Mimbres Apache, pursuing them into the vast recesses and twisting canyons, destroying their crops, killing their animals, and burning their hogans and wikiups. During the war, the First New Mexico Cavalry scouted along Mangas Creek all the way north and west to Rito Quemado and Largo Creek. Scouts were at Zuni Salt Lake and as far west as the headwaters of the Little Colorado River in the White Mountains. One expedition, seeking a wagon road from Fort Craig on the Rio Grande to Fort West on the Gila River, found a creek emptying into the Tularosa River with grains of gold. After spotting the mineral resources of the area, Hispanos in the First New Mexico Cavalry and men in the California Column mapped the creeks and springs where small-scale irrigation was possible, and identified the vast grasslands that would run enormous herds of sheep and cattle.

The Apache, perhaps including Chiricahua chief Mangas Coloradas, had camped for decades in the Mangas Valley. Chiricahua warriors Victorio and Nana had raided the area in the late 1870s and early 1880s, killing, plundering, and taking slaves (mostly Spanish-speaking settlers) of their own. In May 1885, Geronimo sent a scare through the region when he escaped from the San Carlos Apache Indian Reservation. Homesteaders by the hundreds, like Winfield and Quata, had also come here, seeking a respite from the ravages of the Depression that blew their land away and destroyed their lives.

A harsh, yet starkly beautiful landscape of purple mountains set against a brilliant blue sky stretched to the horizon. To the south, the 9,700-foot, aspen-crowned summit of Mangas Mountain towered over the valley like a giant sentinel. Here the dark-green firs on the higher craggy slopes were easily discernable from the light-green ponderosa pines that shrouded the lower hillsides. Well adapted to the semi-arid climate, piñon trees grew in the lower elevations in abundance. Although crooked and gnarly, some were as much as one hundred years old and thirty-five to forty feet tall.

Although only a speck in the distance, the white, glistening lookout on the crest of Mangas Mountain was clearly visible. Knowing that my grandfather was frequently there looking for any sign of smoke and fire gave me great pride. Once, there was a small forest fire burning near the summit of the mountain and I was sure my grandfather was there too. To the west rose the grasslands of the Slaughter and Baca Mesas, where antelope herds roamed the open, rocky expanses. Below Cat Mountain to the east across Mangas Creek, the homes of the Leybas, Bacas, and Olivers were visible, as well as the Thompson house and barn in a grove of piñons.

Below the mountain to the east, beyond Rancho de San José and the old Catholic church, dust devils twirled and raced across the open plains in circling white columns. Several seemed to spiral hundreds of feet into the blue sky only to disappeared and magically form again. Farther east at the foot of Big Alegres were several sharp volcanic cones, or *cerros*. High above, the bigger mountain's rugged west face seemed pathless and unclimbable. Anywhere in the Mangas Valley, you could always look up and see Big Alegres and know where you were.

RATTLESNAKES

Within days, I was off again, this time to attack the barren, rugged, much more difficult south face of the mountain. There near the summit rose a number of small cliffs and volcanic outcroppings. On my green Schwinn with Rusty racing along behind, I headed down the dirt road and across Mangas Creek to the old church that provided the closest access to the mountain. Leaving the bike leaning against a piñon tree that had grown up by the church, I started up the mountain with Rusty. The first hour was easy, though the climb was steep and rocky in places.

Everything came to an abrupt halt about a hundred feet from the summit. At the base of a rocky ledge, amid a pile of boulders, Rusty began to bark furiously. It was a loud, excited bark I had never heard before, one that signaled imminent danger.

Scared that he might have come across a bear or a mountain lion in one of the rocky crevasses, I hurried upward. I envisioned him seriously injured or even killed, and then immediately saw the danger. Neatly coiled, with the upper part of its body in the air and its tongue flicking, was a large rattlesnake. Once you have heard the buzzing of a rattlesnake, the sound is embedded in your brain for the rest of your life. As I grabbed Rusty by the tail and pulled him away, I spotted a second rattler only yards to the left and a third snake to the right. We had climbed into a den of snakes! Half dragging and half carrying Rusty down the mountain, I fled to the church and a bicycle flight home to share my adventures with the family at the dinner table. "You damned well better be careful," was my father's only response.

Being an accomplished mountaineer like Norgay and Hillary, I was determined to climb the south face of Cat Mountain, rattlesnakes be damned! A few weeks later, I was back down the road, past the fallen wooden crosses at the old cemetery, through the piñons, and on the rocky south face of the mountain. Carefully skirting the rattlesnake den, I was nearing the summit when the climbing became exceedingly difficult, at least for a ten-year-old boy. Working my way upward, through the boulders, I reached a place where even an experienced mountaineer would have used a belay. Yet I was no ordinary mountaineer, or so I thought, and I was going to reach the summit.

Less than a hundred feet from the top, I had to climb close to the face of the mountain to keep from falling off. In one place, I had to reach overhead for a handhold before pulling myself upward over a small overhang. Gaining a secure handhold, I stuck my head over the ledge and there in the bright morning light was a coiled rattlesnake, less than two feet from my face, his fierce-looking eyes zeroed in on my forehead and his long, forked tongue swaying about, testing for scent in the breeze. I had no doubt the snake, with his deadly venom, was prepared to strike. For a millisecond, I envisioned being struck squarely in the forehead and falling off the face of the cliff and becoming little more than a pile of broken bones. At the same time, visions of my mother weeping over an open casket before a large hole in the ground swept through my mind.

Rapidly ducking my head, it seemed an eternity before I could regain a secure foothold and release the handhold. This was the snake's mountain, not mine, and I needed no further convincing. His relatives had scared me off the mountain once and he had done it a second time.

With Rusty on my heels, I raced down the mountain, stumbling and falling several times, trembling in fear, skinning my knees, an elbow, before finally reaching the safety of the old church. I sat on the stone steps staring at the cottonwood trees and the ruins of the old ranch house for what must have been an hour or two, still petrified. My heartbeat finally eased, leaving me forever grateful I had survived yet another harrowing adventure. It was only then that I realized I had urinated in my pants. Never had I experienced such fear. I loved the animal kingdom and cringed when my father killed a deer, but I hated those damned rattlesnakes with a passion.

Rusty went down to the springs for a drink of water and returned to lie in the shade of the old church until the sun began setting over Slaughter Mesa. I remember thinking that Hillary and Norgay were lucky there were no rattlesnakes on Mount Everest. That evening over dinner, I was quiet, not wanting to explain the deep, bloody scratches on my arms, the skinned knees, and that I had peed in my pants, a very unmanly thing to do. I certainly did not want a lecture from my grandfather that

Thompsons were brave and did not do such things. Moreover, to reveal what had really happened would, at the insistence of my mother, bring my mountaineering career to an inglorious and abrupt end.

I would return to Cat Mountain several times that summer and in the summers that followed, but never again would I attempt to climb the south face. A vision of that rattlesnake striking me in the face reverberated in my consciousness and in nightmares for years.

I was with my grandmother one day in early summer gathering eggs in the chicken house when she reached under one of the hens to retrieve an egg, only to feel something large and slimy. It was a coiled rattlesnake. With a frightful yell, she fled for my grandfather, who grabbed a pitchfork, jousted the hen off her nest, and with a hoe, cut off the head of the "damned egg-sucking snake," before throwing it out in front of the chicken house, where the chickens pecked it to pieces and ate it.

Rattlesnakes were dangerous, and more than one homesteader and countless domestic animals perished from their venomous bite. About this same time, a surveyor working for the state highway department near Quemado died from a rattlesnake bite. So did one of the Armstrongs north of Quemado. Years later when my father was working for the Forest Service, he was driving home one evening with his partner, Robert Orona, when they spotted a large rattlesnake lying across the road. Orona insisted my father stop, since he wanted to add another set of rattlers to his collection on his hatband. For many cowboys, such buttons were status symbols as much as deer antlers were to hunters. Orona put his boot on the tail of the snake and reached down to cut off the rattler buttons when the snake swung around and bit him on the leg, just above his boot. Later that evening, when his leg began to swell and hurt, Orona was taken by ambulance to the hospital in Springerville. A few days later, I went with my father to see him. Orona was in good spirits, but his leg was swollen to several times its normal size, suspended in an elevated sling above the bed, and black as obsidian.

Another mountain I conquered that summer was a small volcanic *cerrito* a few miles northeast of where we lived. One of the great thrills in the ascent was finding a large spearpoint at least five inches long. Here was another treasure added to the family collection of arrow-heads that grew every summer and during hunting season.

Perhaps more significant was the discovery on the summit of another stone enclosure that had to be a hundred feet in circumference and four feet high. Who toiled endlessly to carry hundreds of black volcanic rocks from the slopes of the mountain to build the structure? I wondered.

MULE MOUNTAIN AND THE THREE SPRUCES

G W hen my grandfather first came to the valley, he made friends with seventy-five-year-old Procopio Leyba, the oldest settler in the valley. Leyba had herded sheep all over the area and lived with his wife, Merencina, and two daughters, Clotilde and Primitiva, in a small, two-room adobe house on the west side of Mangas Creek, across the vega from where we lived. Leyba was "a good and honest man," Winfield proclaimed, which was good enough for me.

Leyba related a story to my grandfather, through an interpreter, of how around the turn of the century he was herding sheep when he came across an old abandoned mine on Mule Mountain, which he speculated was a silver mine dating back to the Spanish era. Mule Mountain was a part of the eastern rimrock of Slaughter Mesa just west of Cat Mountain that jutted out toward the Mangas Valley. From the mine entrance, Leyba said, you could look through the gap between Cat Mountain and Baca Mesa and see the village of Mangas and the water in Mangas Creek. Leyba's son, Prospero, who lived across Mangas Creek to the east and who was married to Josefita Mata—who bore fifteen children—also repeated the story of the lost mine.

LOST SILVER MINE

Years later, the story was enhanced by a deer hunter who told my grandfather he had stumbled across the mine about two-thirds of the way up the mountain. The mineshaft, the hunter said, ran forty to fifty feet into the side of the mountain, and the tailings from the mine were masked by a grove of gamble oaks.

In the early fall, at the end of fire season, we frequently went in search of the mine. Idle thoughts of getting rich seemed to be a characteristic of many who survived the Great Depression. Bouncing along a rutted road past Rancho de San José and a two-track rut that turned west toward the base of the mountain, we spent hundreds of hours and many a weekend searching for the mine. My grandfather was always determined to get to a point on the mountain where you could look through the gap at the north end of Cat Mountain and see Mangas Creek. He never seemed to wonder why, if there really were a silver mine, Leyba or the hunters or the sheepherders had not staked a claim and become wealthy. Over several years, we must have walked over every square foot of Mule Mountain.

Although my grandfather remained just as poor as ever after these expeditions, he was never deterred. The mine had to be there somewhere, he insisted. I sometimes thought it was not the dream of getting rich that compelled him as much as just being out in the mountains. Deep down, I think my grandfather had a little bit of John Muir in him.

APACHE GOLD AND THE LOST ADAMS DIGGINGS

While my grandfather may have been the only individual looking for the silver mine on Mule Mountain, hundreds came in search of the Lost Adams Diggings. Much of this had to do with a talented University of Texas folklorist and Lone Star myth keeper named J. Frank Dobie, who wrote a best-selling book in 1939 entitled *Apache Gold and Yaqui Silver*. Although the book was folklore and based as much on myth and legend as fact, readers devoured it. After all, Dobie was a distinguished professor at the University of Texas. It did not help that during the Depression, the volume of mail in Catron County prompted the Post Office Department to create a new post office northwest of Pie Town called Adams Diggings.

According to Dobie and others, a man named Adams, whose first name has been lost to history, was traveling by wagon train along the Gila Trail from Los Angeles to Tucson during the Civil War. When Apache attacked and burned the wagon train, Adams escaped with a dozen of his horses and made his way to the outpost of Sacaton,

Arizona. There he met a group of twenty-one miners, heading into the goldfields in central Arizona, who were in need of horses. A deal was struck for the horses, and the party set out with a Pima Mexican guide who promised to lead the prospectors to a valley of gold. "I know a place where the canyon walls cry tears of [gold] every day! And those tears are larger than your coins!" the guide allegedly said. The guide had been with a party of Apache who attacked some Pueblo Indians in western New Mexico, at which time he had discovered gold nuggets the size of acorns.

Traveling through the conifer-crowned White Mountains into western New Mexico, within sight of the San Francisco Mountains to the northwest, the guide paused and pointed to two mountains shaped like sugarloaves. "The gold canyon lies at the foot of those peaks," he said. Trekking on, the miners entered a narrow canyon through what Adams said was a "Little Door." The entrance was so narrow that only one rider could enter at a time. Following a twisting trail to the bottom of the canyon, the prospectors found a spring just below a small waterfall.

Within days, the men had collected enough gold to make them all rich. The gold nuggets were so large and numerous that they could pick them off the ground like acorns, just as the guide had said. After getting his share of the gold, the guide departed, but not before offering a warning. The miners should not remain in the canyon for long, for they were in land claimed by Nana, warrior and chief of the Chihenne band of Chiricahua Apache. Sure enough, Nana and thirty warriors appeared not long after the guide left. The area above the falls was sacred, Nana warned, and under no circumstances were the miners to go there.

Several miners continued to gather more gold while others built a log cabin and hid a cache of gold under the cabin's hearthstone. When the miners ran out of supplies, six men set out for Fort Wingate, on the edge of El Malpais, southwest of what is today Grants. When the men had not returned after nine days, Adams climbed out of the canyon and discovered five bodies on the trail. Racing back to camp, he found to his horror that a large party of Apache had raided the camp, killed all the miners, and burned the cabin to the ground. The hearthstone was too hot to move. Thirteen days later, Adams and another miner were rescued by a military patrol out of what Dobie identified as Fort Apache, though he failed to note that Fort Apache did not exist at the time.

After the Apache Wars, Adams settled in California but returned to western New Mexico several times looking for his canyon of gold. He never found it. In 1918, a Socorro County cowpuncher and lawman, Robert W. "Bob" Lewis, claimed he found several skeletons and Adams's abandoned cabin at the mouth of a canyon twenty-five miles northeast of Pie Town. Everything was just as Adams had described it. A Magdalena sheepherder had been there first, Lewis claimed, found the gold, and with his reward bought a ranch near Albuquerque.

A rancher in the Pie Town area, J. M. Johnson, spent his entire adult life looking for the Lost Adams Diggings, as did hundreds of other prospectors. Johnson, who came to the country as a boy in a covered wagon, never lost faith that Adams's gold had to be somewhere in northern Catron County. "Uncle Jimmie," as he was known, shot himself in the head with a .30-30 Winchester at the age of seventy-six.

Many of those who went in search of the Lost Adams Diggings were certain that the gold was in the Zuni Mountains. Others speculated that it was on the Navajo Nation to the northwest, in sight of the San Francisco Mountains. Many others, including my grandfather, were convinced the gold had to be southwest of Pie Town, perhaps in the Mangas or Gallo Mountains, not far from where we lived, but there were certainly no waterfalls there. If not there, it was probably in the Mogollon Mountains to the south, most likely in Whitewater Canyon near where the Civilian Conservation Corps had built the Catwalk in the 1930s, just upstream from Glenwood. But this was a long way from Fort Wingate and not in sight of the San Francisco Mountains. Soldiers out of Fort West near Cliff had discovered gold and silver there about the same time that Adams claimed his gold. Others thought the Datil or Gallinas Mountains were a good place to look. Before he died, Adams spent most of his time searching the headwaters of the San Francisco and Tularosa Rivers near Reserve. For my grandfather and many others, the gold *had* to be there somewhere. After all, Adams and Dobie said it was.

Every summer, a man with a heavy German accent stopped at the house asking for directions. Where did this road lead? Who owned a certain piece of land? Did my father know of other mountains that looked like sugarloaves? Where did this canyon run into that canyon? Every summer, he came to ask more questions, and he and my grandfather would sit and talk for hours. He even stayed overnight once, and he and my grandfather sat talking long after midnight, after everyone else had gone to bed. "He is just another poor, damned fool," my father said, "looking for that damned gold."

Winfield must have dug under the hearthstones of half the abandoned homesteads in northern Catron County. It was obvious, even to me, that these cabins dated from the 1920s and 1930s and could not have been Adams's abandoned cabin. Nevertheless, my grandfather, hoping to find Adams's lost gold and strike it rich, just kept on looking and digging.

As it turns out, Adams probably did have some gold but had actually stolen it from a wagon train in central Arizona. The knowledge of his crime was so common in western New Mexico that once when he was in Reserve, Adams was roughed up. And he was almost killed in Magdalena when a Civil War veteran of the California Column recognized him as the man who had robbed the wagon train.

URANIUM AND THE THREE SPRUCES

In the early 1950s, large deposits of valuable uranium were discovered north of Grants and even small deposits were found northeast of Pie Town. It was the Lost Adams Diggings all over again. My father bought a magazine with the story of a down-on-his-luck uranium prospector in Utah named Charlie Steen. Steen's discovery led to a uranium rush all over the Colorado Plateau. As my father told the story, Steen had been conflicted as to whether he should buy food for his family or a Geiger counter and look for uranium. He chose the latter, went off into the canyonlands near Moab, and on July 6, 1952, struck it rich. If Steen could strike it rich, so could my grandfather.

By the fall of 1953, Winfield had saved enough money to purchase a ninety-nine-dollar Geiger counter, and when the snow melted the next spring, we were off. He would drive to the end of a road some-where, and we would roam the hillsides for miles around, inspecting rocks and cliffs and anything my grandfather thought interesting. We would walk for days and usually found little of interest. Then one day, Winfield drove to the foot of Big Alegres and we walked to some small cliffs that lined the western edge of a high mesa. He put the Geiger counter down on some rocks and the needle on the gadget went off the scale. Excitedly, he turned the controls to another scale, and again the Geiger counter went to the highest reading. The same thing happened on a third, highest scale. The entire outcropping was rich in uranium, and my grandfather could hardly control himself. If he was excited and happy, I was too. He said we needed a name for our mine, which he was certain was equal to or would surpass the Moab mine of Charlie Steen, undoubtedly one of the great uranium deposits in the American West. I suggested Three Spruces for three spruce trees that grew at the foot of the cliff, and he liked the name.

As we sat and ate our bologna sandwiches, Winfield was already calculating how to get the ore down the mountainside and truck it to the railhead at Magdalena. The mountain was so steep that a chute would have to be constructed, he said. It mattered little. We were rich. Winfield said he thought he would purchase a new pickup truck, some-thing he had always wanted. We could hardly wait to share the exciting news with the rest of the family that evening.

Early the next morning, we were off to our Three Spruces mine. Winfield said we would have to keep everything quiet until we had filed a claim at the courthouse in Reserve. Over the next several days, we worked hard to build several rock cairns at the corner of each of our three claims. A mason jar containing the proper claim information was placed in each cairn.

I think it was about a week later that we returned to our mine and my father discovered the readings were lower than before. Not to worry, my grandfather said; the batteries in the Geiger counter prob-ably needed changing. After the batteries were changed that evening, the readings were again lower the next day, and lower the day after that. Then my father discovered something interesting. Even big cow chips and an old piñon log were radioactive. Moreover, day after day, the Geiger counter readings at the claims grew lower and lower, and my grandfather became seriously concerned. Perhaps we weren't rich after all. After a month, there were few readings at all.

Months later, my father and grandfather realized what had happened. We had been in a sea of radiation fallout from one of the aboveground nuclear explosions in Nevada. We just happened to be downwind, and all the radiation had come to earth on that small mesa not far from Big Alegres.

Without realizing it, we had waded around in radioactive dust for weeks, unwitting victims of the government's extensive aboveground nuclear testing. It was amazing we were not dead; indeed, it was later revealed that several individuals had become deathly ill and some had even died after filming scenes for a movie near St. George, Utah.

The uranium boom ended when the government stopped buying the mineral in the 1970s, but my grandfather never gave up hope of striking it rich. He never did get his new pickup truck.

UNIDENTIFIED FLYING OBJECTS

Around this time, Winfield noticed something fascinating and intriguing. As the snow melted along the eastern rim of Baca Mesa, there was one snowbank that did not melt. Examining the spot with his binoculars, my grandfather became convinced that the distant white speck was not snow but a shiny metal object, probably aluminum. That winter, a small plane had gone missing on a flight from Albuquerque to Tucson, and my grandfather had little doubt he had located the crash site three-fourths of the way up the mountain.

Then Winfield thought it might be a crashed UFO. This was the era when UFO sightings were common in New Mexico. Imaginations ran wild after a UFO allegedly crashed near Roswell in the summer of 1947. There were other sightings near Roswell a few years later. It was always amazing to me that somehow extraterrestrials always crashed in New Mexico near Roswell. If Texas and Alaska were larger, why didn't they crash there, or in Canada or Mexico, or Africa or Asia?

Early on a Saturday morning, the sun was still glistening through the trees as we set off for the wreckage site. Halfway down the dirt road to Route 60, Winfield turned the old 1947 flatbed Ford truck west along a rough dirt road and past a creaky windmill, where we parked and walked along a fence line for at least a mile before beginning a steep ascent. The rabbitbrush gave way to scrubby juniper and piñon. At the foot of the mountain, Winfield pulled out his binoculars for a closer glance at the site of the crash and then handed them to me. There was little doubt we had discovered the wreckage of an airplane.

My excitement went wild. Two people had been on board the missing aircraft and we were certain to find their mangled and frozen bodies or, perhaps if the crash were that of a UFO, the remains of little humanlike creatures similar or identical to those found near Roswell. I had never seen a dead body before. During the strenuous hike up the mountain, I became more and more excited, and I think my grandfather did too. This was as exhilarating as climbing Mount Everest. We stopped to rest for a moment and sip water from a canteen my grandfather had brought and then continued the steep climb. After about an hour, we were high on the mountain and we stopped to rest again.

We finally arrived at the crash site, but instead of the wreckage of an airplane or a crashed UFO and the remains of aliens, there was a giant, silver-colored weather balloon lying on the ground and partially draped over a large juniper tree. Attached to the balloon were a bright-orange parachute and some weather instruments. Grandfather figured the device was designed to detach the parachute and the instruments from the balloon at a high altitude, but it had misfired. We carefully rolled the balloon and the parachute into a big bundle and spent the rest of the day carrying, dragging, and pulling it off the mountain.

The small instrument package had an address at White Sands Missile Range in Alamogordo. My grandfather dictated a letter that my grandmother wrote in longhand asking the army if they wanted their missing balloon, saying the parachute and instruments were still attached. A few weeks later, a formal letter arrived saying White Sands was not interested in the recovery of the instruments. My father cut up the balloon and used it to pack some of his poached deer meat, and my grandmother used the parachute to make a couple of shirts and even some underwear.

There were other rewards from all our mountain trekking. I began gathering a large pile of mule deer antlers, which my grandfather stacked into a large Christmas tree that we decorated every year. While searching for uranium near Big Alegres, we once found the skull and remains of a large, twelve-point buck that had starved to death or was killed by coyotes after getting his antlers hung up in a barbed-wire gate. There was one rule everyone abided by: no one carried antlers around during hunting season. My father claimed he once met a hunter from Albuquerque, camped near Mangas, who bragged he was a "sound hunter." Once he heard a sound, he would shoot in the direction of the noise. Only later would he determine if he had killed anything.

RURAL ELECTRIFICATION AUTHORITY

A very special moment came in the early 1950s, when the Rural Electrification Authority (REA), one of FDR's New Deal programs, commenced building an electrical line from Pie Town to Mangas. Created in 1936, the REA brought electricity to rural areas in the country. The isolated areas of Catron County were among the last in the nation to receive the service.

I had no idea at the time what joy and delight electric lights would bring, and what we had been missing for so many years. The Norris brothers from Pie Town cleared the right-of-way through the woods while men from Socorro in big trucks and cranes set tall creosoted poles deep into the ground and strung the wire. Everyone along the route seemed excited.

My father hired a man from Quemado to run wires all through the house, and we anxiously waited for someone to connect the house to the grid. As the family gathered late one afternoon in the living room, my grandmother was given the honor of switching on the lights for the first time. Everyone then took turns flipping the switch on and off. Still in awe several hours later, I kept flicking the lights on and off, until my father put a halt to my exuberance.

To read and do homework, I no longer had to sit by the kerosene lamps my mother lit after dinner, or the flames of the fireplace. We were now part of a bright and exciting new world. As far as the Thompsons were concerned, Lyndon B. Johnson, who had witnessed firsthand the impact the REA had on his family in the Texas Hill Country, was correct when he said in an address in Albuquerque in 1954 that "rural electrification has brought to our country the most profound revolution since our ancestors broke with the British Empire."

Within a few years, with my grandfather and father working regularly, we had an electric stove, a refrigerator, and a small indoor bathroom that my father fashioned. Having to tramp through the snow to the privy on wintry days was now a thing of the past.

COCKFIGHTING

When I was nine or ten, my grandfather became obsessed with cockfighting—a blood sport in which roosters are placed in a ring and fought to the death for the amusement of onlookers who bet on the cocks. Popular in ancient times in India, China, Persia, and other Eastern countries, and introduced to Greece in the time of Themistocles around 500 BC, the "sport" then spread west to Rome and beyond. Magellan had witnessed cockfighting in the Philippines in 1521, and against objections from the Christian clergy, cockfighting was introduced into the North American colonies at an early date.

Although four neighboring states had declared the sport a felony, cockfighting blossomed in New Mexico and by the 1950s became an $80 million industry. In 2007, however, New Mexico became the forty-ninth state to outlaw cockfighting, despite opposition from thousands of citizens and lawsuits by the New Mexico Gamefowl Association, a cockfighting advocacy group. Today, cockfighting is illegal in all fifty states, though the gamecock remains the mascot of more than one university. Even being a spectator at a cockfight today is illegal in forty-three states.

We raised cocks alongside the hens we kept for eggs. Those male birds my grandfather deemed inferior wound up on the dinner table. Winfield would grab the unfortunate bird by the neck and violently twirl its body around until the animal was decapitated, after which its headless body lay on the ground kicking and twisting in an ugly death spiral. Other times, they would be killed when he cut off their heads on a chopping block near the woodpile.

Only the larger, stronger birds were kept and physically trained. The colorfully plumed roosters, often with beautiful black and brown feathers, were separated from the other cocks in wood-and-wire pens and were carefully fed and watered every day, as if they were thoroughbred racehorses. Winfield also built a small glassed-in area next to the chicken house, where he spent hours exercising the roosters, tossing them into the air and forcing them to scurry from side to side.

Several times a year, we journeyed to Hot Springs (the town that became Truth or Consequences), where a man by the name of Herb Lett had converted a large concrete-brick garage into a fighting arena for cockfighting, complete with bleachers. The entrance to the arena was devoted to slot machines. As many as a hundred people, many of questionable moral character and often intoxicated, money in their fists, would crowd around the pit or sit in the stands, drinking, smoking, yelling, and betting on the fights.

With their neck feathers fanned and wings flapping, the birds would jump and parry at each other. They would kick and duel in midair, striking at each other with feet and beaks. The more trauma one of the cocks inflicted on the other, the more frenzied the crowd became. When the fighting waned, handlers would pick up the birds and blow on their backs, yank at their beaks, and hold them beak to beak in an attempt to work them into another frenzy.

Cockfighting was one of the cruelest things I had ever seen. The owners would place their gamecocks in the ring, where they would fight until one of them was critically injured. Matches involved fights between an agreed number of birds, usually five or six, the overall victor being the one who won the majority of fights. Bets on individual fights were anywhere from ten to fifty dollars. Matches were for one hundred dollars or more. Perhaps the cruelest of all was the battle royal, in which several cocks were placed in the pit at the same time and allowed to remain until all but one was dead or disabled.

Although the roosters were bred to fight, it is doubtful they could have killed one another had not razor-sharp, curved, metal spurs called gaffs been strapped to their legs where the cock's natural spur had been partially removed. It was like giving a boxer a pair of gloves outfitted with knives. The gaffs were sharp enough to puncture a lung, pierce an eye, break bones, and inflict maximum injury wherever they landed. Sometimes even the handlers were injured. Once, Winfield had one of the gaffs run through his hand.

Fights could last anywhere from a few seconds to fifteen minutes. Rules did not require a bird to die in order to determine a winner, though death was usually the outcome. Dead birds were thrown in a small alley behind the pit and a second pair would begin their deadly combat. Three or four small boys in torn overalls scurried to grab the dead birds. Those that were still alive would have their necks wrung and be thrown in a big brown tow sack and joyfully carried away, certain to wind up on somebody's dinner plate.

CHEEPER THE FIGHTING ROOSTER

I had taken a special liking to a large rooster my grandfather allowed to run loose and who seemed smarter and gentler than the others. He was always chirping, so I called him Cheeper. His black and brown feathers glistened like a polished car. He was little short of majestic as he came running through the snow, hoping for something to eat. I had purchased a small rack for the back of my green Schwinn, and I taught Cheeper how to jump on and we would ride through the backyard and along the road in front of the house for a mile or more, over the cow pastures and through the trees, or across my grandfather's cornfield. Cheeper seemed to delight in the rides—the rougher the better—and always held on tight. He would spot me on the bicycle and come running for a ride. He quickly became a family favorite that everyone rejoiced in. "Damnedest thing I've ever seen," a visitor once remarked.

Unbeknownst to me, my grandfather took Cheeper to one of the cockfights in Hot Springs, and while I was busy renting seat cushions to people in the stands for 10 cents apiece, my grandfather put Cheeper in the ring. He was killed and discarded like all the other dead birds.

Back home when I missed the rooster and became alarmed, my grandfather confessed what had happened. I pouted and cried for days. Even months later when I thought of Cheeper, tears would roll down my cheeks. Losing Cheeper was like losing a family member. Every time I rode my bicycle, I missed him dearly. My mother and grandmother provided hugs that helped, but deep down inside, I knew they were bitter too. I thought I would never forgive my grandfather. In time, I guess I did, but I never forgot Cheeper, just another dead rooster consumed by one of the poor families in Hot Springs.

A month later, Winfield, who was making some money with his gamecocks, agreed to a match at a larger venue in the Mesilla Valley. Five of my grandfather's best roosters were pitted against those of another cockfighter, with each person putting up $150, a sizeable sum of money. We had made the long drive the day before and rented a cheap motel in Las Cruces while the roosters, with food and water, were left in cages at the cockfighting arena south of Mesilla. The arena was on the edge of a large orchard next to a cotton field. I remember it was late in the evening when we got back to the motel, and the heat was oppressive.

When the contest began the next day, my grandfather's roosters stood motionless when they were attacked. They were not even attempting to fight, and it seemed as if they could not wait to be killed. My grandfather was proud of several of his roosters that had won previous fights at Hot Springs. Something was obviously wrong. After the fifth rooster died quickly, he concluded that someone had entered the building the night before and given the roosters a sedative or some kind of a drug. Angry words were exchanged, accusations were thrown about, and a crowd gathered. For a time, my grandfather refused to give up his $150. My father stood by with clenched fists, and I thought there would be a brawl. "You're damned lucky I don't have a gun or I would blow your fucking head off!" my grandfather yelled at his opponent. It was the first time I had ever heard the "f" word and it was obvious Winfield was furious; his face was as red as a ripe tomato and sweat rolled off his bald head. Before we left with all the empty birdcages, he swore he would never return to Mesilla, and he never did. In fact, his cockfighting days were over.

POKER PLAYING

Besides poaching deer and fighting cocks, my father and grandfather were always involved in illegal poker games. In fact, everyone in the county seemed to poach deer and play cards. When people were arrested for these activities, Catron County juries refused to convict them. The poker games at Pie Town were in a small wooden shack north of the highway, down a rutted road hidden away in some piñon trees, about three blocks behind Tom Weathers's Texaco filling station. The shack's proprietor, a World War I veteran named Claude Rhodes, had settled north of Pie Town during the Depression but had since sold his homestead and moved into town.

One dedicated poker player and World War I veteran was Leslie "Les" Webster Thomas. In 1926, Les and his wife, Beulah, along with their two sons, had driven a wagon with a team of horses all the way from Texas. The family had homesteaded at the foot of Big Alegres, where they built a half dugout and two daughters were born. Seven more children would follow before the family moved to town in 1946.

Another enthusiastic gambler was Wesley "Cap" McCormick, a badly shell-shocked World War I veteran who, in 1931 at the age of thirty-seven, had arrived in a covered wagon from Texas with his mother, sister, and half-brother, Tom Weathers, along with a small herd of cows, some horses, and a few mules. It was rumored that Cap had lost his homestead north of Pie Town while playing poker.

A sink and small pantry sat on one side of the Rhodes hut; a small potbellied stove used for cooking and heating was on another side. In one corner, there was a small bed, and in the middle, the poker table, covered in a dark-green army blanket. Usually about five or six individuals would gather around sunset, and they would play until the sun came up. Some of the gamblers, after losing their money, would depart in the middle of the night. I always tagged along, and in the winter, Rhodes would let me sleep on his small bed. In the warm summer nights, I retreated to my father's car, where it was quieter.

In the smoke-filled room, only draw poker, lowball, and stud poker were allowed. There was always a new deck of cards and alcohol was prohibited. Several of the poker players, I remember, were poor, arriving in their old, beat-up trucks. One man who seemed to lose all the time had several children.

My father talked for years about the time he had a king-high straight flush and bet all his money only to lose to a man who had four aces and the joker. "Damn! What are the odds against that?" he always complained.

On the way home in the early-morning hours, my father and grandfather would discuss their wins and losses, when they should have raised the bet, and when they should have folded. My father, who had played a lot of poker in the army during the war, always seemed to win, often as much as $150; my grandfather always seemed to lose.

MOVIE TIME

Frequently on Saturdays, especially in winter, when my grandfather and father were not working, the family headed to the "picture show" at the Farm Bureau building in Pie Town. As many as thirty people would huddle around a big wooden stove and sit on rough wooden benches. Marvin Few had purchased a movie projector and started showing movies, after which Bill Perry took over the operation, followed by Tom Weathers. Once, in the middle of a movie, the projector fell off the stand and crashed to the floor; it was thirty minutes before the movie resumed. Admission was five cents, but children eight or younger got in free. On rare occasions, there was even popcorn for five cents a bag. Every movie was preceded by a short serial. There was Batman flying through Gotham and getting himself in an unescapable and dangerous predicament, just before the reel ended. The following week, he would miraculously escape, only to get into another jam. There were Dick Tracy, Buck Rogers, and Flash Gordon, and the adventures of Red Ryder, all struggling against evil. I even remember the Purple Monster making his appearance in Pie Town. When I was absent for a week or two, I would seek out a classmate on Monday morning to fill me in on the adventures I had missed.

One movie I will always remember was *Battleground*. It was the first significant American film about World War II, and my father insisted we go since the movie featured the Battle of the Bulge, where he had fought and almost died in the snow and cold of the Ardennes in the winter of 1944–1945. Directed by William Wellman and starring Van Johnson, John Hodiak, and Ricardo Montalbán, the movie told the story of three vulnerable American soldiers who were attached to the 101st Airborne Division and surrounded by the Germans at Bastogne, Belgium. Early in the movie, each soldier seriously considers running away or concocting a scheme that would somehow get him sent to the rear.

In the cold and snow, the soldiers dug in and set up a roadblock. But this did not stop the dastardly Germans from disguising themselves as Americans and infiltrating the American lines. My father thought the movie was accurate, including the December 23, 1944, scene, where some Germans appear with a flag of truce demanding the Americans' surrender and General Anthony McAuliffe responds with his famous "Nuts!" which the Germans seemed unable to translate. After moviegoers celebrated Christmas with the besieged soldiers, who were down to their last few rounds of ammunition, the weather cleared, Allied aircraft took to the skies, and the siege was lifted. With a lively cadence, the survivors proudly marched to the rear, passing their replacements. The good guys won, as they always did in the movies of those days.

I think it was at the end of the first reel when the lights came on and my father looked up to see a buddy of his huddled behind one of the rear seats, shivering and shaking like an aspen leaf. As everyone stood in stunned silence, my father, with compassion and empathy—for which I will always remember him—hugged the veteran, and helped usher him through the dark and cold to his car, as his wife and small children scurried along behind. Iwo Jima and Okinawa, my father said, had been too much for him. Those battles had been all hell, he said.

That marine veteran was one of half a million Americans who endured debilitating post-traumatic stress disorder during and after the war. On the way home, my grandfather talked freely about the pitiful Americans he had seen with "shell shock" in France in 1918. My father, however, was mostly silent, perhaps experiencing flashbacks of his own, saying only that he enjoyed the movie. It was evident, even to a child, that the shadows of the war, even in America and distant Pie Town, were long and at times painful.

WORK REID

One summer when I was about ten and my father was off working building a house near Little Alegres Mountain, my grandfather spotted several fallen piñon logs he said would make excellent wood. After Quata packed our bologna sandwiches, we headed out into the woods in the old truck. For some reason, instead of hauling the wood, my grandfather decided to stack the wood in piles to haul later. I was doing my best to keep up with Winfield, who, despite his age, always worked hard. After a week of sweat, we had several loads of good wood. Grandfather said we should rest for a day or two, and go back and get the wood later.

Sure enough, when we went back a few days later, most of the wood was gone. I had never seen my grandfather so agitated. "Some son of a bitch done stole our wood," he angrily blurted out. "Would you believe that? I think I know who the shithead who done it is." Winfield carefully examined the tire tracks in the soft sand as if he were the Sherlock Holmes of the Mangas Valley and said he had no doubt as to the culprit. There was only one person in the entire valley who would dare do anything like that. "I'll be damned," he complained, as we climbed back into the old truck.

Work Reid, whose real name was Leslie Charles Reid, was a character if there ever was one. Everybody knew him for miles around. Work was a skinny, ruddy-faced, Texas-born World War II veteran who always wore an old, greasy hat and could not have weighed more than 120 pounds, although he was almost six feet tall. He worked as a cowboy almost from the time he left school after the fifth grade in Snyder in Scurry County, Texas.

Work lived in a rundown, two-room shack in a grove of piñon trees less than a half mile off the main road. Through the years, he worked for several ranchers driving cattle along the Livestock Driveway to Magdalena, and he had a small herd of his own. He was such a noted character that Eleanor Williams, a well-known artist who lived on Largo Creek south of Quemado, persuaded him to sit for a portrait. Work had the reputation of being a heavy drinker. Everyone had at least one or two Work Reid stories. Many were embellished, others true. He was undoubtedly the wood thief.

Well-known western New Mexico artist Eleanor Williams made this lifelike oil-on-canvas portrait of "Work" Reid in 1961. Work was content to sit over several days as long as she kept him refreshed with Coors beer, Williams recalled. Courtesy of Helen Cress.

My grandfather was still mad when he arrived at Work's ramshackle homestead, with its crumbling fireplace, a mile or two from the crime scene. I was glad he did not have a gun or I think he would have shot poor Work, who readily, with little embarrassment, admitted to taking the wood. In fact, the freshly cut wood was easily identifiable in his woodpile, and the tires on his old pickup matched my grandfather's detective work. "I needed some good wood for the winter, and somebody just left it there," Work explained. "It's damn good wood. You can always use some good wood for the winter." Few words were exchanged as Winfield backed his truck up to Work's woodpile and stood by as Work loaded the wood into the bed. As we drove off, Winfield said, "Most worthless son of a bitch I ever met. Should have just shot him to put him out of his misery."

As the stories go, many Saturday nights, Work would drive to a bar in Datil, Quemado, or even Springerville—fifty miles across the state line in Arizona—where he would get dead drunk. He allegedly was driving home late one Saturday night, inebriated, when the state police stopped him. "What are you doing, Work?" the policeman inquired. "Oh," Work responded, "just wokin' wond a widdle." "Well," the officer replied, "come with me and you can wok a wond a widdle in the Quemado jail until you sober up." Another time, a state policeman observed Work drinking one too many at the Eagle Guest Ranch in Datil and told the man, "I think I will just take your driver's license away." "No, you won't," Work responded defiantly. "Bob Wellborn [another state policeman in Quemado] already took it."

In 1953, my father saved enough money to buy a new two-door, black Chevrolet Bel Air from Hammond Motor Company in Magdalena for $1,300. I never saw my father take such pride in anything as he did in that car. It was the first new vehicle he had ever owned, and he seemed to spend half his time washing and polishing it. Every time you got into the car, he wanted assurance your shoes were clean.

We went to see Work Reid in the car one day, for some reason I have long since forgotten, and after only a few minutes, my father emerged from the house to find three of Work's goats standing on his new car. Two were on the hood and one was on the very top. "Work!"

my father shouted, "get those goddamned goats of yours off my car!" Back home, my father began his usual polishing. For days, he worried endlessly and complained about the scuff marks on his new car.

The state policeman in Quemado was certain it was only a matter of time before Work was found dead as the result of a serious accident somewhere along US Route 60 or the dirt road leading to Mangas. Sure enough, early one Sunday morning, just as the sun came up, he spotted Work's wrecked pickup at the bottom of a deep arroyo a few miles west of Quemado. It was obvious Work had been doing some drinking in Arizona, as was his habit, and had run off the road on his way home, crashed down the hillside, went through the right-of-way fence, and rolled. The accident was serious, and the policeman thought Work was probably dead.

Cautiously making his way into the arroyo, the policeman found Work. Though he was badly bruised and bloodied, he was sitting upright and gripping the steering wheel of his pickup. There were deep lacerations on his scalp; dried blood covered his face. Although the windshield was shattered, the top of the cab caved in, and the fenders bent, the pickup was upright and pointing up the hill. "Work, you all right?" the policeman yelled out. "Yeah," Work responded. "Just give me a push and I'll drive her out of here."

Another frequently repeated story, undoubtedly exaggerated, if true at all, had Work striding into a bar on Route 60 in downtown Springerville during the annual rodeo celebration on the Fourth of July. "Give me a drink!" he shouted out to the bartender. "I'm a fucker, a fighter, and a wild horse rider!" A man who was standing nearby with his wife took exception to Work's vulgarity, and, half-intoxicated himself, took a swing at Work and caught him squarely on the chin, knocking the old cowboy under a table. Crawling out on all fours, Work made his way back to the bar. "Give me a drink," he said. "I am still a fucker and a wild horse rider." Work Reid died at the age of sixty-eight in September 1978 and was buried at Mangas. ·

WATERMELON

In the fall, people from around Pie Town would caravan to Cedar Hill, near Aztec in the Animas River Valley in the northwestern part of the state. Here they would camp for several days and pick peaches by the bushels.

Many families looked forward every summer to the arrival of fruit trucks that offered delicious fruits and vegetables. On such occasions, my mother and grandmother carefully selected several bushels of fruit, usually peaches and apples, and immediately begin canning the fruit for the winter.

One summer, my grandfather bought a giant green melon for fifty cents from one of the peddlers. I had never seen anything like it. It must have weighed thirty pounds or more. My grandmother grew pumpkins and squash in the garden, but this melon was different. Winfield said it was a watermelon and his family had grown them back in Texas, where they grew well in the heat. The red meat inside was sweet and delicious.

My grandfather said I needed to be exceedingly careful while eating the melon and not to swallow any of the seeds. To do so, he warned, would result in a vine "growing out your ass." For years, I was horrified that I would unknowingly swallow a watermelon seed, a vine would grow out of my rectum, and everyone at Pie Town Elementary School would make fun of me. I must have been well into my teens before I realized my grandfather was joshing and that the story was little more than an old wives' tale.

GREAT DEPRESSION LEGACY

When he had money, my father bought and stored sardines, potted meat, and Vienna Sausage by the case. "You never know what might happen," he would say, parroting my grandfather. If another depression hit, he was ready. He was scornful of anyone who wasted food and seemed upset when people did not eat everything on their plate, often remarking sarcastically, "It looks like your eyes are bigger than your belly."

Following the collapse of the banks during the early years of the Great Depression, and the family's flight west, my grandfather was extremely distrustful of banks, bankers, and anyone who wore a necktie. "They are all a bunch of damned thieves," he insisted, "just waiting to get into your pocket and get your money."

He was deathly afraid of being poor again, and every time he got some money, he placed it in a mason jar and buried it somewhere. I remember going with him late one night with a flashlight to bury sixty dollars under a shock of corn in the cornfield behind the barn. Another time, I held a flashlight as we buried forty dollars under a big piñon tree near the outhouse. Another time, after cashing his Forest Service check, he buried one hundred dollars. With age, Winfield was becoming more and more forgetful, and a few weeks later when he went to retrieve the one hundred dollars, he had forgotten where he had buried it. For weeks, he searched frantically for the money, overturning rocks, digging under trees, and searching around the woodpile and near the barn. For days, he was depressed that he could not find his money. Finally, to Winfield's delight, Rusty dug up the one hundred dollars from my grandmother's asparagus bed behind the garage. If not for Rusty, the money would have been lost forever. "Smart damned dog," my grandfather commented. "I really like him. He is a good dog." In reality, Rusty was just seeking a cool place for an afternoon nap.

COTTON CANDY AND
MOUNTAIN OYSTERS

While I was in elementary school at Pie Town, neighbors frequently stopped to chat with my grandfather. They would sit and talk for hours, especially in the winter, when there was less work to be done. Conversation tended to center around four things: cows, the weather, pickup trucks, and who had killed the biggest buck during hunting season. On some occasions, talk drifted off to the Great Depression and the two world wars. Religion and politics were taboo.

My grandfather became good friends with a man named McKenzie who bought a rather large ranch near Pipe Springs, at the southern end of Little Alegres Mountain. My father and grandfather worked all winter building an attractive log house for McKenzie, and he seemed appreciative. My grandfather knew the land as well as anyone, and every week, McKenzie had questions relating to a particular watering hole, who had homesteaded a piece of property, or if a section or two needed fencing.

McKenzie took great pride in his longhaired black, white, and tan collie dog. Everywhere McKenzie went, the dog went, often sitting on his haunches in the passenger seat of the pickup, his head out the window and hair blowing in the wind. Once, McKenzie drove up to the house and my grandfather went out to greet him. After exchanging handshakes and pleasantries, my grandfather, whose eyesight was growing weak, motioned toward McKenzie's pickup. "Why don't you ask your wife to get down?" With a puzzled look on his face, McKenzie paused for what seemed like a minute or two and then turned to stare at the pickup in disbelief. "Ain't my wife," he calmly responded. "That's my damned dog!" I never saw my grandfather so red faced and embarrassed. The family never let him forget confusing McKenzie's wife for his "damned dog."

There were memorable, sometimes embarrassing, moments with other people who dropped by too. Another frequent visitor was a hardy, hardscrabble homesteader named Lonnie Ebert "Whitey" Reid. Whitey lived with his wife, Jewel Callie Mae, and their six children in a log cabin at the foot of Mangas Mountain. My grandfather and Whitey were both from Texas, worked for the Forest Service on lookouts in the summer, fought forest fires, and had struggled to survive the Great Depression. They seemed to have a lot in common. In the winter, Whitey would stop at the house, and he and my grandfather would sit around the fireplace and talk. Whitey always wore a soiled black cowboy hat that he placed on the floor near the chair where he sat.

The valley was white with snow one day in January as my father, grandfather, and Whitey huddled around the fireplace, trying to keep warm. No one seemed to notice my half-grown tabby cat crawl into Whitey's hat and then poop grandly. When Whitey stood up to leave, putting on his hat, his eyes widened in disbelief and a frown streaked across his face. No one knew what had happened until Whitey blurted out, "Damned cat done shit in my hat." As he attempted to wipe the excrement off his head with his hand, my grandmother rushed into the room from the kitchen with a wet towel and began furiously scrubbing Whitey's head and trying to clean his hat. My grandfather sat stunned, though I noticed a faint smile on my father's face. Everyone in the family offered heartfelt apologies.

After Whitey drove off into the wintry night, my grandfather calmly turned to me: "When someone comes to visit, you need to put that damned cat outside. We can't have cats shitting in people's hats. That was the most disgusting thing I have ever seen. Imagine a cat shitting on your head." My father was never one to joke, but I remember him gently responding with a smile: "Yeah, that was almost as bad as calling McKenzie's wife a dog."

With the passage of time, the tale of Whitey's discomfort became a favorite family story, with even my grandfather telling the tale. A few years later in 1959, Whitey was killed when his horse reared and fell on him. My grandfather lost a good friend.

My father and I pose in our uniforms before a Pie Town baseball game in 1947. Courtesy of the author.

PIE TOWN BASEBALL IN THE ASPIRIN AGE

Beyond the Saturday dances, the greatest excitement when I was growing up in Pie Town was baseball. At that time, there was constant talk of Joe DiMaggio, Bob Feller, Ted Williams, Stan Musial, and my grandfather's hero, Jackie Robinson. As early as 1933, Pie Town had a baseball team that played in the rodeo arena and competed against neighboring villages. "A large crowd attended the Pie Town–Quemado baseball game Sunday afternoon," the *Catron County News* recorded. "The score was 10–7 in favor of Pie Town." The following Sunday the Pie Towners played Atarque at Adams Diggings, and in June, Pie Town beat Quemado, 11–7.

After the war, a field was hacked out of the piñon and juniper trees

Pie Town baseball team before traveling to Reserve for a tournament. In the back row on the far left is my grandmother Quata and standing tall in a white hat second from the far right is my grandfather Winfield. In the back row, second and third from the left, is my mother's aunt and uncle, Lillian and Johnny Cobb. In the front row, I am sitting on the knee of my uncle, Dave Scoggin. Courtesy of the author.

in the soft earth just south of the elementary school. Here as many as fifty to a hundred fans, mostly family members of the players, gathered in the summer once a week on Saturday. My grandmother toiled to make me a uniform that was an exact replica of what my father wore. How proud I was of the bright-red "PT" on the upper-left breast. I even had a baseball cap with "PT" neatly sewn on the front. Scampering after foul balls was tiring but always a great honor.

The team was composed almost entirely of war veterans. My father was the equipment manager and played second base, and my mother kept score. Winfield called balls and strikes. My mother's uncle, Johnny Cobb, played center field and helped manage the team. My only uncle, Dave Scoggin, played third base and frequently pitched. When Dave took over on the mound, Alvin Keelin came in to play third. Harve Hamilton was the catcher (and the bus driver on road trips).

For some reason, Hamilton always showed up with a greasy, old felt cowboy hat instead of a baseball hat. Delbert Perry of Bataan Death March fame also played on the team.

In the summer of 1948, when Glenwood traveled north, Pie Town emerged victorious, 21–16. During the game, one of the Glenwood players got hit on the head and knocked unconscious. Later during the game, Keelin broke a leg while sliding into third base. In the fifth inning, I remember my mother cheering wildly as my father hit a home run that wound up winning the game. Two weeks later, the Pie Towners prevailed in Glenwood, and the week after that, they beat Quemado 15–4.

On overnight trips to Glenwood and Reserve, families packed tents, camping equipment, and bedrolls, and crammed into Hamilton's old school bus. The southern part of the county was always warmer in the summer, and Glenwood at 4,688 feet seemed unbearably hot. When visiting Glenwood, the team camped at the abandoned CCC camp up Whitewater Creek and played on a nearby sandy mesa. At a tournament in Reserve, the team made camp in Lower Frisco in a grove of cottonwood trees where Negrito Creek poured into the San Francisco River. More enjoyable than the games was the camaraderie among the veterans and the social interaction among the various families.

Pie Town could beat every team except Fence Lake, a team that was also made up of veterans and Dust Bowl refugees. Like Pie Town, Fence Lake had been playing baseball since 1933 and played a regular schedule that included teams from Laguna, Gallup, Fort Defiance, and St. Johns, Arizona. Pie Town and Fence Lake were always rivals. Pie Town had once proclaimed itself the pinto bean capital of the United States, whereupon Fence Lake announced it was the pinto bean capital of the world.

Fence Lake had a pitcher named Billy Lenton Vandever who had a blazing fastball, a mean curve, and a slider that seemed to break two feet. As a boy, Vandever, who was the same age as my father, had learned to play baseball in Dallas, Texas, before his family moved to Fence Lake. He was so good that he had once tried out for the minor leagues. Vandever frequently struck out the entire side. Once against

Pie Town, he retired nine batters in a row and came close to pitching a no-hitter. I remember one game when Pie Town scored two runs on Vandever and everyone went crazy, screaming and honking the horn of Hamilton's bus, but Fence Lake still won.

BELOVED BUMS FROM BROOKLYN

At times, Pie Town seemed to be sleeping through the 1950s. I never saw an African American person in the county, and there was little discussion of the civil rights movement sweeping the American South and the rest of the nation. Nor did anyone pay any attention to a nineteen-year-old phenom from Tupelo, Mississippi, who shook his legs while singing, and who my grandfather said was a sissy.

For entertainment, I would sit with my family in the warm summer evenings and listen to Brooklyn Dodgers baseball games. I have no idea what station we were listening to, but it was probably KOB in Albuquerque, the oldest radio station in the state.

Listening to sportscasters Vin Scully and Red Barber made me feel as if I were in the front row at Ebbets Field, and Jackie Robinson was coming to bat in the bottom of the ninth with the Dodgers behind by a run with two out and a runner on third. Scully's dulcet voice was magic. His opening line, "It's time for Dodger baseball," was an indication that something exciting was about to happen. Scully may well have been the greatest baseball broadcaster of all time.

My mother bought me a baseball glove from Sears and Roebuck, and for hours on end, I would throw a baseball up in the air and catch it, or bounce it against the back of the work shed. My father still had his glove from his days with the Pie Town team, but after he had worked all day, he was insensitive to the plea of "Let's play catch." He had also inherited some baseball equipment from the Pie Town team, including a catcher's mitt, a mask, and three or four heavy bats.

I loved Jackie Robinson, especially when he stole a base, but my favorite was the left-hand-hitting center fielder, the Silver Fox, Duke Snider, who was an excellent home-run hitter and frequently batted over .300. The first baseman, Gil Hodges, and the catcher and leadoff hitter, Roy Campanella, were just as good. At shortstop, Pee Wee

Reese was magical. Led by Don Newcombe, all the pitchers, including Preacher Roe, Ralph Branca, and Carl Erskine, were among the best. Although the team's batting averages varied from day to day, I had them all memorized. I also kept a daily count of each player's home runs.

We listened at the edge of our seats as the sprightly Dodgers manager, Leo Durocher, led the team back to defeat the St. Louis Cardinals on the final day in 1949. In his third year at Brooklyn, Jackie Robinson had his finest season that year, leading the National League in hits and stolen bases.

Although the beloved Dodgers fell two games short of the Philadelphia Phillies in 1950, they roared back the following year to tie the crosstown Giants and force a three-game playoff. The teams split the first two games, setting up an epic game 3. When my father and grandfather took off work to listen to the game, the drama seemed intensified. The Dodgers were leading by two runs in the ninth inning when pitcher Ralph Branca came in to face Bobby Thomson with two on base and one out. Thomson proceeded to hit the "Shot Heard 'Round the World" that broke the hearts of all Brooklyn fans. I remember my grandfather walking out of the room and, for years afterward, my father talking about the home run Branca gave up.

The next year, we listened with rapt attention as the Dodgers won the pennant and faced the hated crosstown Yankees in the World Series. The Dodgers won three games and were ahead in the sixth game, but the Yankees rallied to force a decisive game 7. The damned Yankees won the seventh game with a single in the bottom of the ninth, and fans from Brooklyn, Pie Town, and Mangas had to wait another year.

In 1955, the Dodgers took the lead in the National League and won the pennant by thirteen games. Don Newcombe won twenty-seven games, received the Cy Young Award, and was the MVP of the National League. In the World Series, the seemingly invulnerable Yankees took a 2–0 lead. No team had ever won the first two games and lost the World Series. Moreover, the Yankees had beat the Dodgers the last four times they had played and had not lost a World Series since 1942. The Dodgers bounced back, winning the next two games at Ebbets

Field and the next game in the Bronx. The Yankees got five runs in the first inning of game 6 and went on to win 5–1. In the seventh and final game at Yankee Stadium, before sixty-two thousand screaming fans, Johnny Podres shut the Yankees down and the Dodgers won 9–2. It was their first world championship and my grandfather went around smiling for weeks.

When the Dodgers traded Jackie Robinson to the rival Giants in 1956, I sensed the end of an era. Even worse news came the following year, when the Dodgers moved to Los Angeles. My grandfather and I never listened to a Dodgers game again. The magic was over. What Walter O'Malley did was sacrilege, and Brooklyn fans never forgave him. In my eyes, the Dodgers not only lost their identity but their integrity. Chavez Ravine would never be Ebbets Field. I didn't care if the palm trees were waving in the breeze. My Dodgers days were over.

LOBOS, LIBERACE, AND COTTON CANDY

In the autumn of 1954, after my father and grandfather worked all summer, the family decided to attend the state fair in Albuquerque. Even more exciting than the fair, though, was that my beloved University of New Mexico Lobos would be playing the University of Utah Utes in football—and we had tickets. To me, the mighty Lobos were second only to the Brooklyn Dodgers. Mike Prokopiak, a placekicker for the Lobos, had become my biggest hero, more so than even Duke Snider and Jackie Robinson.

I had been delighted two years earlier, in late November 1952, to arrive home one evening to a large manila envelope with my name on it propped up on the kitchen table. The return address read, "Mike Prokopiak, UNM Athletic Department, Albuquerque, New Mex." A short, handwritten letter said the kicker was excited to learn he had a fan in western New Mexico. Moreover, Prokopiak promised to kick a field goal for me at the next game. Enclosed with the letter were two three-by-five, black-and-white photographs of Prokopiak in his Lobo uniform kicking and throwing the football. That very evening, I wrote back saying he was my best friend and I would hold him in my heart forever.

I wondered how Prokopiak had learned a ten-year-old kid in

western New Mexico had become his biggest fan, but he said Jake Hancock, one of the Texas hunters my father guided each year, had written him of my "loyalty" and "interest in football," despite the fact that I had "never seen a football game."

The Lobos left the Border Conference in 1951 to join the Skyline Conference that included University of Utah, Utah State University, Brigham Young University, University of Denver, University of Wyoming, Colorado State University, and University of Montana. Like those of the Dodgers, all the Lobos games were broadcast on an Albuquerque radio station, and they were exciting. I remember listening to a game being played in Missoula, Montana, when the sportscaster kept talking about the six-foot snowdrifts in the end zones and along the sidelines. One year, the Lobos went 7–2 with five shutouts. Every September, I could not wait for the Lobos to begin playing.

When we arrived in Albuquerque in 1954, we checked into a small motel on Central Avenue, halfway between the fairgrounds and the university. I remember my father paying fifteen dollars for a room that had a television. I had never seen a television or even been to Albuquerque. I thought it had to be one of the largest cities in the world, even larger than Magdalena and Socorro. At the fairgrounds, we went to all the exhibits, including one featuring Catron County that was little more than a crude painting of a couple of pine trees and two or three cowboys on horseback. My grandfather said it was embarrassing. I rode the Ferris wheel and my mother bought me some cotton candy. At one of the booths, I won a goldfish that my mother carried around all day in a small bowl.

We went to the rodeo in the evening, and at intermission, they wheeled a large piano into the arena for someone named Wladziu Valentino Liberace, who was dressed in a long, flowing white robe. My mother said she had never heard such beautiful music, but my grandfather said he looked like a sissy.

All week, my mind had been on the Saturday-night football game with the Utes. Finally, sitting on the forty-yard line in the west stands at Zimmerman Field, we watched as the Utes scored a touchdown and went on to win the game 6–0. The inept Lobos did not even come close to scoring. My disappointment knew no bounds. Had Prokopiak not already graduated and been on the team that day, the Lobos would have won, I was sure.

I also distinctly remember huddling around the small black-and-white television in the motel when Willie Mays of the New York Giants made his famous on-the-run, over-the-shoulder, basket catch, 425 feet deep in center field against the Cleveland Indians at the Polo Grounds in New York. The Giants won the game in the tenth inning and went on to sweep the series. My grandfather seemed pleased. Any team winning apart from the Yankees was acceptable.

PIRATE RADIO

When not listening to Dodgers or Lobos games, my grandfather tuned in to XELO at 1010 on the dial. XELO was a border-blaster radio station licensed in Ciudad Juárez, Mexico, and one of several stations on the border that featured quacks, yodelers, psychics, charlatans, and schemers. XELO played country music and offered everything imaginable for sale. The station's mailing address was in Clint, Texas, a small farming community downriver from El Paso.

The great country-and-western singer Johnny Cash said he got his first harmonica from Clint for $2.95. One evening, the XELO announcer offered a device guaranteed to kill rats for only $1. Despite having a number of cats that roamed around the house, we always seemed to have a problem with mice. My grandfather grabbed a pencil and took down the mailing address in Clint, obtained a money order in Pie Town, and sent the order off to Texas. A couple of weeks later, a small package arrived in the mail with an even smaller box inside. The box contained a two-by-four block of wood about five inches long. There was also a small wooden mallet. My grandfather was puzzled until he read the instructions. You were to catch the rat and place it on the board and then hammer the animal over the head with the mallet. If necessary, you were to repeat the process until death ensued. If used properly, the device was guaranteed, as advertised, to kill rats. The entire family laughed for weeks, though my grandfather never thought being duped by a border shyster was that funny.

CLIMBING BIG ALEGRES

By the time I was thirteen, I became tired of climbing Cat Mountain and the small hills around Mangas, and after several weeks of nagging, my father gave in and we were off to "conquer" Big Alegres, just as Hillary and Norgay had conquered Mount Everest. At 10,240 feet, the volcanic, flat-topped promontory was the highest mountain in the northern part of the county, visible for a hundred miles. No matter where you were, you could always look up and see Big Alegres and gain your sense of place and perspective. My father had climbed the mountain as a teenager, as had many homesteaders around Pie Town. Climbers left their names and the date they climbed the mountain on a piece of paper in a glass jar in a small cairn on the western summit.

We set off on a Sunday morning in early August 1954, planning to reach the summit before noon. Then we would start down before monsoon clouds gathered and the lightning and thunder began. Being on top of any mountain during the monsoon season was like dodging bullets.

Although I was young and exuberant, the trek was long and difficult. I thought back to Hillary and Norgay taking months to climb Everest and became even more determined to reach the top. Within a couple of hours, we reached Cabin Springs halfway up the mountain on the northwest side. About 200 feet higher, we edged around some cliffs that framed the rugged western face of the mountain, and the climbing became rocky and much more difficult. Although sawmillers had devastated the lower elevations, the steep upper slopes were beyond their reach. The forest there was majestic and pristine. White-barked aspens abounded in groves in the volcanic soil and rockslides, and there were tall, stately fir and spruce trees stretching well over 150 feet into the endless blue sky. It was August, and as a result of the usual late-summer rains, some of the hillsides were colored with bursts of summer wildflowers.

Parts of the mountain were so steep that we frequently had to reach out and grab a small tree or branch to pull ourselves upward. The higher we went, the more spectacular the scenery became. The atmosphere was crystal clear and the sun brilliant in the turquoise sky.

I was tempted to stop and just sit and gulp in the beauty of the scene and the unspoiled woods. Peering down at the foot of the mountain, we could see what remained of the numerous homesteads and their adjacent bean fields and cornfields, now overgrown with rabbitbrush that dotted the landscape. Looking clearly, I could see the W-Bar Ranch and the schoolhouse at Pie Town.

Across the Continental Divide to the northeast, the naked brown spires and peaks of the Sawtooth Mountains rose abruptly out of the plateau, one resembling a giant sombrero, another the shape of the fabled Matterhorn. Beyond were the gentler blue-green slopes of the Datil Mountains. What had made these mountain ranges so different, yet so close together? I wondered. To the south were the Horse Mountains and to the southwest the pine forests and twisting canyons of the Mangas Mountains, obscuring much of the vast Gila Wilderness that lay beyond. All around were immense ponderosa and piñon forests, the largest in the United States. Overhead was the glare of an endless sky.

My father pointed out where the family had homesteaded in Martin Canyon. Across the Mangas Valley was Slaughter Mesa and the top of Escondido Mountain sticking above Baca Mesa like an Egyptian pyramid. On the far western horizon, if you looked hard enough, you could make out the blueish outline of Escudilla Mountain and the White Mountains of Arizona. The volcanic cones on the edge of the Mangas Valley that I had climbed with such pride appeared as little more than giant anthills.

To the north in the far distance, across the sun-warmed, amber-colored plains and the blackened volcanic malpais, stood the striking 11,306-foot summit of Mount Taylor, or Tsoodził as the Diné call it. The mountain was snow crowned into early summer and looming 2,000 feet over the northern horizon, the timberline clearly visible. Mount Taylor was also one of the four sacred mountains of the Navajo and the highest mountain in the western part of the state, even higher than Big Alegres. When I was older, I thought, I would go there and climb it too.

From a distance, Big Alegres looked like a mesa, flat from one end to the other. On the summit, I was surprised to find a narrow vol-canic ridge, not more than fifteen feet wide in places. Although it had been twenty-five years since my father had climbed the mountain, the cairn was still there. Some climbers had not only written their names but short accounts of their struggles to reach the crest. My father had brought a small piece of paper and a pencil for the grand occasion, and I proudly printed my name beside his. He jotted down the date, and I placed the paper in the jar in the cairn. It was a proud and unforgettable moment. Higher summits on four continents, in ranges from the Himalayas to the Andes, lay ahead for me, but none was ever reached with as much pride as the summit of Big Alegres.

NEAR DEATH FROM THE HEAVENS

It must have been at least fifteen degrees cooler on the summit than at the base of the mountain. There was a light breeze blowing as we walked along the ridge. As it turned out, the eastern end was a few feet higher than the western end. The sunbaked, windswept, steep south face of the mountain stood out. Here naked grayish rockslides dominated the landscape. To the southeast, a lower, flat-topped mountain my father said was nameless was attached to Big Alegres by a high saddle, or col. At the base of the mountain on the southeast side, my father said my grandfather had staked a mining claim during the Depression, but it had never amounted to much.

As we started down, only one small, shiny cloud appeared on the horizon over the Horse Mountains, ten miles to the south. Within five minutes, lightning flashed and a crack of thunder deafened. We hurried as the sky grew dark. Only moments later, less than two hundred feet from the summit, the sky was suddenly ablaze with fire, and there was a deafening roar and a high wind. All I remember is suddenly being flat on my back, unable to move or catch my breath. It felt as if I had been hit over the head with a sledgehammer and violently slammed to the earth. I had been unconscious—for how long? My great fear was that my father had been killed, just like E. Norton and Willis B. Ditmore. Crawling and then scrambling to my feet and gasping for air, I saw my father no more than fifteen yards down the mountain from me, flat on the ground, not moving. I half stumbled down the slope, tears welling up in my eyes. My father began to move. Relief flooded me. He was alive.

The lightning bolt had ripped apart a tall ponderosa snag only yards away. We were lucky not to have been speared by any of the several eight-foot-long splinters that lay scattered on the ground. One or two were implanted in the mountainside like daggers. The smell of smoke rent the air. Reaching my father, I remember him blinking his eyes, looking up. "Oh my God!" he said. "That was really close! Are you all right? We were damned near hit! Let's get off this mountain."

There were more lightning strikes and another roll of thunder as we slid and raced down the mountainside. Only once did we pause for a sip of water from the canteen my father carried. Even when we were safely down, you could still hear the thunder echoing through the canyons and across the mesas. "You realize," my father uttered, "we were damned lucky." Once again, he related the tragic story of E. Norton that had made such a big impression on him when he was young. A gloomy silence followed.

Two weeks after our ascent and death-defying experience on Big Alegres, Cipriano Molina, a fifty-eight-year-old sheepherder from Atrisco, a small village near Albuquerque, was killed by lightning while herding sheep for Frank Hubbell northwest of Pie Town. The previous year, he had also been struck by lightning, while on horseback herding sheep for Hubbell. Although his horse was killed, Molina had miraculously survived, though he was burned badly. To be struck by lightning twice in two years—he had to have been the unluckiest man imaginable. Molina left behind a wife, seven sons, and a daughter.

Once or twice in the years that followed, I mentioned climbing Big Alegres again. "No damned way," my father always retorted. "Do you realize how close we came to being killed? We could wind up in the cemetery with E. Norton." For someone who had almost died at the hands of the Germans several times during the war, he was serious. I took him at his word.

FAMILY TASKS

There seemed to be a sense of teamwork in my family. Each family member performed certain tasks. My mother washed dishes, made beds, washed clothes, ironed, and did most of the sweeping and other cleaning. Monday was always washday, and my mother hung all the clothes on a clothesline in the backyard. In the arid climate, the clothes were dry in minutes. In winter, I remember the clothes sometime freezing solid.

The garden behind the garage was Quata's world. There she spent endless hours during the summer. She always wore a bonnet she had sewn herself, and seemed to toil endlessly, fighting with gophers, grasshoppers, and cutworms, while bragging about her asparagus, squash, and radishes. Winfield and I frequently helped with the watering, hoeing, and hauling manure from the barn and chicken house. Quata also cooked, gathered eggs from the hens, milked the cows, and was in charge of the canning in late summer. On top of all that, Quata was the family seamstress; with her old Singer sewing machine the family had hauled all the way from Texas, she could sew anything. Much of the family clothing, even underwear, was made from colorful flour sacks.

I would frequently go with Quata to the barn to watch her milk. She would patiently sit on a small wooden stool with a milk bucket, squeezing the cow's utter with both hands and squirting milk into the bucket. We had several cats that would follow Quata to the barn, and as soon as she began to milk, they lined up like lemmings. From a distance of several feet, Quata squirted the milk at their mouths. The cats would usually get milk all over their faces and would lick themselves for hours. Although I tried, I never mastered Quata's milking skills, but I would help her carry the milk back to the house.

I also helped her gather eggs from the chicken house. We must have had at least a hundred chickens, and there was a small income to be made selling eggs to grocer Wayne Hickey in Pie Town for fifty cents a dozen

When not working for the Forest Service, Winfield fed the horses, cows, and chickens, cut ice for the animals in the winter, saw to the baby chickens in the spring, carefully tended his fighting roosters, and had the unenviable task of keeping the chicken house clean. Both he and my father cut and carried wood and fed the fireplace. When he was not away somewhere building houses, working on windmills, or drilling wells, my father did most of the carpentry, plumbing, welding, and house repairs. He also took joy in grabbing the double-barreled shotgun he had plundered from a house in Berlin during the war and shooting at chicken hawks.

The winters were severe, and the water pipes from the well to the house frequently froze. My father and grandfather would labor for hours digging through the frozen topsoil to unearth and thaw the pipes with a big blowtorch and then cover them up again. My father built a well house near the windmill. With sawdust-filled walls three feet thick, it also doubled as a meat house.

When the weather was good, my father seemed to devote an inordinate amount of time to washing and polishing his car and making sure it was running properly. For some reason, he spent an exorbitant amount of time checking "the points," whatever those were. The most important part of any day for the family was the evening meal, which usually consisted of deer meat and vegetables from the garden.

MOUNTAIN OYSTERS

In the summers, before the onset of the monsoons, branding time served as a yearly ritual. In the Mangas Valley, the days of sheep and cattle rustling had disappeared, but the ranchers still branded their cattle. My father and grandfather always helped the cattlemen, some of whom ran large heads of cattle. The Thompson men were never paid; everyone just helped everyone else.

The calves would be herded into a pole corral by a couple of cowboys on horseback, roped by another cowboy on horseback, and wrestled to the ground by two or three cowboys on foot. After tying their front and hind feet, the cowboys held the calves to the ground. Branding irons from a roaring fire that was always stoked and kept red hot were set into each hide. The calves would bellow in pain, their tongues flopping into the dirt as their mothers gathered anxiously nearby, the putrid, gray smoke from the burned hide and hair of the animals drifting off into the July morning.

In addition to branding all the calves, the cowboys castrated the males, using pocketknives. To prevent the calves from bleeding to death, they would use a smaller heated iron to sear the wound, and then dab a purplish-looking medicine on it. The bloody testicles were

Branding time in the Mangas Valley in the late 1940s. My grandfather is in the center, kneeling. Courtesy of the author.

tossed on the corral fence. When the poor calves were finally released, they ran out of the corral, bewildered and still bellowing in pain. It only took a minute or two for a calf to be castrated, but the entire process seemed excessively cruel.

Their Wrangler jeans caked in dust, their hats dirtier than before, all the cowboys gathered at the ranch house for a ceremonial midafternoon lunch. I remember going with my grandfather to a branding at the large Mangas Ranch. One of the cowboys announced that as a treat we would be enjoying "mountain oysters" for lunch instead of steak. I had no idea what mountain oysters were, or even real oysters, for that matter. Everyone seemed excited, and one cowboy said he loved oysters better than anything he had ever eaten. The cowboys and their wives sat at a large, long table and the kids at a smaller table in the corner of the room.

It was not until we were back home that evening that my grandfather asked what I thought of the oysters. "Fine," I said. "They tasted just like chicken." He then explained they were really the testicles of the castrated calves. I had watched one of the women remove the testicles from the corral fence, but I thought she planned to feed them to the dogs. It never dawned on me she intended to cook them for human consumption. I was suddenly nauseated and never again ate mountain oysters, though they were available on several occasions. Looking back, I am not sure I was much of a cowboy.

WOOD HAULING

Another yearly ritual was hauling wood, usually in late September or early October during Indian summer when the weather was still warm and the skies clear. "Don't you think we need to get some wood?" my grandfather would say, and that was the signal to begin the task. "You know summer has arrived," he would joke, "when it is time to cut wood for the winter." We had a woodpile that must have been ten feet high and eighty feet across. It was certainly home to a variety of animals, including a family of cottontails and a family of chipmunks. We may have had the largest woodpile in Catron County. We had enough wood to last through a dozen winters, but my grandfather always insisted we needed more. "You never know what might happen," he was fond of saying. "Having wood is like having money in the bank. You can never have enough." On Saturdays and Sundays, early in the morning, he and I would go into the forest to gather wood in our 1947 flatbed Ford truck. My father had bought the Ford after a 1928 Chevrolet truck the family owned had quit working.

Years before chainsaws, my father and grandfather were some of the best woodsmen with double-bladed axes I ever saw. My father kept all the axes as sharp as a razor blade, and I often watched him tear into a green juniper tree and throw out three fence posts within minutes.

For lunch, my mother and grandmother would make egg or bologna sandwiches and pack a can of fruit, a piece of cheese, Vienna Sausages or sardines, and some crackers. Grinding the gears and bouncing along dirt roads, we always headed south. There was typically plenty of dead and fallen ponderosa pine in the nearby Apache National Forest, but the piñon in the lower elevations was richer, burned hotter and longer, and had a pleasant aroma.

Once when we were off to cut wood on the north end of Little Alegres Mountain, we were having lunch under a giant alligator juniper when my father, who delighted in eating sardines, suddenly broke the silence. "I don't believe it," he blurted out. "Shit! Come look at this!" Neatly stacked among the small sardines in the soybean oil was a small lizard, barely three inches long, decapitated and preserved just like the tiny fish. For at least a year, my father refused to eat any more sardines. Afraid of eating a lizard, I, too, declined, but my grandfather did not seem to mind. "When you are hungry, you will eat anything," he remarked. "Remember all those bean pies we ate during the Depression." Another time during a lunch break, my father began reading the contents on a can of deviled ham and said he was going to vomit. "I had no idea all that crap was in there," he said. For several months, he refused to eat any deviled ham or Vienna Sausage.

I remember one Saturday, my father took an old crosscut saw from the toolshed and he and my grandfather spent all day cutting a giant ponderosa tree that had fallen near the Mangas ranger station. They would saw and sweat, and then saw some more, back and forth, back and forth, for hours, as if they were on a miniature seesaw. Then, all day Sunday, they struggled splitting the wood with wedges and a sledgehammer and hauling the wood to our big woodpile, where it was neatly stacked.

Before we got a butane stove, much of the wood helped to feed the fireplace and two old stoves in the bedrooms. Juniper or, as a last resort, oak (both harder than pine), was used in the cooking stove in the kitchen.

One day in Pie Town, my father was talking to the Norris brothers, Granvill and Rex, and they explained how they were having great success using dynamite on large alligator juniper trees. They would simply bore holes in the trunk of a dead tree, Granvill said, stick in some dynamite, light a fuse, and then all you had to do was pick up the pieces.

My father always had plenty of dynamite, which he purchased at the Becker-Mactavish store in Magdalena, and he was always blowing something up, so it was agreed we should take the Norris brothers' advice and save a lot of work. My father spotted a large dead juniper not far from the house that must have been hundreds of years old and at least twenty feet tall. He bore several holes in the tree at different levels, even using a ladder, stuck a half stick of dynamite in each hole, crimped a copper cap on the fuse with a pair of pliers, stuck it in the dynamite, and lit the fuse.

"Perhaps we should get behind the truck," my grandfather suggested. You could see the fuse burning and sputtering along the ground, and then suddenly there was a massive explosion that sent a frightening cloud of white smoke hundreds of feet into the sky. The deafening noise of the blast shook the trees for a hundred yards. Through a cloud of dust and debris, it was obvious the old tree had disintegrated. Nothing remained except a ragged stump and a landscape of tiny splinters, some little more than toothpicks. In the shower of splinters, two small nearby piñon pines looked as if they had been decorated for Christmas.

The concussion from the blast was so severe that it cracked a side window in the old truck. My grandfather had left his felt hat on the bed of the truck and it was blown into the distance and pierced by a large splinter. It would have taken days to gather all the small pieces. "Damnedest thing I ever saw," my grandfather exclaimed, staring at his hat in disbelief. "I do believe you used too much dynamite." Although embarrassed, my father readily agreed. He had misunderstood and used three times as much dynamite as Rex and Granvill had recommended. That was the end of the family's wood-hauling-by-dynamite days.

HUNTING SEASON

Undoubtedly, the most significant fall ritual was hunting season. Each year, thousands of hunters, many from as far away as Texas and Oklahoma, passed through Magdalena on their way into the mountains of Catron County. They returned days or weeks later with as many as two thousand bucks, hundreds of turkeys, and a few bears.

Several hunters from Texas would stay at our house, and my

father and grandfather worked hard to guide them while hunting themselves. The visitors would bring boxes of food and sometimes stay for as long as the hunting lasted. A Texan once arrived with an ice chest full of small crustaceans he called shrimp that I had never seen before, which, when boiled, were delicious. Money was never mentioned, but when the hunters departed every year, they always left a fifty- or one-hundred-dollar bill under their pillow.

The hunters set out every morning before sunup and returned every evening after dusk. There seemed to be a sense of satisfaction and joy in their exhaustion. They would eat and sit around the fireplace, relate their hunting experiences, and debate where they should hunt the next day.

They would hang their kills in the tall piñon trees in the backyard and pose beside the dead animals with their rifles for photographs. My father was excited one year when he killed a big buck in Killion Canyon that had one of the largest antler spreads for a mule deer in the Boone and Crockett records. One of the hunters took the deer head back to Texas for mounting by a taxidermist.

When I tagged along on the hunting excursions, I always went with my grandfather. He was slower and a lot more tolerant than the others. My father had banned me from going with him when I made too much noise stepping on pinecones. Unlike the other hunters, who seemed to compete in killing the largest buck, my grandfather, who had hunted white-tailed deer back in Texas and poached deer in New Mexico during the Depression, didn't seem to care whether he killed a deer or not. His true hunting days were behind him.

Sometimes during hunting season, it would snow and be bitterly cold. I remember one day during a jaunt, my feet were so cold I lost all the feeling in my toes, and I was to the point of tears. On more than one instance, my grandfather would patiently stop and build a fire, and we would warm our feet before walking another mile. I especially remember a particularly cold November morning when we were hiking up a steep ridge toward Mangas Mountain. It was snowing and the wind was blowing out of the north, whipping the snow through the pine trees. My feet were so cold and painful I told my grandfather I could not go on. He stopped, found some rich pine knots and, with some dry pine needles, built a fire.

Once, we spotted two bears, a sow and her half-grown cub, near the summit of Mangas Mountain, and I begged my grandfather not to shoot them. They were related to Smokey Bear, I assured him. Hunters greatly prized killing bears, but my grandfather slowly lowered his .30-30 rifle, and the bears scampered off through the snow across a rockslide and disappeared into an aspen grove.

My grandfather said the bears could not have been related to Smokey Bear, that Smokey lived in the Lincoln National Forest down by Capitan, and had been rescued a few years earlier by a fire crew from Taos Pueblo. Ray Bell, a game warden and a friend of my grandfather's, had taken the three-month-old cub with singed fur and blistered feet and personally flown it to a veterinarian in Santa Fe. He, his wife, Ruth, and their daughter, Judy, cared for the cub until Smokey was taken to the Smithsonian's National Zoo in Washington, DC. His first name was Hot Foot Teddy, Bell said.

Grandfather told the story of his grandson begging him not to shoot the bears around the fireplace that evening. Several hunters were amazed, pronouncing the pleadings little more than those of a whiny kid. They would have killed the sow or perhaps both bears in a second, they said. One even wanted to go up the mountain the next day and look for the bears.

During one hunt, Jake Hancock, the wealthy oilman from Big Springs, Texas, killed a bear near Cat Springs. He skinned the bear and left the carcass hanging beside the deer in the backyard. To me, the body of the bear looked exactly like that of a human. One evening, my grandmother prepared a feast of bear meat, and while trying to eat it, I kept thinking of the bear hanging in the backyard, and the more I chewed the meat, the larger my portion became. It was like chewing on an inner tube.

POACHING

In addition to what Quata grew in her garden, the Thompson family subsisted for a large part of the year on deer meat. In fact, I do not remember anyone ever buying beef.

A few hours before sunset, usually in spring, summer, and early fall, when the roads were passable, my father would grab his .30-06 rifle off the wall and prepare to drive off into the mountains; poaching was always done by automobile, not on foot. If Thanksgiving or Christmas was near, he would sometimes take along his double-barreled shotgun for a turkey. If fact, my father had an arsenal of arms he had shipped home from Germany during the war, including several long rifles and at least three pistols, as well as daggers, bayonets, knives, and plenty of Nazi medals and souvenirs.

My father, frequently with me and my grandfather in tow, took the same route all the time. We headed up San Antonio Canyon along Mangas Creek, past the crumbling ruins of the White House and the Gabaldon Ranch, to the ranger station where I frequently spent the summers. We continued up the narrow canyon to Hairpin Turn, where the road wound west along the crest of the Continental Divide, up a rough, two-track road through tall pines. Halfway along the rocky ridge, I would ask my father to take the shortcut past Cat Springs. It was there on the north slope of Telephone Ridge that the virgin forest had escaped the sawmillers and the old-growth ponderosa pines stood tall and proud. In later summer, Mother Nature seemed to be at her

Grandmother Quata poses while on a picnic at Cat Springs in the foothills of the Mangas Mountains. Courtesy of the author.

most magnificent where a deserted, dilapidated dogtrot cabin built by the CCC still stood at Cat Springs.

Around the turn of the century, the waters from the small spring had been diverted into three long troughs carved out of large ponderosa pines so that several hundred sheep at a time could drink. I always marveled at the labor this must have taken. Grandfather said that sheepherders had done the work with an adze and that it was certain to have taken several workers a week or more. He had once used an adze to hollow out a piñon pine for a pig trough and it took him two days. "You had to be really careful not to chop off a toe or two," he said. A homesteader from near Mangas had once chopped off two of his toes, and Winfield rushed him to the physician in Magdalena. The poor man limped around for the rest of his life.

Each trough was a few inches lower than the one above and the water trickled from one trough into another before seeping off into the forest, where the grass was lush and the dragonflies hovered and butterflies fluttered about. With their distinctive colors and giant eyes, the dragonflies were amazing. Their four wings acted independently, allowing them to hover, dive, and fly backward and even upside down. Grandfather said not to disturb them, that they ate mosquitoes.

I liked to stand under the tall trees as my father and grandfather rested on the steps of the abandoned cabin. There were always turkey and deer tracks and occasionally those of a bobcat or a bear, or even a mountain lion. This was years before the elk flooded into the high country, and at the time, the forest was alive with mule deer and turkey.

From Cat Springs, the narrow, two-track road turned down a picturesque canyon past groves of tall aspen to Slaughter Mesa, where a large herd of pronghorn could be spotted. The road continued across a wide, treeless expanse stretching north toward Escondido Mountain, before turning down the rocky, twisting east face of the rimrock to San Antonio Canyon.

For some reason, my father only killed bucks, never a doe or even a spike. He never shot unless he was certain of his target. Although he killed without mercy, the possibility of wounding an animal seemed to disturb him. My father carried a tarp, a hunting knife, and a hatchet in the trunk of the car, and he could skin and dismember the deer and have it in the trunk in a matter of minutes. The meat was hung from hooks in the well house, where it was always cool, even in summer. On rare occasions, we would meet another hunter from the valley, and it was customary to stop and talk, or at least wave a friendly "hello." Everyone seemed to know what everyone else was doing, but any discussion of poaching was distasteful.

Everyone feared "Bear" Turner, the game warden, who, it was said, would arrest his mother if she were caught poaching. I sensed my father feared arrest, but convictions were almost impossible in Catron County. Prosecutors would sometimes ask for a change of venue to Socorro or Silver City, since it was impossible to find an impartial jury in Catron County.

Poaching deer might get you a hefty fine, but cattle rustling could get you several years in the state penitentiary. When Johnny Cobb moved to California, a big, burly, bearded man by the name of Dan Oliver purchased his ranch. Oliver and my father and grandfather became the best of friends. Oliver seemed to always be calm and collected and in a good mood. He had children, but they had married and moved away, and I would frequently go with him to check on his cows or his windmills. He seemed to enjoy riding around in his pickup truck much more than on horseback. I distinctly recall a conversation late one evening when my father cautioned Oliver to make sure he "put the hide down that old well." It was not until I was older that I figured out what was going on. By this time, Oliver had sold the ranch and moved to Mule Creek, and the crime he and my father had committed had faded into memory.

On one occasion, my father and grandfather were on one of their poaching sojourns and driving up Killion Canyon, near where they had first settled in 1932. "Wasn't it over that ridge where the still was?" my father asked as he pointed east toward Little Alegre Mountain. There was no affirmation of the still being "their" still, but I somehow got that impression. Everyone in the country seemed to have owned a still at one time or another. Home-brewed spirits were common at dances, Saturday-night parties, and other celebrations. Revenue officers frequently roamed through the country looking for the illegal stills, but there were few arrests.

SMOKEY THE HERMIT AND
THE PIE TOWN MARE

$\mathcal{G}$n the 1940s and 1950s, as I attended fourth, fifth, and finally eighth grade at Pie Town Elementary School, I came of age. Some of my experiences undoubtedly paralleled those of other youth growing up after World War II and during the Cold War, but in that small corner of western New Mexico, I think they were unique and irreplaceable.

Medical care in Catron County barely existed, and most people in the northern part of the county went to Springerville or Magdalena. For many years, Amanda Vandevanter, known simply as Grandmother Van, presided over health care in the southern part of the county. Born in Kentucky in 1840, she had come west in 1892 after her second husband died. She and her fifteen-year-old daughter and a four-year-old grandson settled at Reserve. For more than two decades, she was the only physician in the county. Through snow and rain, she traveled by horseback over mountain trails to take care of the sick. "As soon as Grandma was sighted coming over the hill," a resident remembered, "a load seemed to be lifted from our shoulders, for we knew help and sympathy were at hand." One of Grandma Van's last horseback rides was in 1917, when she rode forty miles across rugged mountains to the Blue River in Arizona to visit her grandsons who were going off to war. On the ride, her horse threw her, causing her to break several ribs, yet she was able to complete the journey. She died in Reserve on November 24, 1931.

During the Depression, people in Pie Town and the northern part of the county would see Dr. Michager "Mike" Charles Bell in Quemado. Born in Texas shortly after the Civil War and educated at Tulane and Louisville Medical College, Bell was a captain in the Army Medical Corps during World War I. With his wife, Mattie Josephine Hyatt, and a large family, he came west during the early days of the Depression and homesteaded near Fence Lake, though he maintained an office in Quemado. Bell lost his wife from the flu in April 1936 but continued his medical practice, frequently delivering a baby only to be called to deliver a second right afterward. Bell was known to carry his tire tools in his black bag, along with this pediatric instruments. At age seventy-five, he signed on to carry the mail to Fence Lake by way of Salt Lake and return in the afternoon by way of Trechado. I remember everyone mourning his death in January 1957, when he passed away just shy of his ninetieth birthday. Dr. Bell had the same kind of reputation in the northern part of the county that Grandma Van had in the southern part.

DR. BUMPASS

Anyone in the northern part of the county knew the dentist, Dr. Robert J. Bumpass, who lived alone in a small house on the road to El Malpais, about eighteen miles north of Pie Town. A Texan-born veteran of World War I, Bumpass was a dentist of the old school who did not believe in doing anything to relieve pain. In the Pie Town column in the *Catron County News* in June 1933, it was noted that "Dr. Robert Bumpas[s] was doing some dental work on several people around here."

My father once had a tooth that was excessively painful, and I went with him to see Dr. Bumpass. The tooth extraction began with my father calmly sitting in a chair in the dentist's kitchen, but it ended two hours later with him sitting on a big ponderosa pine log in Bumpass's yard, his mouth all bloody, and Dr. Bumpass trying to pull the tooth with a tooth extractor that resembled a long pair of pliers. Bumpass had one foot on the log for as much leverage as possible. After he finally brought out a chisel and a hammer, the extraction was successful, though my father complained of pain for a week.

SMOKEY THE HERMIT

Less than a half mile west of Pipe Springs, not fifty yards from the dirt road that wound across the Continental Divide to Datil, lived one of the most interesting characters in the entire Mangas Valley, even more fascinating than Work Reid.

The hills around Pipe Springs had been full of homesteaders during the Depression, but everyone except "Smokey" had moved away. Smokey lived in a one-room, wood-frame hut without electricity or running water and with only a small outhouse nearby. He seemed to live off what people gave him and the animals he trapped in the woods. My father said Smokey frequently ate skunk and porcupine, and he once saw him cooking a rattlesnake.

No one that I know of knew his real name, first or last. He was just Smokey, and he seemed to take no offense to the moniker. He had a small wood stove that sat in the middle of his little hut. The stove had no stovepipe, so ash and soot blanketed the interior walls of the small dwelling and much of the exterior as well. His entire house resembled the inside of a fireplace. There were huge cracks in the walls, and I never understood how Smokey did not freeze to death in the winter since he never seemed to have enough wood for his stove. There was a small door at the entrance, but it featured gaping cracks.

Smokey was short, with a long beard that hung down past his waist. He looked as if he had never had a haircut. His clothes were black, his beard was black, and his mop-like hair was black. Sometimes I could tell he had tried to wash his face, but this was rare. He had an old dirty coat he wore in summer and winter, and a pair of farmer overalls. There were holes in his overalls and in his shoes and he never wore any socks.

On one side of his hut, he had a cupboard nailed to the wall, but there was never anything on the shelves. Someone had given him a small calendar from the Eagle Guest Ranch in Datil, but it was outdated. There were no plates, knives, forks—only a small skillet. Smokey was in constant survival mode and seemed to epitomize the concept of fierce individualism that so many in the county adhered to and admired.

Now and then, my father or grandfather would ask Smokey a few questions, but he would never reveal anything personal about himself. No one knew where he came from. My grandfather said he was illiterate and had to be running from the law. At times, Smokey seemed distant and withdrawn. Several lawless characters had taken refuge in the remote recesses of the Mangas and Gallo Mountains during the Depression—perhaps my grandfather was right and he had been one of them.

Smokey did not have a mailbox and he never mailed a letter. While my grandfather was carrying the mail, Smokey would sometimes wait by the roadside, even in the cold of winter, and wave Winfield to a stop. Presenting a dime or two, which my grandfather always refused, he would ask for a loaf of bread from the Eagle Guest Ranch. Once, my grandfather gave him a small jar full of nickels and dimes that the family had saved over several years. Another time, my grandfather gave him a pair of shoes and a box of clothes.

One day in the early 1950s, after my grandfather lost the mail route to Procopio Leyba, we went to check on Smokey to see if he needed anything, but he was gone. We returned to his hut late that evening, and the next day, and the day after that, but he was nowhere to be found. His small, dingy cabin was as it had always been. His dirty bedding was there on his wood-frame cot, along with his few personal possessions. Leyba said he had not seen him in weeks and that he was certain he had not caught a ride to Datil. Had Smokey moved away or had an accident or heart attack and died in the woods? No one lived within five miles of the old man and no one had seen him. There was certainly no reason for anyone to do him harm; he had nothing of value that anyone could conceivably want.

With the help of my father, we searched the hills and steep canyons around Smokey's hut in every direction for days, but there was no sign of the bearded old man. Father said to look for circling buzzards, a sure sign of death, but there were none. My search turned up only an arrowhead and several deer tracks. My grandfather wrote the sheriff in Reserve, but the sheriff never showed up or bothered to respond. No one seemed to care about Smokey's disappearance, and only my grandfather seemed to miss him. He was another victim of the times, perhaps lost somewhere in the mountains. Over the years, Smokey's hut collapsed, and the blackened boards rotted into the dry earth until all that remained were a few rusty tin cans and his iron stove, and then someone took that too.

GI BILL

Corporal Jerry Winfield Thompson Jr. was one of nine million veterans who returned home and took advantage of FDR's GI Bill. The 1944 bill subsidized higher education for veterans in a way that had never been seen before. In Pie Town, more than twenty veterans signed up for what amounted to a fly-by-night vocational course run by the New Mexico College of Agriculture and Mechanic Arts. A professor from Las Cruces drove up once a month to "instruct" the veterans at the Farm Bureau building. Veterans had a choice of enrolling in a class in mechanical arts or in agriculture. For some reason, my father chose agriculture and received a nine-hundred-page book to study. I can't remember him ever opening the book.

The Pie Town veterans were attracted by the monthly stipend more than the education they were to receive. My mother would frequently accompany my father and visit with friends while he went to "school." Several Saturdays, we arrived back at the Farm Bureau building to pick up my father and witnessed an interesting sight: rather than sitting on the handcrafted wooden benches listening to a lecture or discussion, all of the veterans were gambling. The building, thanks to the GI Bill, had become a casino. A few veterans were standing around talking and smoking, but in two corners of the building, there were lively craps games, and at a table near the small stage, four veterans with fists full of dollars were playing poker.

At such gatherings, the veterans readily shared their harrowing war experiences with one another, but rarely did they share those stories with family members. It was not until my father was in his late eighties and near death that he related having narrowly escaped dying at the hands of the Germans several times during the war. The horrors of Buchenwald were something he never forget. The cremation ovens were still hot when the Americans entered the camp, and hundreds of pitiful, forlorn-looking inmates, little more than skin and bones, were walking around in dirty striped uniforms in a daze like ghostly scarecrows.

All the Pie Town veterans seemed to defer to Delbert Perry, a veteran of New Mexico's 200th Coast Artillery. Starved and suffering from disease, Perry and other New Mexicans had held out on the Bataan

Peninsula and at Corregidor in the Philippines for four months in early 1942 before surrendering. For almost four years, Perry had survived the most inhumane treatment imaginable in a Japanese POW camp.

The veterans knew they had been part of the greatest conflict the world had ever seen. Despite all the bloodletting, starvation, suffering, and mindless brutality they had experienced, there was little doubt they had been on the right side. They had somehow survived, gotten their medals, and come home to a gracious nation. As Theodore Roosevelt might have said, they were made of the "right stuff." They had fought the "Good War."

Veterans talked about the horrors of war with other veterans, as if they were the only ones who could understand. I never remember my father talking about the war with my mother, but once he got around another veteran, especially someone who had been in Germany, he could talk for hours. I sometimes heard my father talking to another veteran about the massacre of American prisoners by the German Waffen-SS at Malmedy during the Battle of the Bulge, and how orders had come down for the Americans not to take any German prisoners for two weeks.

Like other veterans, my father sent home from the war a pile of souvenirs. Germans who surrendered were stripped of everything they possessed. My father sent home at least six rifles, three or four handguns, bayonets, medals (including several Iron Crosses), insignia, shoulder patches, and compasses. I was disappointed he had not brought home a flag with a swastika on it, but he said no one should want "one of those damned things." Just seeing a swastika would make him angry. When he was in Berlin at the end of the war, he had stayed in a house that belonged to Hermann Göring's secretary. There was a beautiful grandfather clock at the end of the hall, and my father measured it several times, trying to figure out how to ship it back to New Mexico. Packages were limited to a certain weight and size, and the only thing he could figure out was to saw it in half, but he could not figure out how to glue it back together—and so it stayed in Berlin.

My father came home with a love of the English but great disdain for the French, who he said were elitist and arrogant. If they hadn't been fighting each other, he probably would have liked the Germans better than the French. The Russians, he hated. Witnessing Russian mistreatment of German civilians in Berlin at the end of the war helped to shape his feelings. He told story after story of women fleeing into the American sector of the city after they had been robbed and raped. "Those goddamned Russians were all a bunch of ignorant peasants," he would say. They were "so ignorant they washed their faces in the commodes and thought they were wash basins." I think his hatred of the Russians was also reflective of the growing tensions between the East and the West at the time.

For my father, the memories of war were long. Once when he was alone in the work shed, I heard him singing a song entitled "Lili Marlene." It was a song about love and death penned by a German solider posted to the trenches during World War I that became a favorite of the Allies in World War II and was made famous by the German-born, Nazi-hating actress Marlene Dietrich.

> Outside the barracks
> by the corner light,
> I'll always stand and wait for you at night,
> We will create a world for two,
> I'll wait for you the whole night through.

Another time when my father was alone, I heard him singing something about the "bluebirds over the white cliffs of Dover."

CAUDILL BROTHERS

For draft dodgers, my father had only disdain. This was especially true of some local siblings: four Caudill brothers, Jesse Lee, Preston, Roy Stephen, and Earl Ray. Rather than submit to the draft, the brothers hid out for months in the remote and twisting white-rock confines of León Canyon, beneath the 9,869-foot summit of Escondido Mountain just south of Quemado. Some in in the area referred to the picturesque canyon as Pretty Boy Canyon, since Charles Arthur "Pretty Boy" Floyd allegedly hid out there in the early 1930s before he was gunned down in Ohio in October 1934.

For months in 1943, the Caudill brothers lived on canned vegetables and wild game. They had driven to Quemado, burned their car, and fled into the mountains. But the FBI and state police were always on their heels. After four months of searching and the brothers threatening to kill anyone attempting to apprehend them, the FBI set up operations in Quemado and began a twenty-four-hour watch at strategic points in the area. At the same time, the FBI began negotiating with their father, and it was finally agreed that the sons would surrender peacefully.

After several miles of trekking, the father led twelve agents into the boxlike canyon, which was accessible only by foot. At the narrow entrance to the canyon, only one person at a time could enter; the brothers had cut down several trees at this threshold to barricade it. The FBI found three trap guns nailed to trees or hidden between rocks, each with a trigger attached to a trip wire. The brothers assured the agents the guns were for wild animals and not humans, but the agents had no doubt the brothers had been planning to shoot it out. Several agents were certain to have died if that had come to pass. Inside the canyon, the brothers had taken up residence in a series of caves. One cave atop a high cliff served as a lookout, where the brothers could watch for anyone attempting to enter the canyon.

Two other caves were so well camouflaged you could stand on top of the trapdoor entrance into them and never discover the door until digging into the dry earth. Another cave featured a fireplace, a tier of four bunks with bedrolls, and foodstuffs including canned vegetables and fruit. Enough frozen deer meat to feed the brothers for months was hanging in one of the caves, and outside twelve deer heads lay in the dirt. The Caudills also had several cases of ammunition, another indication they had been willing to shoot it out with anyone attempting to apprehend them.

Arraigned in Albuquerque, each of the brothers was placed under $25,000 bond. All except Earl Ray posed for a photograph with their captors. After the war, I remember being at a rodeo in Magdalena and watching my father become furious when it was announced that one of the brothers was a "hero home from the war." Rather than serve a prison term, at least one of the brothers had enlisted. Earl Ray, the youngest of the four, was pardoned by President Harry Truman in 1947.

CHASING COMMUNISTS

When we were not listening to Dodgers games or comedy programs, my family and I tuned in to dramas. Although we were remote, and far from Washington, DC, radio programs brought us to the front lines of the Cold War and the struggle between the democratic, freedom-loving Americans and the dictatorial, dastardly Russians and their authoritarian empire. The intense rivalry raised serious questions across the country about whether communist sympathizers, or "Reds," might actively be working as Soviet spies in the United States.

FBI director J. Edgar Hoover equated any kind of protest with communist subversion, and in 1947 President Truman issued an executive order to determine whether federal employees were sufficiently loyal to the government. Much of the pioneering efforts to root out communists came from the House Un-American Activities Committee (HUAC), which had been formed before World War II.

The committee worked hard to identify subversive elements in the leftist Hollywood film industry. Blacklists were compiled that barred suspected radicals from employment. These fears seemed justified when, in 1949, twelve members of the Communist Party of the United States were sent to prison for attempting to overthrow the US government. Then, in 1951, Julius Rosenberg and his wife, Ethel, were found guilty of conspiring to pass atomic secrets to the Soviets, and they were executed two years later by electric chair at Sing Sing prison in New York.

Of course, not all of the fear and anxiety was justified. At the forefront of the Red Scare was Senator Joseph R. McCarthy of Wisconsin, who used hearsay and intimidation to establish himself as an enemy of anyone who disagreed with him, especially intellectuals and celebrities. As the McCarthy witch hunts came into full swing in the early 1950s, no one seemed willing to challenge the senator. The Russians testing a nuclear bomb and the Communists taking over

China, followed by the Korean War, agitated Americans further. There was a real fear that the "Reds" would take over the United States too. The Supreme Court went so far as to declare that the free-speech rights of accused communists could be restricted because they presented a clear and present danger to the government. At school, we learned a new version of the Pledge of Allegiance that included the words "under God." McCarthy and HUAC took center stage in news reports and radio broadcasts, and fear and repression seemed to rule the land.

In the evenings, my grandfather would tune in to *I Was a Communist for the FBI*, a radio series starring Dana Andrews that ran for seventy-eight episodes in 1952 and 1953. The story followed Matt Cvetic (a communist-sounding name if there ever was one), who worked in a Pittsburgh steel mill and infiltrated a local communist party for nine years while reporting to the FBI. The entire Thompson family sat spellbound as Cvetic became emotionally involved with a communist schoolteacher disillusioned with the party.

The show was ultrapatriotic, with tinges of racism and fear of a totalitarian power such as the Soviet Union. The Thompsons, like most American families, easily concluded that the communists were little more than a bunch of violent thugs trying to subjugate the world. McCarthy said there were communists in the State Department and both my father and grandfather, caught up the airwaves of propaganda, agreed.

I Was a Communist for the FBI was such a success that it was followed by *I Led 3 Lives* on television, which was loosely based on the life of Herbert Philbrick, a Boston advertising executive who had infiltrated the Communist Party of the United States on behalf of the FBI. That show lasted 117 episodes.

I listened to the radio show every week, following the story of the immoral communists as they plotted to assassinate their political enemies. They referred to one another as *comrade*, as if they were in the days of the Paris Commune or the Russian Revolution. In the anti-communist hysteria of the 1950s, there seemed to be "Reds under the bed" in almost every community.

COMRADES IN PIE TOWN

When I was in the fifth grade, the Baptist preacher from Pie Town, in an attempt to supplement his meager income, took over driving the bus on the Mangas route. All previous drivers had allowed the passengers a brief stop after school once a week at Keele's grocery store to purchase a candy bar. But not the reverend. Candy was bad for us, he said. I thought he was nasty and impolite. A "Good morning, sir" was received with an irritated grunt. Moreover, he stunk up the bus with his chain-smoking. Only on rare occasions did he appear without a cigarette hanging out of the corner of his mouth.

On the way home one evening, I was crawling under one of the seats in the front of the bus and I found a letter addressed to the bus driver. At first, I thought of throwing the letter out the window as some kind of retribution, but I decided to open it instead. It was then that things really got exciting. The letter opened with "Dear Comrade." The only place I had heard that was on the radio, and I knew only communists referred to one another as "comrade." There was little doubt I was on the trail of something that might endanger national security, certainly something the FBI should know about. Somehow, someway, I concluded the bus driver had to be a communist who was conspiring to blow up Pie Town Elementary School. For what reason I did not dare speculate. All I knew was that he had to be stopped and soon. Perhaps he should be executed at Sing Sing, just like the Rosenbergs.

That evening after dinner, as the fire grew dim in the fireplace, and everyone had gone to bed except my father, I revealed the plot to blow up the school and implored him to contact the FBI as soon as possible. Pulling the letter out of my backpack as evidence, I handed it to him as if I were testifying before HUAC. He quietly read the letter and handed it back to me with orders to return the letter to the bus driver the next day and apologize for taking it. As it turned out, the Veterans of Foreign Wars was inviting the driver to one of their chapter meetings in Socorro. He had fought in North Africa and Italy during the war and had been wounded at Salerno, my father said. Years later, I would reflect back and wonder how the Red Scare could have had such a profound influence on a ten-year-old elementary school student in the mountains of western New Mexico.

ARMY-MCCARTHY HEARINGS

The Wisconsin senator went too far with his baseless charges in 1954, when he took on the army, accusing it of "coddling" communists. During the lengthy and highly publicized Army-McCarthy hearings, McCarthy came across as a demagogue and a fraud, and the Senate voted to censure him, effectively ending his career and eradicating his influence. In the following years, McCarthy turned increasingly to alcohol, and he died of hepatitis at the age of forty-eight in May 1957. Even at Pie Town Elementary School, his reign of terror was over.

During the McCarthy era, every student at Pie Town learned to fear a nuclear attack by the dreaded Russians, or "Russkies," as my father called them. Everyone had seen the unearthly, moonlike photographs of Hiroshima and Nagasaki, and even children were aware of the devastation a nuclear bomb would cause. In response to the possibility of a nuclear attack, some of the people around Pie Town turned their Depression-era dugouts into fallout shelters. One man who lived a few miles south of town told my father he had stored up enough food and water to keep his family alive for two months. My father asked him what he planned to do after he emerged from the shelter into a nuclear landscape. There would be no animals, plants, or unpolluted water on which to survive, and it was likely he and his family would starve to death or die a painful death from radiation poisoning. "Damn. I never thought of that," the man replied.

When the Soviet Union detonated its first nuclear device at a remote site in Kazakhstan in August 1949, it signaled a new and terrifying phase in the Cold War. Instead of the bomb being an exclusively American asset, the weapon could now be used against the American people. As part of President Truman's Federal Civil Defense Administration program, almost every week we went through a duck-and-cover drill at Pie Town, just like Bert the Turtle, who retreated into his shell after an explosion. We hid under tables, our desks, even the teacher's desk. We practiced placing our hands firmly on our knees and bending our head forward as far as possible, tightly covering our face or placing our hands on the back of our neck. What we were really doing, we joked at recess, was kissing our ass goodbye.

In the 1950s, although Americans were generally better off than they had ever been before, McCarthy and the Cold War had filled them with anxiety. It was a time of great fear. In October 1957, a bleep in the sky turned out to be a beach ball–sized Russian satellite called *Sputnik*. Shock waves reverberated across the country. America had lost the missile race, and the shadow of communism seemed to lurk even larger and behind every bush. The Russians even sent a second satellite with a dog named Laika into orbit. Not knowing Laika died on the fourth orbit when the satellite overheated, I named one of my tabby cats after the dog. The Americans tried to put a satellite into orbit, but the rocket blew up on the launchpad, and everyone called it Kaputnik.

WORLD OF TOMORROW

In the 1950s, my mother came across the wonders of something called DDT, a colorless, tasteless, and almost odorless chemical. The discovery of DDT had brought one scientist the Nobel Prize; the chemical was used widely during World War II, especially in the Pacific, to control malaria and typhus. After the war, it was widely promoted by the US government for use against household pests. Produced by fifteen chemical companies as an agricultural and household insecticide, it was part of the bright, new "world of tomorrow."

My mother poured DDT into a small spray can and sprayed flies or any insect she thought undesirable. She sprayed the deadly chemical on the kitchen table and screen doors, anywhere there was a fly or a bug. Once, she spotted a fly on my shirt and began furiously pumping. Another time, she sprayed a bowl of radishes on the dinner table. Sometimes she just sprayed the DDT into the air as a deterrent. Any time there was a fly or a spider, or any insect at all, my mother came to the rescue. She was the official family exterminator.

The publication in 1962 of Rachel Carson's *Silent Spring*, a seminal text in the environmental movement, revealed the deadly impact of the use of DDT, and there was widespread public outcry. Not only did the chemical cause cancer, but it was also a threat to wildlife, especially birds, including the bald eagle and the peregrine falcon, both of which were on the brink of extinction in the contiguous United States. Pregnant women's exposure to DDT was also linked to spontaneous miscarriages and the development of autism in their children. Billions of pounds of the substance had been dumped into the environment, some of it by my mother.

4-H CAMP

When I was in the fifth grade, I joined the 4-H club. At one time or another, almost all of the twenty small, one-room log schoolhouses in the northern part of the county had a 4-H club. The four Hs in the club's name stood for "Head, Heart, Hands, and Health." The club promised that if you joined—and almost all the students did—you would do better in school, be motivated to help others, improve your self-esteem, and gain new friends. I joined because everyone else was joining. There was also the promise of a summer camp that sounded exciting since I had never been away from home.

Once you joined 4-H, you had to choose one of almost two hundred projects to take on in animal science, horticulture, creative arts, or home economics. Most of the girls signed up for baking and sewing. I chose raising chickens since that was the only thing I knew anything about. My grandfather helped put in an order for baby chickens, and a few weeks later, several boxes arrived with chicks chirpings away. I was amazed that you could send chickens through the mail.

The most exciting event came in early summer when my mother said I could sign up for the 4-H summer camp at Glenwood. For several years, the 4-H clubs in Catron County had held three-day camps at the old CCC camp in the towering pines on the south bank of the Tularosa River at Apache Creek, but after so many people moved away after World War II, there weren't enough members and the annual encampment was combined with Grant County's.

Mother helped me make up a bedroll complete with a pillow and an extra set of clothes, and my grandfather took me to Pie Town, where, along with three or four other students, I jumped on an old school bus that took us to Datil to pick up two more students. We then drove down the Tularosa Basin to Reserve, where at least ten other students joined. By noon, we were already across Saliz Pass and through the mountains and pulling in to the old CCC camp at Glenwood. I could not believe how hot it was.

Hundreds of students from Grant County arrived, none of whom seemed overly friendly. I was assigned to a room in one of the old barracks with a tall, redheaded, freckle-faced kid from Cliff, who bragged endlessly about how many cows his father owned, what a great baseball player he was, and how the Cliff Cowboys were dominant in basketball. He did not seem very impressed when I tried to explain my chicken project.

Everything went well until I woke up in the middle of the first night with a great need to urinate. It was pitch dark outside and there were no lights or electricity in the old barracks, and I had no idea where the restrooms were. It was a terrifying moment for someone as insecure and scared of the dark as I was. If I ventured out of the barracks, who knows? I could get lost and a bear would eat me. Or the bogeyman might carry me off into the nearby Mogollon Mountains. I had to do something, and I had to do it quick. I have no idea what caused me to do it, but I grabbed one of my roommate's shoes and urinated in it.

The next morning, we were awakened early for breakfast and the obnoxious redheaded kid went to put on his shoes. Suddenly he stopped and began to carefully examine one of them. Here comes trouble, I thought. "Damn," the kid proclaimed, "it must have rained last night and the roof leaked." I wholeheartedly agreed. "I thought I heard it raining," I said. Although the earth was bone dry outside, it was certain to have rained in the night and there was a leak in the roof.

The kids from Grant County outnumbered the 4-Hers from Catron County by at least ten to one and they dominated all the activities. It was not until the third day that I was invited to join a softball team. At the camp, I remember learning only one thing—where the restrooms were, so the redheaded kid from Cliff no longer became a victim of the "rain."

RODEO DAYS AND THE PIE TOWN MARE

Once or twice a year, we would go to a rodeo, usually in Quemado, Pie Town, Datil, Magdalena, or Springerville. During the Great Depression, the Pie Town Rodeo during the second week of September featured what the *Catron County News* said was a "girl's pony race" and an "old men's calf roping" contest for ropers fifty-five years of age or older.

The Pie Town Rodeo had been going on for over two decades. One of the more popular Pie Town Rodeos, in 1936, featured free barbecue. H. Lindsey and Bee Julian were responsible for organizing the rodeo, one of the best ever staged in Catron County, it was said. At the time of the rodeo, there were agricultural exhibits in Harmon Craig's beanery and at the Farm Bureau building, mostly hosted by county 4-H clubs. As part of the festivities, Quemado High School arrived for a basketball game on the town's dirt court and prevailed 47–7. Hundreds of attendees were entertained with a dance on Friday and Saturday evening.

In 1937, the rodeo was on the weekend of September 24–25, as part of the Northern Catron County Fair. Once again, there was free barbecue, and "everyone was happy and ate heartily." Numerous vegetables, fresh and canned, were on exhibit. Keeping with the town tradition, fifty pies were on display, and there was a singing contest at

For several years, the Pie Town Rodeo, with no arena, was part of the Northern Catron County Fair. Photograph by Russell Lee. Courtesy of the Library of Congress, Prints & Photographs Division, Farm Security Administration / Office of War Information Color Photographs; call number LC-USF35-355.

the Baptist church. In the evening, there was a bonfire and dancing, and a platform with a public address system. Livestock and poultry exhibits attracted attention, as did all kinds of farm produce. Ribbons awaited the winners.

The rodeo was for amateurs only, and featured calf roping for both men and boys, bareback bronc riding, wild-cow milking, wild-cow riding, a girls' pony race, and, in conclusion, a free-for-all quarter-mile horse race. The Thompson family enjoyed the festivities immensely, the *Catron County News* reported. Beginning in 1938, Harmon Craig and Joe Keele took responsibility for the fair and rodeo. At the slightest pretense, Craig would rush off to Santa Fe, sometimes dragging Keele along with him, to promote the rodeo and the small community.

By 1939, the fair had become an annual affair with a thousand people attending. That year, two bean farmers, Sam Norris and Harve Hamilton, exhibited some tobacco they had grown. They also displayed some tobacco stalks at Craig and Keele's store. Tobacco could become a cash crop in the area, it was argued. Norris and Hamilton even showed off their tobacco at the state fair in Albuquerque. That year, Sam Norris, Bill Elmore, and Cyrus West won the state grain-judging contest in Albuquerque and received an all-expenses-paid trip to compete at the National Grain and Feed Association Convention in Chicago.

The granddaddy of all the rodeos was the Round-Up in Magdalena on Labor Day weekend. The rodeo started in 1926 and grew in size throughout the Depression and war years. Magdalena was still an active community into the 1950s, with several fine department stores. Although they rarely bought anything, my mother and grandmother used the occasion to go shopping.

The celebration opened with a grand parade featuring marching bands from as far away as Albuquerque. The town was colorfully decorated, and there were dances every evening. In 1935, more than three hundred cars were on the rodeo grounds, and the daily attendance was well over a thousand. The windup to the rodeo was always the horse races on Sunday afternoon. The one rodeo I remember was in the early 1950s when Bee Julian's Pie Town Mare was matched against an Indian pony from the Alamo Navajo reservation. In three years, the

Pie Town Mare had never lost a race; she had become legendary in the northern part of the county. My father and grandfather had little doubt the mare would again prevail. The betting on the race was heavy, and they bet eighty-five dollars, every cent they had. As hundreds of people lined the raceway north of the rodeo arena, the mare got off to a good start and led by more than a length, but just before the finish line, the pony from Alamo nosed her out.

My father and grandfather lost all their money. It was a financial blow the family could ill afford. Moreover, as a result of the loss, my mother and grandmother did not have enough money for the family to enjoy the traditional hamburger and soft drink at Evett's drugstore afterward. We just left for home. "That's the way it is," my grandfather said. "You win some and you lose some, and today we lost."

CALVES, STEERS, AND BULLS

In the early summer when I was nine or ten, the family attended a kids' rodeo in Quemado. Rodeo competition seemed to be part of the DNA of every real cowboy, and participating was the highlight of any summer. If you were not a contestant in the rodeo, you were nobody. Registration was at a bar on California Street, the main east–west artery, though the arena was down a dusty dirt road, a mile to the northwest, near the town cemetery. There was barrel racing for the girls, calf roping and steer riding for the high school boys, and calf riding for elementary school boys. It did not take much begging on my part for my grandfather to come up with the $2.50 entrance fee for the calf-riding contest.

On a cloudless, bright July afternoon, there must have been fifty people in attendance. Most of the families sat in a small wooden grandstand on the south side of the arena, though a few remained in their cars and pickups that lined the arena on the north side. A tall, wobbly-looking announcer's stand rose above the chutes on the east side of the arena.

I was shown how to hold the rigging, or surcingle, that fastened tightly around the calf's girth with my right hand while holding my left hand high in the air. The loudspeaker announced my name, and in a heartbeat, the chute swung open, and away I went. The Hereford calf did not buck as I expected but ran around in circles. Within seconds, I lost my balance but held on as tightly as I could and managed to survive the required eight seconds before tumbling headfirst into the soft earth.

When the rodeo concluded, all the participants gathered at the announcer's booth anxiously awaiting the judges' decision. First-place winners received a blue ribbon and ten dollars, those finishing second got a red ribbon and five dollars, and third place received a white ribbon and three dollars. When my name came over the loudspeaker as the third-place winner, my pride knew no bounds. It did not matter that there were only four contestants. The white ribbon seemed to symbolize another step in coming of age in the cowboy culture of Catron County.

Family legend holds that during a Fourth of July celebration back in Odessa, Texas, my grandfather rode a bucking horse down Main Street. In New Mexico, my aunt Twauna made the local newspaper as the only girl to ride a steer at a rodeo at Oak Springs, across the Continental Divide from Mangas. That sunny day in Quemado, it was obvious the mantle had been passed to another generation, and I was on my way to becoming a real rodeo cowboy.

At the time, Quemado, Reserve, and Springerville all had rodeos for young people. During the Depression, there had been rodeos at Pipe Springs, Greens Gap, Adams Diggings, Fence Lake, Oak Springs, and Mangas, but when the homesteaders moved away, these had disappeared.

A few years later, I advanced to the steer-riding category, and every summer there were more ribbons and more accolades. Once, I even got my name in the *Catron County News*, just like Aunt Twauna. My grandfather wove a special bull-rigging surcingle and painted a cowbell with my initials on it. The bell acted as a weight that allowed the rope to fall off the animal at the conclusion of the ride. He even bought me a pair of spurs like the real cowboys wore. Winfield also tied a barrel between two piñon trees in the backyard to simulate the bucking of a bull. The surcingle and a saddle blanket were tied to the barrel, and all it took was someone to jerk on the ropes, and I could practice my riding skills. When family members cooperated, I practiced for hours

Learning to ride with my grandfather at an early age. Courtesy of the author.

on end. I was determined to become the best bull rider in the county and get one of the highly coveted silver-plated belt buckles I saw the real cowboys wearing, which seemed to always impress the cowgirls.

Once a cowboy registered for the rodeo, he was given a small piece of loincloth with a number painted on it that was pinned to the back of his shirt or the lower part of his pant leg. These were highly prized status symbols that were kept as souvenirs. Real cowboys wore chaps, had a wad of tobacco in their cheek, and a plug of Days O Work or Red Man in their shirt pocket.

Often the girls gathered in the stands as the cowboys paraded by, as if it were a fashion show. The cowboys pretended they were going to the refreshment stand, spurs jingling and chaps flapping, but they were really trying ever so subtly to catch some female's attention.

Boys from ranching families always had horses and entered the calf-roping contest. Riding calves or steers seemed beneath them. They would park their pickups and horse trailers near the arena chutes. The pickups would sometimes have the names of the ranchers and their ranches painted on the side, as if to say, "Look at me."

When I was fifteen, the rodeo in Springerville was around the Fourth of July on a Saturday and Sunday. My father and grandfather were working at the time, so I hitched a ride with the George Adams family. I always felt a special attachment to Springerville, since it was where I had been born in November 1942.

Independent and proud, I had little doubt that I was one of the better steer riders in western New Mexico. The Springerville rodeo would be an opportunity to show off my skills in Arizona. No ID was required, so I entered an older age bracket. In addition to fifty dollars for first place, what I really wanted was one of those shiny belt buckles.

A BRUISED AND DEFLATED EGO

When I arrived at the grounds, I was astounded to see the older cowboys I was to compete against were riding bulls. This was long before TV cowboys wore gloves, helmets, chaps, flak jackets, and advertising on their vests, and threw their hats in the air after a successful ride. I drew a fierce-looking, cream-colored Brahman bull with sawed-off horns. He was snorting and stomping in the chute before I even got near him. When I was safely seated and holding on as tightly as I could, the chute swung open. The bull lurched forward in one giant leap, slamming his front hooves into the ground, violently kicking his rear feet high in the air, and twisting his two-thousand-pound body in a giant contortion in one direction and then abruptly in the other. Off I went, headfirst into the arena, not fifteen feet from the chute. In less than two seconds, I was on the ground.

The bull did not run away or try to stick a horn in me, as they sometimes did. Instead, he stood over me in triumph, as if to pound his nemesis into the manure-infested Arizona earth, stomping and snorting. In the bigger rodeos like this, brightly attired clowns rushed forward to lure the bull away, pretending they were bullfighters, before jumping to safety into a big rubber barrel that the bulls battered about the arena. This bull was different. He was not in the least bit distracted by the clown. I tried to protect myself by throwing my hands over my head, but there was little I could do to save myself from the beast. In seconds, I felt a numbing dizziness, and then everything went dark.

I have no idea how long I lay in the Arizona sun. Finally gaining consciousness, I looked up to see a clown with a brightly painted face and a big, red fake nose staring down at me. "Are you OK, kid?" I remember him saying. "Can you hear me?" he kept asking. Several cowboys circled around, one of whom threw some water in my face from a canteen he was carrying. Finally struggling to my feet and trying to regain my senses and manliness and as much strength as I could, I mumbled that I was fine, that I had been bucked off before. I was a tough cowboy. I could take it. As I was half dragged out of the arena like a dead gladiator, several people in the stands quietly clapping in sympathy, winning the silver belt buckle was the least of my worries.

There was no doubt I had suffered a concussion. There is a lot I cannot remember, but one thing was for sure: although that bull might have wound up as hamburger at some point, this was his day. The back of my head was hurting and badly bleeding from the bull's hooves. My shirt was ripped, my pants—and even my underwear—were torn, my back was bleeding, and one of my legs was badly bruised. Moreover, my pride had taken a fatal blow. Dizzy, with a throbbing headache, I lay quiet and still in the grandstands, flat on my back, before becoming violently sick and throwing up. There was little doubt the sudden illness was from the furious pounding my body had taken. Although I was reluctant to admit it, no cowboy could take what that bull had dished out, even the tough ones. It was not until later that I realized I had swallowed a big wad of tobacco.

That evening, my mother put Mercurochrome on my wounds, repaired my shirt and pants, and did as much as she could to comfort my badly bruised ego. My father was less sympathetic. "I have been telling you those rodeos can be dangerous," he said. "What on earth were you doing trying to ride a bull?" A bit calmer several minutes later, he asked, "What are you going to do now?"

"When I get to be eighteen, I think I will join the marines," I responded quietly. "You are right, Dad. Those damned bulls can kill you!"

My father thought joining the marines was about the dumbest thing he had ever heard, and concluded I might have suffered permanent brain damage. There was one thing for sure: my rodeo days were over.

END OF AN ERA

The eighth-grade graduation ceremony at Pie Town Elementary School was a big event for the small community. For entertainment, the tradition was for the graduates to present a one-act play. It was hard to find a one-act play for four graduates, as was the case in 1956, so we presented a series of skits instead.

There must have been at least forty parents and relatives in attendance at the old Farm Bureau building when the curtain went up that evening in late May. The skits were overly simple, not well rehearsed, and not entertaining. Yet everyone seemed pleased, especially the parents of the graduates. At the conclusion of the ceremony, we stood on the stage to receive handshakes, hugs, and a small blue diploma signed by the county school superintendent and the president of the school board, my father.

In 1965, less than a decade after I graduated from Pie Town Elementary School, so few students were attending the school that it was closed and the property reverted to Theora and Harmon Craig, the original owners. In turn, the Craigs sold the property to a couple of schoolteachers from the Texas Hill Country, Karl and Esther Hartmann, who turned the building into a summer home.

When I was arguing with a colleague many years later, he became overly agitated, jammed his finger in my chest, and blurted out, "Do you realize I have a PhD from Harvard?" I could think of only one response: "Do you realize I graduated from Pie Town Elementary School?"

Sometimes when the light begins to fade in the late afternoon, or at night when it is quiet, I reflect back on those days of my youth, the sun glistening off the snow, the wind whistling through the pines, high on the Continental Divide in the mountains of western New Mexico, to that little school in Pie Town.

EPILOGUE

While I was a graduate student at the University of New Mexico in Albuquerque in 1967, I frequently visited my grandfather, who was at the Veterans Affairs hospital in the city after having undergone a heart operation. In the evenings, he would be sitting on the side of his bed, all alone, frail and weak. The hospital was sad and depressing, like most hospitals. There never seemed to be a nurse or attendant on duty, much less a physician, and many of the old veterans who stumbled through the narrow corridors seemed to be close to death. I frequently found them playing dominoes or sitting around smoking and telling war stories or complaining about the lack of medical care. In many ways, the place resembled a poorhouse from the previous century. Any joy or excitement in their lives had long since faded into oblivion. Many were just waiting to die. "I think I am getting close to the end," Winfield told me one evening. I knew he was right, but it was still depressing to hear, and what he said haunted me for days.

Winfield badly wanted to return home to Mangas. Finally released that fall, he died a few months later, two days after Christmas in 1967, from a heart attack while sitting on the old couch in front of the fireplace. It was there that we had spent many precious hours together awaiting the opening pitch at Ebbets Field, listening excitedly as the University of New Mexico Lobos took the field, or tuning in as the FBI chased a few communists.

A snowstorm had swept across the county a few weeks earlier, so a four-wheel-drive vehicle had to pull the hearse to the cemetery in Quemado. There, on a frigid day, Jerry Winfield Thompson Sr. was buried on the hillside beneath Sloan's Peak. Quata was never the same again. She suffered a debilitating stroke a few years later and was bound to a wheelchair. My mother and father tried to take care of her, but it was almost impossible since they were both working at the time, so she wound up in a nursing home in Aztec, close to where my aunt lived. The last time I saw her, I expected the usual joyous hug, but she lay rolled up in a small bed not much larger than a crib. Her dementia was so severe that she did not recognize me. It was all so very sad. I felt so much remorse for not having spent more time with her in the last decade of her life. What a terrible way to leave the world, I thought. Quata Veta Thompson died on January 27, 1973, and was buried in the soft, dry earth beside Winfield on the hillside at Quemado. At the gravesite, my father planted two piñon trees.

My mother smoked all her life and began suffering from emphysema in the late 1970s. The disease progressed slowly at first, but she eventually became bedridden and dependent on oxygen. At every opportunity, I flew to Albuquerque from Laredo, Texas, and then drove out to Quemado to see her. At the same time, I worried about my father, who was still working full time for the Forest Service. After laboring all day, he would wake up several times at night to care for my mother before going off to work early the next morning. My mother's aunt, Lillian Cobb, helped take care of my mother for almost a year and then Aunt Twauna moved down from Aztec to assume the duties. My mother, Jo Lee Thompson, the orphan girl from Oklahoma with the mysterious past, died a painful death on March 28, 1982. A few weeks later, I found in the bottom drawer of an old dresser the shoebox full of letters that unraveled the tragic story of her troubled youth. In 2019, after ten years of research, the story of her mixed-blood Cherokee outlaw father, who robbed countless banks and trains and spent fourteen years in Leavenworth, and who I did not know even existed, was published as *Wrecked Lives and Lost Souls: Joe Lynch Davis and the Last of the Oklahoma Outlaws* by the University of Oklahoma Press.

My father outlived my mother by twenty-eight years, passing away on April 25, 2010. Living alone, he arose early one morning to feed Big Tom, his favorite cat, and then sat down on the couch, where a neighbor later found him dead. Only days earlier, I had flown out to help him celebrate his ninetieth birthday with a few of his friends. For several years, I had urged him to move to Texas with me, to a lower elevation, where he could have better medical care. "Hell no! This is where I belong and I am not going anywhere," he responded, obstinate to the end. The phone call from the neighbor saying that he was dead was heart wrenching.

Today, Pie Town is only a shell of its former self. Weeds grow on the playground where children once played cowboys and Indians. Craig and Keele's general store, the beanery, and the hotel on the dike have long since disappeared. Of the original village, only the teacherage and the Farm Bureau building still stand. Travelers speed past on Route 60 not knowing the place even exists. In distant Washington, DC, Russell Lee's treasured photographs survive in a vault at the Library of Congress.

Go out to Pie Town. Turn off Route 60, make your way down past the old Farm Bureau building, listen quietly, and you can hear the faint voices of Depression-era bean farmers, perhaps a cowboy or two galloping past, the joyous cries of children playing, or even the bounce of a basketball on the dry, cold earth. In the coolness of the evening, there is likely a whiff of piñon smoke in the air, and in the night, the barking of coyotes. Drive south down the dirt road past the old W-Bar Ranch, through the dike, and turn west to Mangas. Here, beneath the summit of Big Alegres Mountain, the land and its peaks and valleys will likely enter your soul. Climb up Cat Mountain and, in the shade of a piñon tree, you can just sit and marvel at the beauty of the natural environment, the quietness and vastness of the unspoiled land. Pick a few piñons, linger on the past for a while, and watch the world go by.

ANNOTATED BIBLIOGRAPHY

Any study of Pie Town must begin and end with Kathryn McKee Roberts's *From the Top of the Mountain: Pie Town, New Mexico and Neighbors!* (Albuquerque: Bishop Printing, 1990). The book contains invaluable family recollections of the Pie Town homesteaders and their trials and tribulations. The book also has 230 significant photographs. Roberts's *From Dust to Dust: Cemeteries in Northern Catron County* (Bosque Farms: printed by the author, 2006), has a chapter on the Pie Town cemetery, Juniper Haven, with numerous biographical sketches of individuals buried there, as well as information on other cemeteries in the northern part of the county.

When Catron County was created in 1921, a newspaper was established at the county seat entitled the *Reserve Advocate*, but it lasted for only a few years. For several years during the Great Depression, the *Quemado News* and the *Catron County News* were published every Friday in Magdalena. Much of the contents was from the wider-circulating Magdalena newspaper. These newspapers featured societal columns from small hamlets in the northern part of the county including Pie Town, Datil, Horse Springs, Mangas, Divide, Mesa, Tres Lagunas, Pipe Springs, Omega, Adams Diggings, and even Fox Mountain and Bear Canyon. Many of the columns, although largely gossip, are valuable in reconstructing a social history of these predominantly homesteading communities.

Much of the information on the Melquiades Aragon and Pedro Gabaldon families is derived from census records (1900, 1910, 1920). Interviews with Tina Koranda, Eva Aragon Oroña, Cristine Romero Ellis, and Frank Awalt helped to retell the life of the sheep baron José

Ygnacio Aragon. A lot of information on the families and the early history of Rito Quemado and Mangas is from the *Las Vegas Gazette*. Numerous conversations with Eliseo Baca, first at Mangas and later at Quemado, beginning in the 1970s and ending around 2001, were invaluable. No one knew as much about the history of the area as Eliseo did.

Perhaps the best Depression-era recollections of Pie Town are those of Doris Caudill, as told by Joan Myers, in *Pie Town Woman: The Hard Life and Good Times of a New Mexico Homesteader* (Albuquerque: University of New Mexico Press, 2001). The book has thirty-three of Russell Lee's best photographs. Before she passed away at the age of ninety-three in 2011, I asked my beloved elementary school teacher Colita Schalbar, who knew the history of Pie Town and its people as well as anyone, to read *Pie Town Woman*. Schalbar was able to correct several mistakes in the book, not only in the spelling of names, but factual errors.

Russell Lee's images of Pie Town remain a uniquely rare window into the lives of its homesteaders on the eve of World War II. These photographs are discussed thoroughly in F. Jack Hurley's *Portrait of a Decade* (Baton Rouge: Louisiana State University Press, 1972). A number of Lee's best Pie Town photographs are in Marta Weigle's *Women of New Mexico: Depression Era Images* (Santa Fe: Ancient City Press, 1993). *Far from Main Street: Three Photographers in Depression-Era New Mexico* by Russell Lee, John Collier Jr., and Jack Delano (Santa Fe: Museum of New Mexico Press, 1994) also has several of Lee's Pie Town images. Lee's Pie Town photographs are also discussed in an excellent article by Paul Hendrickson entitled "Savoring Pie Town" in the February 2005 issue of *Smithsonian* magazine. A supplement to the *Albuquerque Tribune* (August 22, 1996) contains a feature story by Ollie Reed Jr. with several contemporary photographs of Pie Town by Kay Lynn Deveney.

All of the Lee quotes are from his letters from Pie Town to his superiors in Washington, DC. These were published in Jerry Thompson, "Bean Farmers and Thunder Mugs: Russell Lee's 1940 Farm Security Administration Photographs and Letters of Pie Town and Catron County," *New Mexico Historical Review* (Fall 2009).

In 1986, Jean Smith Lee donated a portfolio of her husband's Pie Town photographs to the Southwestern Writers Collection at the Alkek Library at what is today Texas State University. In the summer of 1991, Francine Carraro, distinguished art historian and museum director, along with Eric Weller, professor of art and design, lead a team of students from Texas State University to Pie Town. Their extended stay resulted in a large number of photographs and valuable videotape interviews with such pioneer homesteaders as Maudie Belle and Roy McKee, Granvill and Rex Norris, Colita Schalbar, and Bob, Sam, and Opal McKee. The vitality of these photographs became the basis of a research project, photographic exhibition, and publication entitled *Retracing Russell Lee's Steps: A New Documentary* (1992). Typescripts and the original recordings are available at the archives at the Alkek Library. Also of interest is *Russell Lee: A Centenary Exhibition* (San Marcos, TX: Wittliff Gallery of Southwestern & Mexican Photography, 2003). *American Heritage* published an article by Larry Meyer entitled simply "Pie Town" in the February/March 1980 issue that is illustrated with some of Lee's best Kodachrome images. A must-read is Lee's own article "Life on the American Frontier—1941 Version," in the October 1941 issue of *U.S. Camera*, which featured forty-five of what he judged to be his best photographs. "The Great Pie Town Show Down" by Candace Walsh features the Pie Town Pie Festival (*New Mexico Magazine*, August 2013). The article includes an homage to Russell Lee by photographer Arthur Drooker, who made four visits to the village between 2011 and 2013. Drooker's photographs depict several descendants of the original Pie Town homesteaders holding iconic Russell Lee Kodachrome images of their predecessors. In 2015, Drooker published a book, *Pie Town Revisited*, with a foreword by F. Jack Hurley, an authority on Lee (Albuquerque: University of New Mexico Press).

The *New Yorker* featured a number of Lee's images in August 2014 in "A Slice of America in 1940: Pie Town, New Mexico" by Siobhán Bohnacker. In 2011, Brooklyn-based artist Debbie Grossman took some of Lee's photographs, especially those of Faro, Doris, and Josie Caudill, along with the Norris, Whinery, and Hutton families, and in a powerful statement about feminism and lesbianism, manipulated the images using Photoshop in an attempt "to make the history I wish was real." In *My Pie Town*, Lee's classic images became lesbian relationships. Grossman's images were displayed at several leading American art museums to create an imaginary world—a Pie Town populated exclusively by women. The males in the original images were digitally reimagined and re-sexed. A few of the images are featured in Jesse Green's article "The Revisionists: How Today's Queer Artists Are Revising History" (*New York Times Style Magazine*, December 8, 2019). A number of art museums, including the New Mexico Museum of Art, continue to feature Lee's iconic images.

Marta Weigle's "Pie Town: A Slice of Homestead Life," in *New Mexico Magazine* (November 1996) has a short history of the town centered on the recollections of Doris Caudill. Anne Sullivan also provides a brief history of the community in her "Memories of a Pie Town Original" in the same issue of *New Mexico Magazine*. The article features Roy and Maudie Bell McKee and includes a wonderful photograph of Roy posed by his tractor.

Several interviews with Colita Schalbar were invaluable. An interview with a Pie Town Elementary School classmate, Bobby Ray McKinley, perhaps one of the better Catron County cowmen, was also beneficial. So were interviews with schoolmates Merle Lee Schalbar and Jeannie Chadwell.

In 1936, Clay W. Vaden, a fieldworker in the New Mexico Federal Writers' Project of the WPA, passed through Pie Town and Quemado. Vaden wrote a short piece entitled "Plains of San Augustine." After talking to Harmon Craig in Pie Town, Vaden wrote a far more valuable piece, "Profitable Piñon Picking near Pie Town." In Quemado, he interviewed Felipe Padilla, who was a boy during Nana's 1881 raid and recorded Padilla's recollections as "Mexican Boy Captured by Apache Indians." All three reports are on the internet. Similar records are at the New Mexico State Records Center and Archives in Santa Fe. In 1997, the *Magdalena Mountain Mail* published a number of recollections of area residents that were helpful.

Although she never liked or sympathized with the Pie Town homesteaders, Agnes Morley Cleaveland's best seller, *No Life for a Lady*

(1941), remains a classic. Darlis A. Miller's biography of Cleaveland, *Open Range* (Norman: University of Oklahoma Press, 2010) is exceptionally well researched, makes for superb reading, and is highly recommended. Although centered on Quemado and largely fictionalized, Pat Kilmer's *Dough, Ray and Me: The Adventures of a Family Who Gave up Social Security for Home on the Range* (New York: William Sloane Associates, 1957), is undoubtedly one of the best-written and interesting of the homesteader recollections. Ira McKinley, a well-known rancher in the Pie Town area for several decades, has left us a set of lively accounts, *My Saddle and I* (New York: Carlton Press, 1978).

Jim Hogg's *Pioneer Pride: We Came, We Struggled, We Survived* (Albuquerque: LMC Printing Service, 1988), is one of the more insightful homesteader recollections, although it has more to do with Quemado than Pie Town. Undoubtedly, the best of the homesteading records is that of Etta Rose Knox, *Homesteading on Grasshopper Flats: A True Story of 1930's Pioneers on New Mexico's Continental Divide* (Alameda, CA: Drollery Press, 1984). In the rimrock country northeast of Zuni Salt Lake and west of Trechado, Knox relates an unforgettable story of suffering that included near starvation, unendurable cold, and spousal abuse. Langford Johnston and Eve Ball's "A House by the Side of the Road" (*True West*, June 1982) tells the compelling story of Lawrence and Ida Parsons, who staked out a claim at the mouth of Alamosa Creek, northeast of Pie Town, in 1913. Bonnie L. Armstrong's *Homesteader's Daughter* (self-published, CreateSpace, 2012) is also of interest. Curt Moyer's "The Frank A. Hubbell Company, Sheep and Cattle," in the *New Mexico Historical Review* (January 1979), was helpful.

Susan E. Lee has two perceptive chapters on Catron County, one entitled, "La Tierra de Mañana y Ayer," in her self-published *These Also Served: Brief Histories of Pioneers; Short Stories and Pictures Relative to Catron, Grant, Sierra, Socorro, and Valencia Counties of New Mexico* (Los Lunas, NM: printed by the author, 1960). Gary Tietjen's *Mustangs and Wild Cows* (self-published, Xlibris, 2017), an informative set of recollections of cattle ranching in the Zuni Mountains and Ray Morley's Drag A Ranch in the Datil Mountains, is highly recommended. Among the more animated recollections of ranchers in northern Catron County in the early twentieth century is Langford Ryan Johnston's *Old Magdalena Cow Town* (Albuquerque: Cottonwood Printing, 1983). Johnston's reminiscence of the death of Henry Coleman is particularly significant. Undoubtedly, the best study of Coleman is Eleanor Williams's (using the pseudonym Mel Jewell) series of eight articles in *New Mexico Electric News* entitled "Outlaw Born Too Late" (August 1964–March 1965). Although taken almost word for word from Williams's work, Oscar Caudill's recollections (as told to Eve Ball) of Coleman in "Hell on the Largo," in *Frontier Times* (January 1972), is of some value. Also worth a read is "The Posse That Killed" by Ben W. Kemp (as told to Eve Ball) (*True West*, April 1982).

Recollections of the church service at Aragon that the CCC men attended is from an interview Richard Melzer conduced with T. J. Duffy of Philadelphia, Pennsylvania, in 1991. Melzer's thoroughly researched and nicely crafted *Coming of Age in the Great Depression: The Civilian Conservation Corps Experience in New Mexico, 1933–1942* (Las Cruces, NM: Yucca Tree Press, 2000), told partly in the words of former enrollees, is highly recommended. The book features several photographs of the CCC camp at Glenwood, including the image on the jacket of the book.

The story of the draft-dodging Caudill brothers is based on accounts from the *Albuquerque Journal* (February 9, 1944) and the *Santa Fe New Mexican* (February 9, 1944). The pardon for Earl Ray is recorded in the December 24, 1947, issue of the *Albuquerque Journal*.

The story of what was thought to have been the last grizzly bear in New Mexico is based on Montague Stevens's *Meet Mr. Grizzly: A Saga on the Passing of the Grizzly Bear* (Silver City, NM: High Lonesome Books, 2002). First published in 1943, the book has gone through four editions. Besides *Meet Mr. Grizzly*, Montague Stevens left behind his financial records, legal documents, and business correspondence, which are available in the Special Collections at the University of Arizona Libraries. A few other Stevens documents are in the Center for Southwest Research and Special Collections at the Zimmerman Library at the University of New Mexico.

Robert N. Watt details the Chihenne Apache warrior Nana's raid through the San Francisco Mountains area in his meticulously researched *'With My Face to My Bitter Foes': Nana's War 1889–1881* (Havertown, PA: Helion and Co., 2019), the third volume of his impressive study of the Victorio War.

Edwin A. Tucker and George Fitzpatrick's *Men Who Matched the Mountains: The Forest Service in the Southwest* (Washington, DC: US Government Printing Office, 1972), remains one of the best sources on the subject. Many Forest Service records from the first half of the twentieth century are at the National Archives in Washington, DC, and have yet to be thoroughly studied. I searched endlessly and unsuccessfully for a photograph of the old wooden lookout tower on Mangas Mountain my father often described.

From 2018 to 2020, the Catron County Historical Society presented a number of speakers who reflected on their family recollections during the Depression and in the years that followed. Recorded and available today, these include those of the Barbara Hogsett and Bub Adams families, along with Marvin Magee's recollections of Pie Town. Bonnie Armstrong Dfoor helped in recalling some of the events in Quemado.

There have been several attempts to write a history of Magdalena. Most efforts have been fragmented and incomplete. David Wallace Adams's highly engaging *Three Roads to Magdalena: Coming of Age in a Southwest Borderland, 1890–1990* (Lawrence: University Press of Kansas, 2016) is an exception. In clear prose, Adams relates the dramatic story of how Alamo Diné, Hispanics, and Anglos negotiated the social and cultural dynamics of the small livestock and mining community.

INDEX